Expert C Programming

Deep C Secrets

Peter van der Linden

SunSoft Press
A Prentice Hall Title

Library of Congress Cataloging-in-Publication Data
Van der Linden, Peter
Expert C Programming! / Peter van der Linden.
p. cm.
Includes index.
ISBN 0-13-177429-8
1. C (Computer program language) I. Title.
QA76.73.C15V356 1994
005.13'3--dc20 94-253
CIP

The publisher offers discounts on this book when ordered in bulk quantities. For more information, contact: Corporate Sales Department, PTR Prentice Hall, 113 Sylvan Avenue, Englewood Cliffs, NJ 07632, Phone: 201-592-2863, Fax: 201-592-2249

Editorial/production supervision and interior design: *Camille Trentacoste*; Illustrator: *Gail Cocker-Bogusz*
Manufacturing manager: *Alexis Heydt*
Acquisitions editor: *Michael Meehan*; Editorial assistant: *Nancy Boylan*
Cover designer: *Doug DeLuca*
Cover photo: *Coelacanth/Lloyd Ullberg, Special Collections, California Academy of Sciences*

The cover depicts a coelacanth (pronounced C-la-canth), a butt-ugly fish that ichthyologists thought had been extinct for 70 million years. Then, in 1938, a specimen was caught off the coast of South Africa and taken to the local museum curator for identification. She recognized the significance of the find, and called in the experts—but not in time to prevent the fisherman stuffing and mounting his unique trophy! A second specimen was not caught until 1952. The limb-like fins of the coelacanth make this fish a "missing link" between ocean- and land-dwelling vertebrates. It is one vile-looking piece of seafood though.

Printed in the United States of America

13 14 15 16 17 18 19 20

ISBN 0-13-177429-8

SunSoft Press
A Prentice Hall Title

Warning

Do not unscrew the cover of this book—there are no user-serviceable parts inside.

Typo's and Errors

At least one statement in this book is wrong (but it may be this one).

There's a bounty of $1 per error to the first person who brings a technical correction to the author's attention, so it can be corrected in future printings.

Please send your correction by e-mail to linden@eng.sun.com or by mail to the author c/o Prentice Hall, 113 Sylvan Ave., Englewood Cliffs, NJ 07632.

Dedication

I hereby dedicate this book to pizza, Dalmatian dogs, Sunday afternoons in a hammock, and comedy. The world would be a lot better off if there were more of these. I plan to become reacquainted with them all now the book is done.

In fact, I think I'll spend next Sunday afternoon swinging in a hammock, and laughing at my Dalmatian dog's attempts to eat pizza.

I would also like to acknowledge the fine products of the Theakston Brewing Company, Yorkshire, England.

Contents

Preface

Browsing in a bookstore recently, I was discouraged to see the dryness of so many C and C++ texts. Few authors conveyed the idea that anyone might enjoy programming. All the wonderment was squeezed out by long boring passages of prose. Useful perhaps, if you can stay awake long enough to read it. But programming isn't like that!

Programming is a marvellous, vital, challenging activity, and books on programming should brim over with enthusiasm for it! This book is educational, but also interesting in a way that puts the *fun* back into *functions*. If this doesn't seem like something you'll enjoy, then please put the book back on the shelf, but in a more prominent position. Thanks!

OK, now that we're among friends, there are already dozens and dozens of books on programming in C—what's different about this one?

Expert C Programming should be every programmer's *second* book on C. Most of the lessons, tips, and techniques here aren't found in any other book. They are usually pencilled in the margin of well-thumbed manuals or on the backs of old printouts, if they are written down at all. The knowledge has been accumulated over years of C programming by the author and colleagues in Sun's Compiler and Operating System groups. There are many interesting C stories and folklore, like the vending machines connected to the Internet, problems with software in outer space, and how a C bug brought down the entire AT&T long-distance phone network. Finally, the last chapter is an easy tutorial on C++, to help you master this increasingly-popular offshoot of C.

The text applies to ANSI standard C as found on PCs and UNIX systems. Unique aspects of C relating to sophisticated hardware typically found on UNIX platforms (virtual memory, etc.) are also covered in detail. The PC memory model and the Intel 8086 family are fully described in terms of their impact on C code. People who have already mastered the basics of C will find this book full of all the tips, hints and shortcuts that a programmer usually picks up over a period of many years. It covers topics that many C programmers find confusing:

- What does `typedef struct bar {int bar;} bar;` actually mean?
- How can I pass different-sized multidimensional arrays to one function?
- Why, oh why, doesn't `extern char *p;` match `char p[100];` in another file?
- What's a bus error? What's a segmentation violation?
- What's the difference between `char *foo[]` and `char(*foo)[]` ?

If you're not sure about some of these, and you'd like to know how the C experts cope, then read on! If you already know all these things and everything else about C, get the book anyway to reinforce your knowledge. Tell the bookstore clerk that you're "buying it for a friend."

PvdL, Silicon Valley, Calif.

Acknowledgments

This isn't one of those lame little acknowledgment sections that you see in most other books: a string of feeble tributes to everyone the author ever borrowed money from, starting with his grade school buddies, proceeding through all his spouse's relatives, and ending with a grovelling but blatant attempt to curry favor with his thesis advisor ("and lastly to the great and powerful Professor Oz, whose work on whether the toilet paper should hang at the front of the roll or the back has done so much to resolve this crucial question"). No way! *This* is a genuine list of people who really and truly helped while I was writing this book. Everyone listed here has actually earned their acknowledgment. And you can bet that as I spend my leisurely days, and the princely royalty payments, on a beach in Tahiti I'll be thinking of them. Really I will!

I'd like to start with a special acknowledgment of the help given by Phil Gustafson and Brian Scearce, who read the entire manuscript in draft form and suggested many corrections and improvements. The effort was so intense that they have now deeded their bodies to science.

Thanks, too, to the friends and colleagues who read large parts of the work-in-progress:

Lee Bieber,

Keith Bierman (whose business card reads "Rabble-Rouser" for his title, and he is certainly the right man for the job),

Robert Corbett,

Rod Evans,

Doug Landauer,

Joseph McGuckin,

Walter Nielsen,

Charlie Springer (who taught me to count on my fingers in binary—you can count up to 1023 that way!),

Nicholas Sterling,

Panos Tsirigotis,

Richard Tuck,

who read parts of the manuscript and generously shared their candid, not to say blunt, views.

And I'm very grateful to the people who generally helped, often by patiently answering a stream of endless questions:

Chris Aoki,

Arindam Banerji,

Mark Brader,

Brent Callaghan (who hacked the audio feature into snoop),

David Chase,

Joseph T. Chew,

Adrian Cockcroft,

Sam Cramer,

Steve Dever,

Derek Dongray,

Joe Eykholt,

Roger Faulkner,

Mike Federwisch,

Dave Ford,

Burkhard Gerull of Sun Germany,

Rob Gingell,

Cathy Harris (for the plentiful supply of common sense),

Bruce Hildenbrand (and his amazing flying bicycle trick),

Mike Kazar,

Bob Jervis,

Diane Kelly,

Charles Lasner,

Bil Lewis,

Greg Limes,

Tim Marsland,

Marianne Mueller,

Eugene N. Miya,

Chuck Narad,

Bill Petro (for his inspiring and non-stop history lessons),

Trelford Pinkerton,

Alex Ramos,

Fred Sayward,

Bill Shannon,

Mark D. Smith,

Kathy Stark,

Dan Stein,

Steve Summit,

Paul Tomblin,

Wendy van der Linden (who came up with the bob-for-apples inheritance example for C++, and improved the rhythm of the "two 'l' null" verse),

Dock Williams,

Nigel "Gag Me" Witherspoon,

Brian Wong,

Tom Wong.

I'm grateful to editor Karin Ellison who let me mix metaphors, and several times poured midnight oil onto troubled waters on my behalf; to Astrid Julienne, who answered a lot of questions about Framemaker, and to Peter Van Coutren in the Sun Library.

I appreciate the knowledgeable help of the Prentice Hall staff, including Mike Meehan, Camille Trentacoste, Susan Aumack, Eloise Starkweather, and Nancy Boylan.

I'd also like to acknowledge the following people who didn't make a nuisance of themselves while I was working on this book. They generally stayed out of my hair, and they didn't screw anything up too badly. They're OK kinds of people, I guess:

Dirk Wibble-O'Dooley,

P. A. G. Embleton,

snopes.

Some of the material in this book was inspired by conversations, e-mail, net postings, and suggestions of colleagues in the industry. I have credited these sources where known, but if I have overlooked anyone, please accept my apologies.

PvdL, Silicon Valley, Calif.

Introduction

C code. C code run. Run code run...please!

—Barbara Ling

All C programs do the same thing: look at a character and do nothing with it.

—Peter Weinberger

Have you ever noticed that there are plenty of C books with suggestive names like *C Traps and Pitfalls*, or *The C Puzzle Book*, or *Obfuscated C and Other Mysteries*, but other programming languages don't have books like that? There's a very good reason for this!

C programming is a craft that takes years to perfect. A reasonably sharp person can learn the basics of C quite quickly. But it takes much longer to master the nuances of the language and to write enough programs, and enough different programs, to become an expert. In natural language terms, this is the difference between being able to order a cup of coffee in Paris, and (on the Metro) being able to tell a native Parisienne where to get off. This book is an advanced text on the ANSI C programming language. It is intended for people who are already writing C programs, and who want to quickly pick up some of the insights and techniques of experts.

Expert programmers build up a tool kit of techniques over the years; a grab-bag of idioms, code fragments, and deft skills. These are acquired slowly over time, learned from looking over the shoulders of more experienced colleagues, either directly or while maintaining code written by others. Other lessons in C are self-taught. Almost every beginning C programmer independently rediscovers the mistake of writing:

```
if (i=3)
```

instead of:

```
if (i==3)
```

Once experienced, this painful error (doing an assignment where comparison was intended) is rarely repeated. Some programmers have developed the habit of writing the literal first, like this: `if (3==i)`. Then, if an equal sign is accidentally left out, the compiler will complain about an "attempted assignment to literal." This won't protect you when comparing two variables, but every little bit helps.

The $20 Million Bug

In Spring 1993, in the Operating System development group at SunSoft, we had a "priority one" bug report come in describing a problem in the asynchronous I/O library. The bug was holding up the sale of $20 million worth of hardware to a customer who specifically needed the library functionality, so we were extremely motivated to find it. After some intensive debugging sessions, the problem was finally traced to a statement that read:

```
x==2;
```

It was a typo for what was intended to be an assignment statement. The programmer's finger had bounced on the "equals" key, accidentally pressing it twice instead of once. The statement as written compared x to 2, generated true or false, and discarded the result.

C is enough of an expression language that the compiler did not complain about a statement which evaluated an expression, had no side-effects, and simply threw away the result. We didn't know whether to bless our good fortune at locating the problem, or cry with frustration at such a common typing error causing such an expensive problem. Some versions of the lint program would have detected this problem, but it's all too easy to avoid the automatic use of this essential tool.

This book gathers together many other salutary stories. It records the wisdom of many experienced programmers, to save the reader from having to rediscover everything independently. It acts as a guide for territory that, while broadly familiar, still has some unexplored corners. There are extended discussions of major topics like declarations and arrays/pointers, along with a great many hints and mnemonics. The terminology of ANSI C is used throughout, along with translations into ordinary English where needed.

Programming Challenge

OR

Handy Heuristic

Sample Box

Along the way, we have **Programming Challenges** outlined in boxes like this one.

These are suggestions for programs that you should write.

There are also **Handy Heuristics** in boxes of their own.

These are ideas, rules-of-thumb, or guidelines that work in practice. You can adopt them as your own. Or you can ignore them if you already have your own guidelines that you like better.

Convention

One convention that we have is to use the names of fruits and vegetables for variables (only in small code fragments, not in any real program, of course):

```
char pear[40];
double peach;
int mango = 13;
long melon = 2001;
```

This makes it easy to tell what's a C reserved word, and what's a name the programmer supplied. Some people say that you can't compare apples and oranges, but why not—they are both hand-held round edible things that grow on trees. Once you get used to it, the fruit loops really seem to help. There is one other convention—sometimes we repeat a key point to emphasize it. In addition, we sometimes repeat a key point to emphasize it.

Like a gourmet recipe book, *Expert C Programming* has a collection of tasty morsels ready for the reader to sample. Each chapter is divided into related but self-contained sections; it's equally easy to read the book serially from start to finish, or to dip into it at random and review an individual topic at length. The technical details are sprinkled with many true stories of how C programming works in practice. Humor is an important technique for mastering new material, so each chapter ends with a "light relief" section containing an amusing C story or piece of software folklore to give the reader a change of pace.

Readers can use this book as a source of ideas, as a collection of C tips and idioms, or simply to learn more about ANSI C, from an experienced compiler writer. In sum, this book has a collection of useful ideas to help you master the fine art of ANSI C. It gathers all the information, hints, and guidelines together in one place and presents them for your enjoyment. So grab the back of an envelope, pull out your lucky coding pencil, settle back at a comfy terminal, and let the fun begin!

Some Light Relief—Tuning File Systems

Some aspects of C and UNIX are occasionally quite lighthearted. There's nothing wrong with well-placed whimsy. The IBM/Motorola/Apple PowerPC architecture has an E.I.E.I.O. instruction[1] that stands for "Enforce In-order Execution of I/O". In a similar spirit, there is a UNIX command, `tunefs`, that sophisticated system administrators use to change the dynamic parameters of a filesystem and improve the block layout on disk.

The on-line manual pages of the original `tunefs`, like all Berkeley commands, ended with a "Bugs" section. In this case, it read:

```
Bugs:
This program should work on mounted and active file systems, but it
doesn't. Because the superblock is not kept in the buffer cache, the
program will only take effect if it is run on dismounted file systems; if
run on the root file system, the system must be rebooted.
You can tune a file system, but you can't tune a fish.
```

Even better, the word-processor source had a comment in it, threatening anyone who removed that last phrase! It said:

```
Take this out and a UNIX Demon will dog your steps from now until the
time_t's wrap around.
```

1. Probably designed by some old farmer named McDonald.

When Sun, along with the rest of the world, changed to SVr4 UNIX, we lost this gem. The SVr4 manpages don't have a "Bugs" section—they renamed it "Notes" (does that fool anyone?). The "tuna fish" phrase disappeared, and the guilty party is probably being dogged by a UNIX demon to this day. Preferably lpd.

Programming Challenge

Computer Dating

When will the `time_t`'s wrap around?

Write a program to find out.

1. Look at the definition of `time_t`. This is in file `/usr/include/time.h`.
2. Code a program to place the highest value into a variable of type `time_t`, then pass it to `ctime()` to convert it into an ASCII string. Print the string. Note that `ctime` has nothing to do with the language C, it just means "convert time."

For how many years into the future does the anonymous technical writer who removed the comment have to worry about being dogged by a UNIX daemon? Amend your program to find out.

1. Obtain the current time by calling `time()`.
2. Call `difftime()` to obtain the number of seconds between now and the highest value of `time_t`.
3. Format that value into years, months, weeks, days, hours, and minutes. Print it.

Is it longer than your expected lifetime?

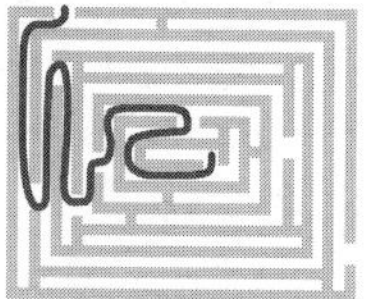

Programming Solution

Computer Dating

The results of this exercise will vary between PCs and UNIX systems, and will depend on the way time_t is stored. On Sun systems, this is just a typedef for long. Our first attempted solution is

```
#include <stdio.h>
#include <time.h>

int main() {
  time_t biggest = 0x7FFFFFFF;

  printf("biggest = %s \n", ctime(&biggest) );
  return 0;
}
```

This gives a result of:

```
   biggest = Mon Jan 18 19:14:07 2038
```

However, this is not the correct answer! The function `ctime()` converts its argument into *local* time, which will vary from Coordinated Universal Time (also known as Greenwich Mean Time), depending on where you are on the globe. California, where this book was written, is eight hours behind London, and several years ahead.

We should really use the `gmtime()` function to obtain the largest UTC time value. This function doesn't return a printable string, so we call `asctime()` to get this. Putting it all together, our revised program is

```
#include <stdio.h>
#include <time.h>

int main() {
  time_t biggest = 0x7FFFFFFF;
```

Computer Dating (Continued)

```
  printf("biggest = %s \n", asctime(gmtime(&biggest)) );
  return 0;
}
```

This gives a result of:

```
biggest = Tue Jan 19 03:14:07 2038
```

There! Squeezed another eight hours out of it!

But we're *still* not done. If you use the locale for New Zealand, you can get 13 more hours, assuming they use daylight savings time in the year 2038. They are on DST in January because they are in the southern hemisphere. New Zealand, because of its easternmost position with respect to time zones, holds the unhappy distinction of being the first country to encounter bugs triggered by particular dates.

Even simple-looking things can sometimes have a surprising twist in software. And anyone who thinks programming dates is easy to get right the first time probably hasn't done much of it.

C Through the Mists of Time 1

C is quirky, flawed, and an enormous success.

—Dennis Ritchie

the prehistory of C...the golden rule for compiler-writers... early experiences with C...the standard I/O library and C preprocessor... K&R C...the present day: ANSI C...it's nice, but is it standard?... the structure of the ANSI C standard...reading the ANSI C standard for fun, pleasure, and profit...how quiet is a "quiet change"?...some light relief—the implementation-defined effects of pragmas

The Prehistory of C

The story of C begins, paradoxically, with a failure. In 1969 the great Multics project—a joint venture between General Electric, MIT, and Bell Laboratories to build an operating system—was clearly in trouble. It was not only failing to deliver the promised fast and convenient on-line system, it was failing to deliver anything usable at all. Though the development team eventually got Multics creaking into action, they had fallen into the same tarpit that caught IBM with OS/360. They were trying to create an operating system that was much too big and to do it on hardware that was much too small. Multics is a treasure house of solved engineering problems, but it also paved the way for C to show that small is beautiful.

As the disenchanted Bell Labs staff withdrew from the Multics project, they looked around for other tasks. One researcher, Ken Thompson, was keen to work on another operating system, and made several proposals (all declined) to Bell management. While waiting on official approval, Thompson and co-worker Dennis Ritchie amused themselves porting Thompson's "Space Travel" software to a little-used PDP-7. Space Travel simulated the major bodies of the solar system, and displayed them on a graphics screen along with a space craft that could be piloted and landed on the various planets. At the same time, Thompson worked intensively on providing the PDP-7 with the rudiments of a new operating system, much simpler and lighter-weight than Multics. Everything was written in assembler language. Brian Kernighan coined the name "UNIX" in 1970, parodying the lessons now learned from Multics on what not to do. Figure 1-1 charts early C, UNIX, and associated hardware.

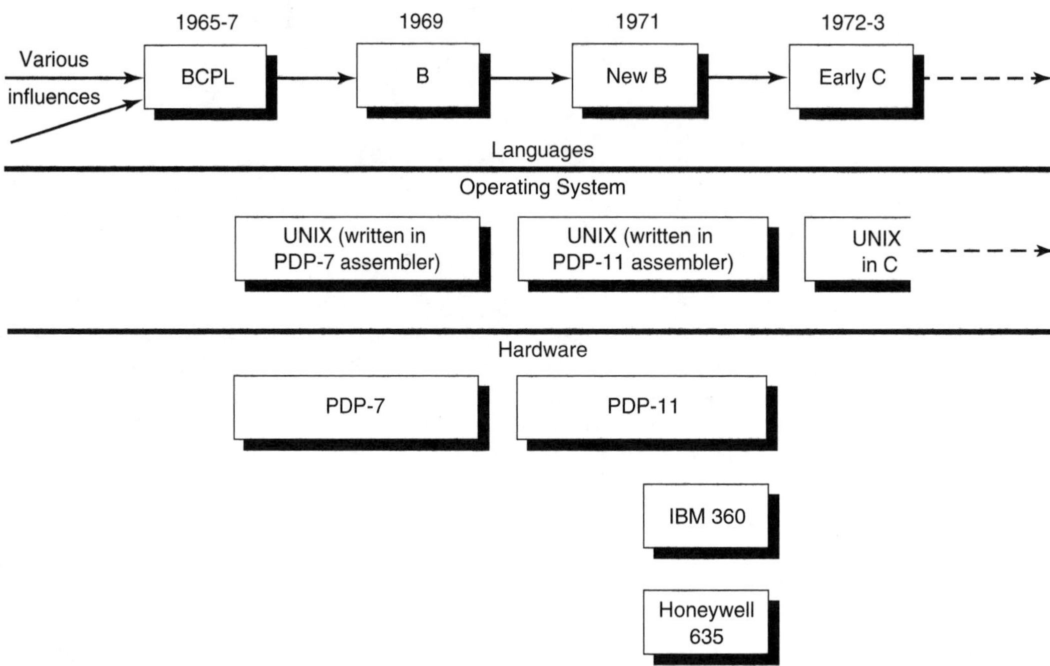

Figure 1-1 Early C, UNIX, and Associated Hardware

In this potential chicken-and-egg situation, UNIX definitely came well before C (and it's also why UNIX system time is measured in seconds since January 1, 1970—that's when time began). However, this is the story not of poultry, but of programming. Writing in assembler proved awkward; it took longer to code data structures, and it was harder to debug and understand. Thompson wanted the advantages of a high-level implementation language, but without the PL/I[1] performance and complexity problems that he had seen on Multics. After a brief and unsuccessful flirtation with Fortran, Thompson created the language B by simplifying the research language BCPL[2] so its interpreter would fit in the PDP-7's 8K word memory. B was never really successful; the hardware memory limits only provided room for an interpreter, not a compiler. The resulting slow performance prevented B from being used for systems programming of UNIX itself.

1. The difficulties involved in learning, using, and implementing PL/I led one programmer to pen this verse:
IBM had a PL/I / Its syntax worse than JOSS / And everywhere this language went / It was a total loss.
JOSS was an earlier language, also not noted for simplicity.

Software Dogma

The Golden Rule of Compiler-Writers:
Performance Is (almost) Everything.

Performance is almost everything in a compiler. There are other concerns: meaningful error messages, good documentation, and product support. These factors pale in comparison with the importance users place on raw speed. Compiler performance has two aspects: runtime performance (how fast the code runs) and compile time performance (how long it takes to generate code). Runtime performance usually dominates, except in development and student environments.

Many compiler optimizations cause longer compilation times but make run times much shorter. Other optimizations (such as dead code elimination, or omitting runtime checks) speed up both compile time and run time, as well as reducing memory use. The downside of aggressive optimization is the risk that invalid results may not be flagged. Optimizers are very careful only to do safe transformations, but programmers can trigger bad results by writing invalid code (e.g., referencing outside an array's bounds because they "know" that the desired variable is adjacent).

This is why performance is *almost* but not quite everything—if you don't get accurate results, then it's immaterial how fast you get them. Compiler-writers usually provide compiler options so each programmer can choose the desired optimizations. B's lack of success, until Dennis Ritchie created a high-performance compiled version called "New B," illustrates the golden rule for compiler-writers.

B simplified BCPL by omitting some features (such as nested procedures and some looping constructs) and carried forward the idea that array references should "decompose" into pointer-plus-offset references. B also retained the typelessness of BCPL; the only operand was a machine word. Thompson conceived the ++ and -- operators and added them to the B compiler on the PDP-7. The popular and captivating belief that they're in C because the PDP-11 featured corresponding auto-increment/decrement addressing modes

2. "BCPL: A Tool for Compiler Writing and System Programming," Martin Richards, Proc. AFIPS Spring Joint Computer Conference, 34 (1969), pp. 557-566. BCPL is not an acronym for the "Before C Programming Language", though the name *is* a happy coincidence. It is the "Basic Combined Programming Language"—"basic" in the sense of "no frills"—and it was developed by a combined effort of researchers at London University and Cambridge University in England. A BCPL implementation was available on Multics.

is wrong! Auto increment and decrement predate the PDP-11 hardware, though it is true that the C statement to copy a character in a string:

```
*p++ = *s++;
```

can be compiled particularly efficiently into the PDP-11 code:

```
movb (r0)+,(r1)+
```

leading some people to wrongly conclude that the former was created especially for the latter.

A typeless language proved to be unworkable when development switched in 1970 to the newly introduced PDP-11. This processor featured hardware support for datatypes of several different sizes, and the B language had no way to express this. Performance was also a problem, leading Thompson to reimplement the OS in PDP-11 assembler rather than B. Dennis Ritchie capitalized on the more powerful PDP-11 to create "New B," which solved both problems, multiple datatypes, and performance. "New B"—the name quickly evolved to "C"—was compiled rather than interpreted, and it introduced a type system, with each variable described in advance of use.

Early Experiences with C

The type system was added primarily to help the compiler-writer distinguish floats, doubles, and characters from words on the new PDP-11 hardware. This contrasts with languages like Pascal, where the purpose of the type system is to protect the programmer by restricting the valid operations on a data item. With its different philosophy, C rejects strong typing and permits the programmer to make assignments between objects of different types if desired. The type system was almost an afterthought, never rigorously evaluated or extensively tested for usability. To this day, many C programmers believe that "strong typing" just means pounding extra hard on the keyboard.

Many other features, besides the type system, were put in C for the C compiler-writer's benefit (and why not, since C compiler-writers were the chief customers for the first few years). Features of C that seem to have evolved with the compiler-writer in mind are:

- **Arrays start at 0 rather than 1.** Most people start counting at 1, rather than zero. Compiler-writers start with zero because we're used to thinking in terms of offsets. This is sometimes tough on non-compiler-writers; although `a[100]` appears in the definition of an array, you'd better not store any data at `a[100]`, since `a[0]` to `a[99]` is the extent of the array.

- **The fundamental C types map directly onto underlying hardware.** There is no built-in complex-number type, as in Fortran, for example. The compiler-writer does not have to invest any effort in supporting semantics that are not directly provided by the hardware. C didn't support floating-point numbers until the underlying hardware provided it.

- **The `auto` keyword is apparently useless.** It is only meaningful to a compiler-writer making an entry in a symbol table—it says *this storage is automatically allocated on entering the block* (as opposed to global static allocation, or dynamic allocation on the heap). Auto is irrelevant to other programmers, since you get it by default.

- **Array names in expressions "decay" into pointers.** It simplifies things to treat arrays as pointers. We don't need a complicated mechanism to treat them as a composite object, or suffer the inefficiency of copying everything when passing them to a function. But don't make the mistake of thinking arrays and pointers are always equivalent; more about this in Chapter 4.

- **Floating-point expressions were expanded to double-length-precision everywhere.** Although this is no longer true in ANSI C, originally real number constants were always doubles, and float variables were always converted to double in all expressions. The reason, though we've never seen it appear in print, had to do with PDP-11 floating-point hardware. First, conversion from float to double on a PDP-11 or a VAX is really cheap: just append an extra word of zeros. To convert back, just ignore the second word. Then understand that some PDP-11 floating-point hardware had a mode bit, so it would do either all single-precision or all double-precision arithmetic, but to switch between the two you had to change modes.

  Since most early UNIX programs weren't floating-point-intensive, it was easier to put the box in double-precision mode and leave it there than for the compiler-writer to try to keep track of it!

- **No nested functions (functions contained inside other functions).** This simplifies the compiler and slightly speeds up the runtime organization of C programs. The exact mechanism is described in Chapter 6, "Poetry in Motion: Runtime Data Structures."

- **The `register` keyword.** This keyword gave the compiler-writer a clue about what variables the programmer thought were "hot" (frequently referenced), and hence could usefully be kept in registers. It turns out to be a mistake. You get better code if the compiler does the work of allocating registers for individual uses of a variable, rather than reserving them for its entire lifetime at declaration. Having a `register` keyword simplifies the compiler by transferring this burden to the programmer.

There were plenty of other C features invented for the convenience of the C compiler-writer, too. Of itself this is not necessarily a bad thing; it greatly simplified the language, and by shunning complicated semantics (e.g., generics or tasking in Ada; string handling in PL/I; templates or multiple inheritance in C++) it made C much easier to learn and to implement, and gave faster performance.

Unlike most other programming languages, C had a lengthy evolution and grew through many intermediate shapes before reaching its present form. It has evolved through years of practical use into a language that is tried and tested. The first C compiler appeared circa 1972, over 20 years ago now. As the underlying UNIX system grew in popularity, so C was carried with it. Its emphasis on low-level operations that were directly supported by the hardware brought speed and portability, in turn helping to spread UNIX in a benign cycle.

The Standard I/O Library and C Preprocessor

The functionality left out of the C compiler had to show up somewhere; in C's case it appears at runtime, either in application code or in the runtime library. In many other languages, the compiler plants code to call runtime support implicitly, so the programmer does not need to worry about it, but almost all the routines in the C library must be explicitly called. In C (when needed) the programmer must, for example, manage dynamic memory use, program variable-size arrays, test array bounds, and carry out range checks for him or herself.

Similarly, I/O was originally not defined within C; instead it was provided by library routines, which in practice have become a standardized facility. The portable I/O library was written by Mike Lesk[3] and first appeared around 1972 on all three existing hardware platforms. Practical experience showed that performance wasn't up to expectations, so the library was tuned and slimmed down to become the standard I/O library.

The C preprocessor, also added about this time at the suggestion of Alan Snyder, fulfilled three main purposes:

- String replacement, of the form "change all *foo* to *baz*", often to provide a symbolic name for a constant.
- Source file inclusion (as pioneered in BCPL). Common declarations could be separated out into a header file, and made available to a range of source files. Though the ".h" convention was adopted for the extension of header files, unhappily no convention arose for relating the header file to the object library that contained the corresponding code.

3. It was Michael who later expressed the hilariously ironic rule of thumb that "designing the system so that the manual will be as short as possible minimizes learning effort." (Datamation, November 1981, p.146). Several comments come to mind, of which "Bwaa ha ha!" is probably the one that minimizes learning effort.

- Expansion of general code templates. Unlike a function, the same macro argument can take different types on successive calls (macro actual arguments are just slotted unchanged into the output). This feature was added later than the first two, and sits a little awkwardly on C. White space makes a big difference to this kind of macro expansion.

```
#define a(y) a_expanded(y)
a(x);
```

expands into:

```
a_expanded(x);
```

However,

```
#define a (y)   a_expanded (y)
a(x);
```

is transformed into:

```
(y)   a_expanded (y)(x);
```

Not even close to being the same thing. The macro processor could conceivably use curly braces like the rest of C to indicate tokens grouped in a block, but it does not.

There's no extensive discussion of the C preprocessor here; this reflects the view that the only appropriate use of the preprocessor is for macros that don't require extensive discussion. C++ takes this a step further, introducing several conventions designed to make the preprocessor completely unnecessary.

Software Dogma

C Is Not Algol

Writing the UNIX Version 7 shell (command interpreter) at Bell Labs in the late 1970's, Steve Bourne decided to use the C preprocessor to make C a little more like Algol-68. Earlier at Cambridge University in England, Steve had written an Algol-68 compiler, and found it easier to debug code that had explicit "end statement" cues, such as `if ... fi` or `case ... esac`. Steve thought it wasn't easy enough to tell by looking at a "`}`" what it matches. Accordingly, he set up many preprocessor definitions:

```
#define STRING char *
#define IF if(
#define THEN ){
#define ELSE } else {
#define FI ;}
#define WHILE while (
#define DO ){
#define OD ;}
#define INT int
#define BEGIN {
#define END }
```

This enabled him to code the shell using code like this:

```
INT  compare(s1, s2)
     STRING s1;
     STRING s2;
BEGIN
     WHILE *s1++ == *s2
     DO IF *s2++ == 0
          THEN return(0);
          FI
     OD
     return(*--s1 - *s2);
END
```

C Is Not Algol (Continued)

Now let's look at that again, in C this time:

```
int compare(s1, s2)
        char * s1, *s2;
{
        while (*s1++ == *s2) {
                if (*s2++ == 0) return (0);
        }
        return (*--s1 - *s2);
}
```

This Algol-68 dialect achieved legendary status as the Bourne shell permeated far beyond Bell Labs, and it vexed some C programmers. They complained that the dialect made it much harder for other people to maintain the code. The BSD 4.3 Bourne shell (kept in /bin/sh) is written in the Algol subset to this day!

I've got a special reason to grouse about the Bourne shell—it's my desk that the bugs reported against it land on! Then I assign them to Sam! And we do see our share of bugs: the shell doesn't use malloc, but rather does its own heap storage management using sbrk. Maintenance on software like this too often introduces a new bug for every two it solves. Steve explained that the custom memory allocator was done for efficiency in string-handling, and that he never expected anyone except himself to see the code.

The Bournegol C dialect actually inspired The International Obfuscated C Code Competition, a whimsical contest in which programmers try to outdo each other in inventing mysterious and confusing programs (more about this competition later).

Macro use is best confined to naming literal constants, and providing shorthand for a few well-chosen constructs. Define the macro name all in capitals so that, in use, it's instantly clear it's not a function call. Shun any use of the C preprocessor that modifies the underlying language so that it's no longer C.

K&R C

By the mid 1970's the language was recognizably the C we know and love today. Further refinements took place, mostly tidying up details (like allowing functions to return structure values) or extending the basic types to match new hardware (like adding the keywords `unsigned` and `long`). In 1978 Steve Johnson wrote *pcc*, the portable C compiler. The source was made available outside Bell Labs, and it was very widely ported, forming a common basis for an entire generation of C compilers. The evolutionary path up to the present day is shown in Figure 1-2.

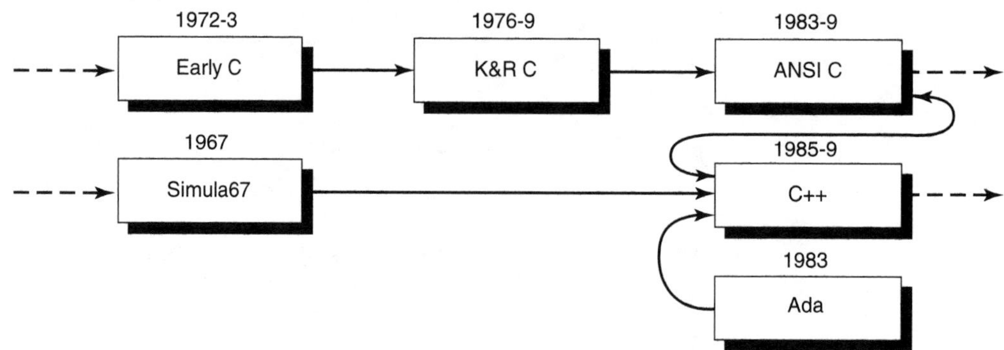

Figure 1-2 Later C

Software Dogma

An Unusual Bug

One feature C inherited from Algol-68 was the assignment operator. This allows a repeated operand to be written once only instead of twice, giving a clue to the code generator that operand addressing can be similarly thrifty. An example of this is writing `b+=3` as an abbreviation for `b=b+3`. Assignment operators were originally written with assignment first, not the operator, like this: `b=+3`. A quirk in B's lexical analyzer made it simpler to implement as *=op* rather than *op=* as it is today. This form was confusing, as it was too easy to mix up

```
b=-3; /* subtract 3 from b */
```

and

```
b= -3; /* assign -3 to b */
```

The feature was therefore changed to its present ordering. As part of the change, the code formatter `indent` was modified to recognize the obsolete form of assignment operator and swap it round to operator assignment. This was very bad judgement indeed; no formatter should ever change anything except the white space in a program. Unhappily, two things happened. The programmer introduced a bug, in that almost anything (that wasn't a variable) that appeared after an assignment was swapped in position.

If you were "lucky" it would be something that would cause a syntax error, like

```
epsilon=.0001;
```

being swapped into

```
epsilon.=0001;
```

An Unusual Bug (Continued)

But a source statement like

```
valve=!open; /* valve is set to logical negation of open */
```

would be silently transmogrified into

```
valve!=open; /* valve is compared for inequality to open */
```

which compiled fine, but did not change the value of `valve`.

The second thing that happened was that the bug lurked undetected. It was easy to work around by inserting a space after the assignment, so as the obsolete form of assignment operator declined in use, people just forgot that indent had been kludged up to "improve" it. The indent bug persisted in some implementations up until the mid-1980's. Highly pernicious!

In 1978 the classic C bible, *The C Programming Language,* was published. By popular acclamation, honoring authors Brian Kernighan and Dennis Ritchie, the name "K&R C" was applied to this version of the language. The publisher estimated that about a thousand copies would be sold; to date (1994) the figure is over one and a half million (see Figure 1-3). C is one of the most successful programming languages of the last two decades, perhaps the most successful. But as the language spread, the temptation to diverge into dialects grew.

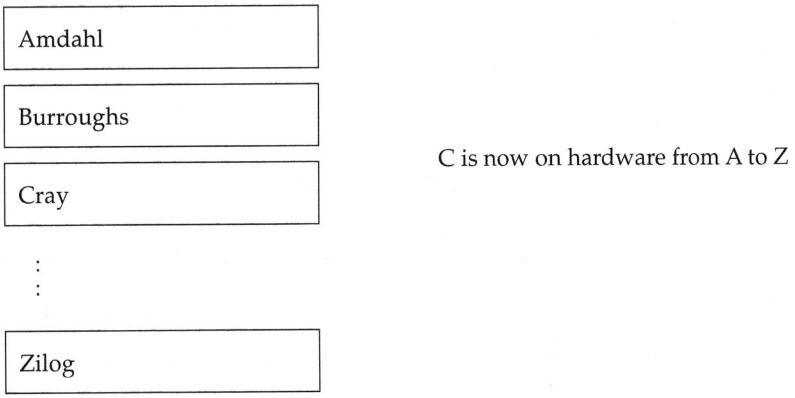

Figure 1-3 Like Elvis, C is Everywhere

The Present Day: ANSI C

By the early 1980's, C had become widely used throughout the industry, but with many different implementations and changes. The discovery by PC implementors of C's advantages over BASIC provided a fresh boost. Microsoft had an implementation for the IBM

PC which introduced new keywords (`far`, `near`, etc.) to help pointers to cope with the irregular architecture of the Intel 80x86 chip. As many other non-pcc-based implementations arose, C threatened to go the way of BASIC and evolve into an ever-diverging family of loosely related languages.

It was clear that a formal language standard was needed. Fortunately, there was much precedent in this area—all successful programming languages are eventually standardized. However, the problem with standards manuals is that they only make sense if you already know what they mean. If people write them in English, the more precise they try to be, the longer, duller and more obscure they become. If they write them using mathematical notation to define the language, the manuals become inaccessible to too many people.

Over the years, the manuals that define programming language standards have become longer, but no easier to understand. The Algol-60 Reference Definition was only 18 pages long for a language of comparable complexity to C; Pascal was described in 35 pages. Kernighan and Ritchie took 40 pages for their original report on C; while this left several holes, it was adequate for many implementors. ANSI C is defined in a fat manual over 200 pages long. This book is, in part, a description of practical use that lightens and expands on the occasionally opaque text in the ANSI Standard document.

In 1983 a C working group formed under the auspices of the American National Standards Institute. Most of the process revolved around identifying common features, but there were also changes and significant new features introduced. The `far` and `near` keywords were argued over at great length, but ultimately did not make it into the mildly UNIX-centric ANSI standard. Even though there are more than 50 million PC's out there, and it is by far the most widely used platform for C implementors, it was (rightly in our view) felt undesirable to mutate the language to cope with the limitations of one specific architecture.

Handy Heuristic

Which Version of C to Use?

At this point, anyone learning or using C should be working with ANSI C, not K&R C.

The language standard draft was finally adopted by ANSI in December 1989. The international standards organization ISO then adopted the ANSI C standard (unhappily removing the very useful "Rationale" section and making trivial—but very annoying—formatting and paragraph numbering changes). ISO, as an international body, is technically the senior organization, so early in 1990 ANSI readopted ISO C (again excluding the Rationale) back in place of its own version. In principle, therefore, we should say that the C standard adopted by ANSI is ISO C, and we should refer to the language as ISO C. The Rationale is a useful text that greatly helps in understanding the standard, and it's published as a separate document.[4]

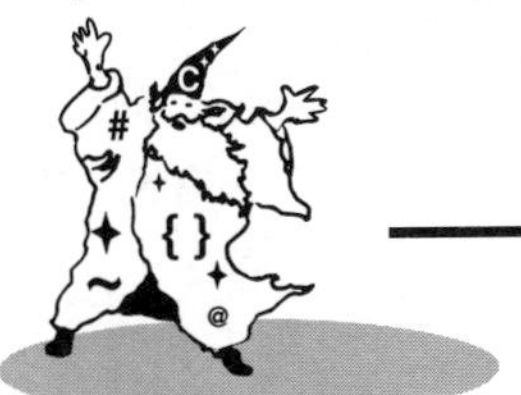

Handy Heuristic

Where to Get a Copy of the C Standard

The official name of the standard for C is: ISO/IEC 9899-1990. ISO/IEC is the International Organization for Standardization International Electrotechnical Commission. The standards bodies sell it for around $130.00. In the U.S. you can get a copy of the standard by writing to:

American National Standards Institute
11 West 42nd Street
New York, NY 10036
Tel. (212) 642-4900

Outside the U.S. you can get a copy by writing to:

ISO Sales
Case postale 56
CH-1211 Genève 20
Switzerland

Be sure to specify the English language edition.

Another source is to purchase the book *The Annotated ANSI C Standard* by Herbert Schildt, (New York, Osborne McGraw-Hill, 1993). This contains a photographically reduced, but complete, copy of the standard. Two other advantages of the Schildt book are that at $39.95 it is less than one-third the price charged by the standards bodies, and it is available from your local bookstore which, unlike ANSI or ISO, has probably heard of the twentieth century, and will take phone orders using credit cards.

In practice, the term "ANSI C" was widely used even before there was an ISO Working Group 14 dedicated to C. It is also appropriate, because the ISO working group left the technical development of the initial standard in the hands of ANSI committee X3J11.

---

4. The ANSI C Rationale (only) is available for free by anonymous ftp from the site ftp.uu.net, in directory /doc/standards/ansi/X3.159-1989/.
(If you're not familiar with anonymous ftp, run, don't walk, to your nearest bookstore and buy a book on Internet, before you become <insert lame driving metaphor of choice> on the Information Highway.)
The Rationale has also been published as a book, *ANSI C Rationale*, New Jersey, Silicon Press, 1990. The ANSI C standard itself is not available by ftp anywhere because ANSI derives an important part of its revenue from the sale of printed standards.

Toward the end, ISO WG14 and X3J11 collaborated to resolve technical issues and to ensure that the resulting standard was acceptable to both groups. In fact, there was a year's delay at the end, caused by amending the draft standard to cover international issues such as wide characters and locales.

It remains ANSI C to anyone who has been following it for a few years. Having arrived at this good thing, everyone wanted to endorse the C standard. ANSI C is also a European standard (CEN 29899) and an X/Open standard. ANSI C was adopted as a Federal Information Processing Standard, FIPS 160, issued by the National Institute of Standards and Technology in March 1991, and updated on August 24, 1992. Work on C continues—there is talk of adding a complex number type to C.

It's Nice, but Is It Standard?

Save a tree—disband an ISO working group today.

—Anonymous

The ANSI C standard is unique in several interesting ways. It defines the following terms, describing characteristics of an implementation. A knowledge of these terms will aid in understanding what is and isn't acceptable in the language. The first two are concerned with unportable code; the next two deal with bad code; and the last two are about portable code.

Unportable Code:

implementation-defined—The compiler-writer chooses what happens, and has to document it.

Example: whether the sign bit is propagated, when shifting an int right.

unspecified—The behavior for something correct, on which the standard does not impose any requirements.

Example: the order of argument evaluation.

Bad Code:

undefined—The behavior for something incorrect, on which the standard does not impose any requirements. Anything is allowed to happen, from nothing, to a warning message to program termination, to CPU meltdown, to launching nuclear missiles (assuming you have the correct hardware option installed).

Example: what happens when a signed integer overflows.

a constraint—This is a restriction or requirement that must be obeyed. If you don't, your program behavior becomes *undefined* in the sense above. Now here's an amazing thing: it's easy to tell if something is a constraint or not, because each topic in the standard has a subparagraph labelled "Constraints" that lists them all. Now here's an even more amazing thing: the standard specifies[5] that compilers only have to produce error messages for violations of syntax and constraints! This means that any semantic rule that's not in a constraints subsection can be broken, and since the behavior is *undefined,* the compiler is free to do anything and doesn't even have to warn you about it!

> Example: the operands of the `%` operator must have integral type. So using a non-integral type with `%` must cause a diagnostic.
>
> Example of a rule that is not a constraint: all identifiers declared in the C standard header files are reserved for the implementation, so you may not declare a function called `malloc()` because a standard header file already has a function of that name. But since this is not a constraint, the rule can be broken, and the compiler doesn't have to warn you! More about this in the section on "interpositioning" in Chapter 5.

Software Dogma

Undefined Behavior Causes CPU Meltdown in IBM PC's!

The suggestion of undefined software behavior causing CPU meltdown isn't as farfetched as it first appears.

The original IBM PC monitor operated at a horizontal scan rate provided by the video controller chip. The flyback transformer (the gadget that produces the high voltage needed to accelerate the electrons to light up the phosphors on the monitor) relied on this being a reasonable frequency.

However, it was possible, in software, to set the video chip scan rate to zero, thus feeding a constant voltage into the primary side of the transformer. It then acted as a resistor, and dissipated its power as heat rather than transforming it up onto the screen. This burned the monitor out in seconds. Voilà: undefined software behavior causes system meltdown!

---

5. In paragraph 5.1.1.3, "Diagnostics", if you must know. Being a language standard, it doesn't say something simple like *you've got to flag at least one error in an incorrect program.* It says something grander that looks like it was drawn up by a team of corporate lawyers being paid by the word, namely, *a conforming implementation shall*[*] *produce at least one diagnostic message (identified in an implementation-dependent manner) for every translation unit that contains a violation of any syntax rule or constraint. Diagnostic messages need not be produced in other circumstances.*

* Useful rule from Brian Scearce[†]—if you hear a programmer say "shall" he or she is quoting from a standard.

† Inventor of the nested footnote.

Portable Code:

strictly-conforming—A *strictly-conforming* program is one that:

- only uses *specified* features.
- doesn't exceed any implementation-defined limit.
- has no output that depends on *implementation-defined, unspecified,* or *undefined* features.

This was intended to describe maximally portable programs, which will always produce the identical output whatever they are run on. In fact, it is not a very interesting class because it is so small compared to the universe of conforming programs. For example, the following program is not strictly conforming:

```
#include <limits.h>
#include <stdio.h>
int main() { (void) printf("biggest int is %d", INT_MAX); return 0;}

/* not strictly conforming: implementation-defined output! */
```

For the rest of this book, we usually don't try to make the example programs be strictly conforming. It clutters up the text, and makes it harder to see the specific point under discussion. Program portability is valuable, so you should always put the necessary casts, return values, and so on in your real-world code.

conforming—A conforming program can depend on the nonportable features of an implementation. So a program is *conforming* with respect to a specific implementation, and the same program may be nonconforming using a different compiler. It can have extensions, but not extensions that alter the behavior of a strictly-conforming program. This rule is not a constraint, however, so don't expect the compiler to warn you about violations that render your program nonconforming!

The program example above is conforming.

Translation Limits

The ANSI C standard actually specifies lower limits on the sizes of programs that must successfully translate. These are specified in paragraph 5.2.4.1. Most languages say how many characters can be in a dataname, and some languages stipulate what limit is acceptable for the maximum number of array dimensions. But specifying lower bounds on the sizes of various other features is unusual, not to say unique in a programming language standard. Members of the standardization committee have commented that it was meant to guide the choice of minimum acceptable sizes.

Every ANSI C compiler is required to support at least:

- 31 parameters in a function definition
- 31 arguments in a function call
- 509 characters in a source line
- 32 levels of nested parentheses in an expression
- The maximum value of `long int` can't be any less than 2,147,483,647, (i.e., long integers are at least 32 bits).

and so on. Furthermore, a conforming compiler must compile and execute a program in which all of the limits are tested at once. A surprising thing is that these "required" limits are not actually constraints—so a compiler can choke on them without issuing an error message.

Compiler limits are usually a "quality of implementation" issue; their inclusion in ANSI C is an implicit acknowledgment that it will be easier to port code if definite expectations for some capacities are set for all implementations. Of course, a really good implementation won't have any preset limits, just those imposed by external factors like available memory or disk. This can be done by using linked lists, or dynamically expanding the size of tables when necessary (a technique explained in Chapter 10).

The Structure of the ANSI C Standard

It's instructive to make a quick diversion into the provenance and content of the ANSI C standard. The ANSI C standard has four main sections:

Section 4: An introduction and definition of terminology (5 pages).

Section 5: Environment (13 pages). This covers the system that surrounds and supports C, including what happens on program start-up, on termination, and with signals and floating-point operations. Translator lower limits and character set information are also given.

Section 6: The C language (78 pages) This part of the standard is based on Dennis Ritchie's classic "The C Reference Manual" which appeared in several publications, including Appendix A of *The C Programming Language*. If you compare the Standard and the Appendix, you can see most headings are the same, and in the same order. The topics in the standard have a more rigid format, however, that looks like Figure 1-4 (empty subparagraphs are simply omitted).

General Form of a Paragraph in the ANSI C Standard	Example Paragraph in the ANSI C Standard
Paragraph-Number Topic	**6.4 Constant Expressions**
Syntax *Syntax diagrams*	**Syntax** constant expression: conditional expression:
Description *A general description of the feature*	**Description** A *constant expression* can be evaluated during translation rather than runtime, and accordingly may be used in any place that a constant may be.
Constraints *The compiler must emit an error message if any rules in here are broken*	**Constraints** Constant expressions shall not contain assignment, increment, decrement, function-call, or comma operators, except when they are contained within the operand of `sizeof` operator. Each constant expression shall evaluate to a constant that is within the range of representable values for its type.
Semantics *What the feature means or does*	**Semantics** An expression that evaluates to a constant is required in several contexts. If a floating expression is evaluated in the translation environment, the arithmetic precision and...
Example *A fragment of code showing the feature*	...

Figure 1-4 How a Paragraph in the ANSI C Standard Looks

The original Appendix is only 40 pages, while this section of the standard is twice as long.

Section 7: The C runtime library (81 pages). This is a list of the library calls that a conforming implementation must provide—the standard services and routines to carry out essential or helpful functions. The ANSI C standard's section 7 on the C runtime library is based on the /usr/group 1984 standard, with the UNIX-specific parts removed. "/usr/group" started life as an international user group for UNIX. In 1989 it was renamed "UniForum", and is now a nonprofit trade association dedicated to the promotion of the UNIX operating system.

UniForum's success in defining UNIX from a behavioral perspective encouraged many related initiatives, including the X/Open portability guides (version 4, XPG/4 came out in October 1992), IEEE POSIX 1003, the System V Interface Definition, and the ANSI C libraries. Everyone coordinated with the ANSI C working group to ensure that all their draft standards were mutually consistent. Thank heaven.

The ANSI C standard also features some useful appendices:

Appendix F: Common warning messages. Some popular situations for which diagnostic messages are not required, but when it is usually helpful to generate them nonetheless.

Appendix G: Portability issues. Some general advice on portability, collected into one place from throughout the standard. It includes information on behavior that is unspecified, undefined, and implementation-defined.

Software Dogma

Standards Are Set in Concrete, Even the Mistakes

Just because it's written down in an international standard doesn't mean that it's complete, consistent, or even correct. The IEEE POSIX 1003.1-1988 standard (it's an OS standard that defines UNIX-like behavior) has this fun contradiction:

"[A pathname] ... consists of at most PATH_MAX bytes, including the terminating null character."—section 2.3

"PATH_MAX is the maximum number of bytes in a pathname (not a string length; count excludes a terminating null)."—section 2.9.5

So PATH_MAX bytes both *includes* and *does not include* the terminating null!

An interpretation was requested, and the answer came back (IEEE Std 1003.1-1988/INT, 1992 Edition, Interpretation number: 15, p. 36) that it was an inconsistency and both can be right (which is pretty strange, since the whole point is that both *can't* be right).

The problem arose because a change at the draft stage wasn't propagated to all occurrences of the wording. The standards process is formal and rigid, so it cannot be fixed until an update is approved by a balloting group.

This kind of error also appears in the C standard in the very first footnote, which refers to the accompanying Rationale document. In fact, the Rationale no longer accompanies the C Standard—it was deleted when ownership of the standard moved to ISO.

Handy Heuristic

Differences between K&R C and ANSI C

Rest assured that if you know K&R C, then you already know 90% of ANSI C. The differences between ANSI C and K&R C fall into four broad categories, listed below in order of importance:

1. The first category contains things that are new, very different, and important. The only feature in this class is the prototype—writing the parameter types as part of the function declaration. Prototypes make it easy for a compiler to check function use with definition.

2. The second category is new keywords. Several keywords were officially added: `enum` for enumerated types (first seen in late versions of pcc), `const`, `volatile`, `signed`, `void`, along with their associated semantics. The never-used `entry` keyword that found its way into C, apparently by oversight, has been retired.

3. The third category is that of "quiet changes"—some feature that still compiles, but now has a slightly different meaning. There are many of these, but they are mostly not very important, and can be ignored until you push the boundaries and actually stumble across one of them. For example, now that the preprocessing rules are more tightly defined, there's a new rule that adjacent string literals are concatenated.

4. The final category is everything else, including things that were argued over interminably while the language was being standardized, but that you will almost certainly never encounter in practice, for example, token-pasting or trigraphs. (Trigraphs are a way to use three characters to express a single character that a particularly inadequate computer might not have in its character set. Just as the digraph `\t` represents "tab", so the trigraph `??<` represents "open curly brace".)

The most important new feature was "prototypes", adopted from C++. Prototypes are an extension of function declarations so that not just the name and return type are known, but also all the parameter types, allowing the compiler to check for consistency between parameter use and declaration. "Prototype" is not a very descriptive term for "a function name with all its arguments"; it would have been more meaningful to call it a "function signature", or a "function specification" as Ada does.

Software Dogma

The Protocol of Prototypes

The purpose of prototypes is to include some information on parameter types (rather than merely giving the function name and return value type) when we make a forward declaration of a function. The compiler can thus check the types of arguments in a function call against the way the parameters were defined. In K&R C, this check was deferred till link time or, more usually, omitted entirely. Instead of

```
char * strcpy();
```

declarations in header files now look like this:

```
char * strcpy(char *dst, const char *src);
```

You can also omit the names of the parameters, leaving only the types:

```
char * strcpy(char * , const char * );
```

Don't omit the parameter names. Although the compiler doesn't check these, they often convey extra semantic information to the programmer. Similarly, the definition of the function has changed from

```
char * strcpy(dst, src)
      char *dst, *src;
{ ... }
```

to

```
char * strcpy(char *dst, const char *src) /* note no semi-colon! */
{ ... }
```

Instead of being ended with a semicolon, the function header is now directly followed by a single compound statement comprising the body of the function.

Prototype everything new you write and ensure the prototype is in scope for every call. Don't go back to prototype your old K&R code, unless you take into account the default type promotions—more about this in Chapter 8.

Having all these different terms for the same thing can be a little mystifying. It's rather like the way drugs have at least three names: the chemical name, the manufacturer's brand name, and the street name.

Reading the ANSI C Standard for Fun, Pleasure, and Profit

Sometimes it takes considerable concentration to read the ANSI C Standard and obtain an answer from it. A sales engineer sent the following piece of code into the compiler group at Sun as a test case.

```
1 foo(const char **p) { }
2
3 main(int argc, char **argv)
4 {
5         foo(argv);
6 }
```

If you try compiling it, you'll notice that the compiler issues a warning message, saying:

```
line 5: warning: argument is incompatible with prototype
```

The submitter of the code wanted to know why the warning message was generated, and what part of the ANSI C Standard mandated this. After all, he reasoned,

argument `char *s` matches parameter `const char *p`

This is seen throughout all library string functions.

So doesn't argument `char **argv` match parameter `const char **p` ?

The answer is no, it does not. It took a little while to answer this question, and it's educational in more than one sense, to see the process of obtaining the answer. The analysis was carried out by one of Sun's "language lawyers,"[6] and it runs like this:

The Constraints portion of Section 6.3.2.2 of the ANSI C Standard includes the phrase:

> Each argument shall have a type such that its value may be assigned to an object with the unqualified version of the type of its corresponding parameter.

This says that argument passing is supposed to behave like assignment.

Thus, a diagnostic message must be produced unless an object of type `const char **` may be assigned a value of type `char **`. To find out whether this assignment is legal,

6. *The New Hacker's Dictionary* defines a language lawyer as "a person who will show you the five sentences scattered through a 200-plus-page manual that together imply the answer to your question 'if only you had thought to look there.'" Yep! That's exactly what happened in this case.

flip to the section on simple assignment, Section 6.3.16.1, which includes the following constraint:

> One of the following shall hold:...
>
> - Both operands are pointers to qualified or unqualified versions of compatible types, and the type pointed to by the left has all the qualifiers of the type pointed to by the right.

It is this condition that makes a call with a `char *` argument corresponding to a `const char *` parameter legal (as seen throughout the string routines in the C library). This is legal because in the code

```
char * cp;
const char *ccp;
ccp = cp;
```

- The left operand is a pointer to "char qualified by const".
- The right operand is a pointer to "char" unqualified.
- The type `char` is a compatible type with `char`, and the type pointed to by the left operand has all the qualifiers of the type pointed to by the right operand (none), plus one of its own (const).

Note that the assignment cannot be made the other way around. Try it if you don't believe me.

```
cp = ccp;    /* results in a compilation warning */
```

Does Section 6.3.16.1 also make a call with a `char **` argument corresponding to a `const char **` parameter legal? It does not.

The Examples portion of Section 6.1.2.5 states:

> The type designated "const float *" is not a qualified type—its type is "pointer to const-qualified float" and is a pointer to a qualified type.

Analogously, `const char **` denotes a pointer to an unqualified type. Its type is a pointer to a pointer to a qualified type.

Since the types `char **` and `const char **` are both pointers to unqualified types that are not the same type, they are not compatible types. Therefore, a call with an argument of type `char **` corresponding to a parameter of type `const char **` is not allowed. Therefore, the constraint given in Section 6.3.2.2 is violated, and a diagnostic message must be produced.

This is a subtle point to grasp. Another way of looking at it is to note that:

- the left operand has type FOO2—a pointer to FOO, where FOO is an unqualified pointer to a character qualified by the const qualifier, and
- the right operand has type BAZ2—a pointer to BAZ, where BAZ is an unqualified pointer to a character with no qualifiers.

FOO and BAZ are compatible types, but FOO2 and BAZ2 differ other than in qualification of the thing *immediately* pointed to and are therefore not compatible types; therefore the left and right operands are unqualified pointers to types that are not compatible. Compatibility of pointer types is not transitive. Therefore, the assignment or function call is not permitted. However, note that the restriction serves mainly to annoy and confuse users. The assignment is currently allowed in C++ translators based on cfront (though that might change).

Handy Heuristic

Const Isn't

The keyword `const` doesn't turn a variable into a constant! A symbol with the `const` qualifier merely means that the symbol cannot be used for assignment. This makes the value read-only *through that symbol*; it does not prevent the value from being modified through some other means internal (or even external) to the program. It is pretty much useful only for qualifying a pointer parameter, to indicate that this function will not change the data that argument points to, but other functions may. This is perhaps the most common use of `const` in C and C++.

A `const` can be used for data, like so:

```
const int limit = 10;
```

and it acts somewhat as in other languages. When you add pointers into the equation, things get a little rough:

```
const int * limitp = &limit;
int i=27;
limitp = &i;
```

This says that `limitp` is a pointer to a constant integer. The pointer cannot be used to change the integer; however, the pointer itself can be given a different value at any time. It will then point to a different location and dereferencing it will yield a different value!

Const Isn't (Continued)

The combination of `const` and `*` is usually only used to simulate call-by-value for array parameters. It says, "I am giving you a pointer to this thing, but you may not change it." This idiom is similar to the most frequent use of `void *`. Although that could theoretically be used in any number of circumstances, it's usually restricted to converting pointers from one type to another.

Analogously, you can take the address of a constant variable, and, well, perhaps I had better not put ideas into people's heads. As Ken Thompson pointed out, "The `const` keyword only confuses library interfaces with the hope of catching some rare errors." In retrospect, the `const` keyword would have been better named `readonly`.

True, this whole area in the standard appears to have been rendered into English from Urdu via Danish by translators who had only a passing familiarity with any of these tongues, but the standards committee was having such a good time that it seemed a pity to ruin their fun by asking for some simpler, clearer rules.

We felt that a lot of people would have questions in the future, and not all of them would want to follow the process of reasoning shown above. So we changed the Sun ANSI C compiler to print out more information about what it found incompatible. The full message now says:

```
Line 6: warning: argument #1 is incompatible with prototype:
  prototype: pointer to pointer to const char : "barf.c", line 1
  argument : pointer to pointer to char
```

Even if a programmer doesn't understand *why,* he or she will now know *what* is incompatible.

How Quiet is a "Quiet Change"?

Not all the changes in the standard stick out as much as prototypes. ANSI C made a number of other changes, usually aimed at making the language more reliable. For instance, the "usual arithmetic conversions" changed between ye olde originale K&R C and ANSI C. Thus, where Kernighan and Ritchie say something like:

> Section 6.6 Arithmetic Conversions
>
> A great many operators cause conversions and yield result types in a similar way. This pattern will be called the "usual arithmetic conversions."

First, any operands of type char or short are converted to int, and any of type float are converted to double. Then if either operand is double, the other is converted to double and that is the type of the result. Otherwise, if either operand is long, the other is converted to long and that is the type of the result. Otherwise, if either operand is unsigned, the other is converted to unsigned and that is the type of the result. Otherwise, both operands must be int, and that is the type of the result.

The ANSI C manual has closed the loopholes by rewriting this as:

Section 6.2.1.1 Characters and Integers (the integral promotions)

A char, a short int, or an int bit-field, or their signed or unsigned varieties, or an enumeration type, may be used in an expression wherever an int or unsigned int may be used. If an int can represent all the values of the original type, the value is converted to an int; otherwise it is converted to an unsigned int. These are called the integral promotions.

Section 6.2.1.5 Usual Arithmetic Conversions

Many binary operators that expect operands of arithmetic type cause conversions and yield result types in a similar way. The purpose is to yield a common type, which is also the type of the result. This pattern is called the "usual arithmetic conversions."

First, if either operand has type long double, the other operand is converted to long double. Otherwise, if either operand has type double, the other operand is converted to double. Otherwise, if either operand has type float, the other operand is converted to float. Otherwise the integral promotions [refer to section 6.2.1.1 for the integral promotions] are performed on both operands. Then the following rules are applied.

If either operand has type unsigned long int, the other operand is converted to unsigned long int. Otherwise, if one operand has type long int and the other has type unsigned int, if a long int can represent all values of an unsigned int the operand of type unsigned int is converted to long int; if a long int cannot represent all the values of an unsigned int, both operands are converted to unsigned long int. Otherwise, if either operand has type long int, the other operand is converted to long int. Otherwise, if either operand has type unsigned int, the other operand is converted to unsigned int. Otherwise, both operands have type int.

The values of floating operands and of the results of floating expressions may be represented in greater precision and range than that required by the type; the types are not changed thereby.

In English (complete with loopholes and lack of precision), the ANSI C version would mean something like:

Operands with different types get converted when you do arithmetic. Everything is converted to the type of the floatiest, longest operand, signed if possible without losing bits.

The *unsigned preserving* approach (K&R C) says that when an unsigned type mixes with an int or smaller signed type, the result is an unsigned type. This is a simple rule, independent of hardware, but, as in the example below, it does sometimes force a negative result to lose its sign!

The *value preserving* approach (ANSI C) says that when you mix integral operand types like this, the result type is signed or unsigned depending on the relative sizes of the operand types.

The following program fragment will print a different message under ANSI and pre-ANSI compilers:

```
main() {
  if ( -1 < (unsigned char) 1 )
      printf("-1 is less than (unsigned char) 1: ANSI semantics ");
  else
      printf("-1 NOT less than (unsigned char) 1: K&R semantics ");
}
```

Depending on whether you compile it under K&R or ANSI C, the expression will be evaluated differently. The same bitpatterns are compared, but interpreted as either a negative number, or as an unsigned and hence positive number.

Software Dogma

A Subtle Bug

Even though the rules were changed, subtle bugs can and do still occur. In this example, the variable d is one less than the index needed, so the code copes with it. But the if statement did not evaluate to true. Why, and what, is the bug?

```
int array[] = { 23, 34, 12, 17, 204, 99, 16 };
#define TOTAL_ELEMENTS (sizeof(array) / sizeof(array[0]))

main()
{
    int d= -1, x;
    /* ... */

    if (d <= TOTAL_ELEMENTS-2)
        x = array[d+1];
    /* ... */
}
```

A Subtle Bug (Continued)

The defined variable `TOTAL_ELEMENTS` has type unsigned int (because the return type of sizeof is "unsigned"). The test is comparing a signed int with an unsigned int quantity. So d is promoted to unsigned int. Interpreting -1 as an unsigned int yields a big positive number, making the clause false. This bug occurs under ANSI C, and under K&R C if `sizeof()` had an unsigned return type in a given implementation. It can be fixed by putting an int cast immediately before the `TOTAL_ELEMENTS`:

```
if (d <= (int) TOTAL_ELEMENTS - 2)
```

Handy Heuristic

Advice on Unsigned Types

Avoid unnecessary complexity by minimizing your use of unsigned types. Specifically, don't use an unsigned type to represent a quantity just because it will never be negative (e.g., "age" or "national_debt").

Use a signed type like `int` and you won't have to worry about boundary cases in the detailed rules for promoting mixed types.

Only use unsigned types for bitfields or binary masks. Use casts in expressions, to make all the operands signed or unsigned, so the compiler does not have to choose the result type.

If this sounds a little tricky or surprising, it is! Work through the example using the rules on the previous page.

Finally, just so that we don't see this code appear as a bad example in a future edition of *The Elements of Programming Style*[7], we'd better explain that we used

```
#define TOTAL_ELEMENTS (sizeof(array) / sizeof(array[0]))
```

instead of

```
#define TOTAL_ELEMENTS (sizeof(array) / sizeof(int))
```

because the former allows the base type of the array to change (from, say, `int` to `char`) without needing a change to the `#define`, too.

7. *The Elements of Programming Style*, Kernighan (yes, that Kernighan) and Plauger, New York, McGraw-Hill, 1978. A thundering good read, credible plot, great little book—buy it, read it, live it!

The Sun ANSI C compiler team felt that moving from "unsigned preserving" to "value preserving" was a totally unnecessary change to C's semantics that would surprise and dismay anyone who encountered it unexpectedly. So, under the "principle of least astonishment," the Sun compiler recognizes and compiles ANSI C features, unless the feature would give a different result under K&R C. If this is the case, the compiler issues a warning and uses the K&R interpretation by default. In situations like the one above, the programmer should use a cast to tell the compiler what the final desired type is. Strict ANSI semantics are available on a Sun workstation running Solaris 2.x by using the compiler option `-Xc`.

There are plenty of other updates to K&R C in ANSI C, including a few more so-called "quiet changes" where code compiles under both but has a different meaning. Based on the usual programmer reaction when they are discovered, these really should be called "very noisy changes indeed". In general, the ANSI committee tried to change the language as little as possible, consistent with revising some of the things that undeniably needed improvement.

But that's enough background on the ANSI C family tree. After a little light relief in the following section, proceed to the next chapter and get started on code!

Some Light Relief— The Implementation-Defined Effects of Pragmas . . .

The Free Software Foundation is a unique organization founded by ace MIT hacker Richard Stallman. By the way, we use "hacker" in the old benevolent sense of "gifted programmer;" the term has been debased by the media, so outsiders use it to mean "evil genius." Like the adjective *bad*, "hacker" now has two opposing meanings, and you have to figure it out from the context.

Stallman's Free Software Foundation was founded on the philosophy that software should be free and freely available to all. FSF's charter is "to eliminate restrictions on copying, redistribution, understanding and modification of computer programs" and their ambition is to create a public-domain implementation of UNIX called GNU (it stands for "GNU's Not UNIX." Yes, really.)

Many computer science graduate students and others agree with the GNU philosophy, and have worked on software products that FSF packages and distributes for free. This pool of skilled labor donating their talent has resulted in some good software. One of FSF's best products is the GNU C compiler family. gcc is a robust, aggressive optimizing compiler, available for many hardware platforms and sometimes better than the manufacturer's compiler. Using gcc would not be appropriate for all projects; there are questions of maintenance and future product continuity. There are other tools needed besides a compiler, and the GNU debugger was unable to operate on shared libraries for a long time. GNU C has also occasionally been a little, shall we say, giddy in development.

When the ANSI C standard was under development, the pragma directive was introduced. Borrowed from Ada, #pragma is used to convey hints to the compiler, such as the desire to expand a particular function in-line or suppress range checks. Not previously seen in C, pragma met with some initial resistance from a gcc implementor, who took the "implementation-defined" effect very literally—in gcc version 1.34, the use of pragma causes the compiler to stop compiling and launch a computer game instead! The gcc manual contained the following:

> The "#pragma" command is specified in the ANSI standard to have an arbitrary implementation-defined effect. In the GNU C preprocessor, "#pragma" first attempts to run the game "rogue"; if that fails, it tries to run the game "hack"; if that fails, it tries to run GNU Emacs displaying the Tower of Hanoi; if that fails, it reports a fatal error. In any case, preprocessing does not continue.
>
> —Manual for version 1.34 of the GNU C compiler

And the corresponding source code in the preprocessor part of the compiler was:

```
/*
 * the behavior of the #pragma directive is implementation defined.
 * this implementation defines it as follows.
 */
do_pragma ()
{
 close (0);
 if (open ("/dev/tty", O_RDONLY, 0666) != 0)
                    goto nope;
 close (1);
 if (open ("/dev/tty", O_WRONLY, 0666) != 1)
                    goto nope;
 execl ("/usr/games/hack", "#pragma", 0);
 execl ("/usr/games/rogue", "#pragma", 0);
 execl ("/usr/new/emacs", "-f", "hanoi", "9", "-kill", 0);
 execl ("/usr/local/emacs", "-f", "hanoi", "9", "-kill", 0);
nope:
 fatal ("You are in a maze of twisty compiler features, all different");
}
```

Especially droll is the fact that the description in the user manual is wrong, in that the code shows that "hack" is tried before "rogue".

It's Not a Bug, It's a Language Feature

2

Bugs are by far the largest and most successful class of entity, with nearly a million known species. In this respect they outnumber all the other known creatures about four to one.

—Professor Snopes' *Encyclopedia of Animal Life*

why language features matter...sins of commission: switches let you down with fall through...available hardware is a crayon?...too much default visibility...sins of mission: overloading the camel's back..."some of the operators have the wrong precedence"...the early bug `gets()` the Internet worm...sins of omission: mail won't go to users with an "f" in their username...space–the final frontier...the compiler date is corrupted... lint should never have been separated out... some light relief—some features really are bugs

Why Language Features Matter— The Way the Fortran Bug Really Happened!

The details of a programming language really matter. They matter because the details make the difference between a reliable language and an error-prone one. This was dramatically revealed in Summer 1961 by a programmer at NASA, testing a Fortran subroutine used to calculate orbital trajectories.[1] The subroutine had already been used for several brief Mercury flights, but it was mysteriously not providing the precision that was expected and needed for the forthcoming orbital and lunar missions. The results were close, but not quite as accurate as expected.

1. The story is very widely misreported, and inaccurate versions appear in many programming language texts. Indeed, it has become a classic urban legend among programmers. The definitive account, from Fred Webb who worked at NASA at the time and saw the actual source code, can be seen in "Fortran Story—The Real Scoop" in *Forum on Risks to the Public in Computers and Related Systems*, vol. 9, no. 54, ACM Committee on Computers and Public Policy, December 12, 1989.

After checking the algorithm, the data, and the expected results at great length, the engineer finally noticed this statement in the code:

```
DO 10 I=1.10
```

Clearly, the programmer had intended to write a `DO` loop of the form:

```
DO 10 I=1,10
```

In Fortran, blank characters are not significant and can even occur in the middle of an identifier. The designers of Fortran intended this to help cardpunch walloppers and to aid the readability of programs, so you could have identifiers like `MAX Y`. Unfortunately, the compiler quite correctly read the statement as `DO10I = 1.10`

Variables do not have to be declared in Fortran. The statement as written caused the value 1.1 to be assigned to the implicitly declared floating point variable `DO10I`. The statements in the body of the intended loop were executed once instead of ten times, and a first approximation of a calculation took place instead of an iterative convergence. After correcting the period to a comma, the results were correct to the expected accuracy.

The bug was detected in time and never caused a Mercury space flight to fail as many versions claim (a different bug, in the Mariner flights, described at the end of the chapter, did have this effect), but it does graphically illustrate the importance of language design. C has all-too-many similar ambiguities or near-ambiguities. This chapter describes a representative sample of the most common ones, and how they typically show up as bugs. There are other problems that can arise in C; for example, any time you encounter the string `malloc(strlen(str));` it is almost always sure to be an error, where `malloc(strlen(str)+1);` was meant. This is because almost all the other string-handling routines include the room needed for the trailing nul terminator, so people get used to not making the special provision for it that `strlen` needs. The malloc example is an error in the programmer's knowledge of a library routine, whereas this chapter concentrates on problematic areas in C itself, rather than the programmer's use of it.

One way of analyzing the deficiencies in a programming language is to consider the flaws in three possible categories: things the language does that it shouldn't do; things it doesn't do that it should; and things that are completely off the wall. For convenience, we can call these "sins of commission," "sins of omission," and "sins of mission," respectively. The following sections describe C features in these categories.

This chapter isn't meant as fatal criticism of C. C is a wonderful programming language with many strengths. Its popularity as the implementation language of choice on many platforms is well-deserved. But, as my grandmother used to say, you can't run a superconducting supercollider without smashing a few atoms, and you can't analyze C without looking at the flaws as well as the high points. Reviewing areas for improvement is one of the factors that gradually improves the science of software engineering and the art of programming language design. That's why C++ is so disappointing: it does nothing to address some of the most fundamental problems in C, and its most important addition (classes) builds on the deficient C type model. So with the spirit of enquiry dedicated to improving future languages, here are some observations and case histories.

Handy Heuristic

The One 'l' nul and the Two 'l' null
Memorize this little rhyme to recall the correct terminology for pointers and ASCII zero: The one "l" `NUL` ends an ASCII string, The two "l" `NULL` points to no thing. Apologies to Ogden Nash, but the three "l" nulll means check your spelling. The ASCII character with the bit pattern of zero is termed a "NUL". The special pointer value that means the pointer points nowhere is "NULL". The two terms are not interchangeable in meaning.

Sins of Commission

The "sins of commission" category covers things that the language does, that it shouldn't do. This includes error-prone features like the switch statement, automatic concatenation of adjacent string literals, and default global scope.

Switches Let You Down with Fall Through

The general form of a switch statement is:

```
switch (expression) {
  case constant-expression: zero-or-more-statements
                  default: zero-or-more-statements
  case constant-expression: zero-or-more-statements
     }
```

Each case is introduced by triplets of the keyword `case`, followed by an integer-valued constant or constant expression, followed by a colon. Execution starts at the case that matches the expression. The default case (if present) can appear anywhere in the list of cases, and will be executed if none of the cases match. If there's no default case and none of the cases match, nothing is done by this statement. Some people have suggested that it might be better to have a runtime error for the "no match" case, as does Pascal. Runtime error checking is almost unknown in C—checking for dereferencing an invalid pointer is about the only case, and even that limited case can't be fully done under MS-DOS.

Handy Heuristic

Runtime Checking in MS-DOS

Invalid pointers can be the bane of a programmer's life. It's just too easy to reference memory using an invalid pointer. All virtual memory architectures will fault a process that dereferences a pointer outside its address space as soon as this happens. But MS-DOS doesn't support virtual memory, so it cannot catch the general case at the instant of failure.

However, MS-DOS can and does use a heuristic to check the specific case of dereferencing a null pointer, after your program has finished. Both Microsoft and Borland C, before entering your program, save the contents of location zero. As part of their exit code, they check whether it now contains a different value. If it does, it's a pretty fair bet that your program stored through a null pointer, and the runtime system prints the warning "null pointer assignment".

More about this in Chapter 7.

Runtime checking goes against the C philosophy that the programmer knows what he or she is doing and is always right.

The cases and the default can come in any order, though by convention the default case is usually the last one. A conformant C compiler must permit at least 257 case labels for a switch statement (ANSI C Standard, section 5.2.4.1). This is to allow a switch on an 8-bit character (256 possible values, plus EOF).

Switch has several problems, one of which is that it is too relaxed about what it accepts in the cases. For example, you can declare some local storage by following the switch's opening curly brace with a declaration. This is an artifact of the original compiler—most of the same code that processed any compound statement could be reused to process the braces-enclosed part of a switch. So a declaration is naturally accepted, though it's futile to add an initial value as part of a declaration in a switch statement, as it will not be executed—execution starts at the case that matches the expression.

Handy Heuristic

Need Some Temporary Store? Be the First on Your Block!

It is always the case in C that where you have some statements opening a block

```
{
    statements
```

you can always add some declarations in between, like this:

```
{
    declarations
    statements
```

You might use this if allocating memory was expensive, and hence avoided if possible. A compiler is free to ignore it, though, and allocate the space for all local blocks on calling a function. Another use is to declare some variables whose use is really localized to this block.

```
if ( a>b )
    /* swap a, b */
  {
    int tmp = a;
    a = b; b = tmp;
  }
```

C++ takes this a step further still, and allows arbitrary intermingling of statements and declarations, and even embedding declarations in the middle of "for" statements.

```
for (int i=0; i<100; i++) { . . .
```

If not used with restraint, that can quickly lead to confusion.

Another problem is that any statements inside a switch can be labelled and jumped to, allowing control to be passed around arbitrarily:

```
switch (i) {
  case 5+3: do_again:
  case 2: printf("I loop unremittingly \n"); goto do_again;
  default : i++;
  case 3: ;
}
```

The fact that all the cases are optional, and any form of statement, including labelled statements, is permitted, means that some errors can't be detected even by lint. A colleague of mine once mistyped `defau1t` for the default label (i.e., mistyped a digit "1" for the letter "l"). It was very hard to track this bug down, and it effectively removed the default case from the switch statement. However, it still compiled without errors, and even a detailed review of the source showed nothing untoward. Most lints don't catch this one.

By the way, since the keyword `const` doesn't really mean constant in C,

```
const int two=2;

switch (i) {
  case 1: printf("case 1 \n");
  case two: printf("case 2 \n");
**error** ^^^ integral constant expression expected

  case 3: printf("case 3 \n");
  default: ;
}
```

the code above will produce a compilation error like the one shown. This isn't really the fault of the switch statement, but switch statements are one place the problem of constants not being constant shows up.

Perhaps the biggest defect in the switch statement is that cases don't break automatically after the actions for a case label. Once a case statement is executed, the flow of control continues down, executing all the following cases until a break statement is reached. The code

```
switch (2) {
  case 1: printf("case 1 \n");
  case 2: printf("case 2 \n");
  case 3: printf("case 3 \n");
  case 4: printf("case 4 \n");
  default: printf("default \n");
}
```

will print out

```
case 2
case 3
case 4
default
```

This is known as "fall through" and was intended to allow common end processing to be done, after some case-specific preparation had occurred. In practice it's a severe misfeature, as almost all case actions end with a `break;`. Most versions of lint even issue a warning if they see one case falling through into another.

Software Dogma

Default Fall Through Is Wrong 97% of the Time

We analyzed the Sun C compiler sources to see how often the default fall through was used. The Sun ANSI C compiler front end has 244 switch statements, each of which has an average of seven cases. Fall through occurs in just 3% of all these cases.

In other words, the normal switch behavior is ***wrong*** 97% of the time. It's not just in a compiler—on the contrary, where fall through was used in this analysis it was often for situations that occur more frequently in a compiler than in other software, for instance, when compiling operators that can have either one or two operands:

Default Fall Through Is Wrong 97% of the Time (Continued)

```
switch( operator->num_of_operands ) {
    case 2: process_operand( operator->operand_2 );
              /* FALLTHRU */
    case 1: process_operand( operator->operand_1 );
    break;
}
```

Case fall through is so widely recognized as a defect that there's even a special comment convention, shown above, that tells lint "this really is one of the 3% of cases where fall through was desired." The inconvenience of default fall through is borne out in many other programs.

We conclude that default fall through on switches is a design defect in C. The overwhelming majority of the time you don't want to do it and have to write extra code to defeat it. As the Red Queen said to Alice in *Through the Looking Glass*, you can't deny that even if you used both hands.

Another Switch Problem—What Does `break` Break?

This is a replica of the code that caused a major disruption of AT&T phone service throughout the U.S. AT&T's network was in large part unusable for about nine hours starting on the afternoon of January 15, 1990. Telephone exchanges (or "switching systems" in phone jargon) are all computer systems these days, and this code was running on a model 4ESS Central Office Switching System. It demonstrates that it is too easy in C to overlook exactly which control constructs are affected by a "break" statement.

```
network code()
{
  switch (line) {

    case THING1:
      doit1();
      break;

    case THING2:
      if (x == STUFF) {
          do_first_stuff();

          if (y == OTHER_STUFF)
              break;
```

Another Switch Problem—What Does `break` Break? (Continued)

```
            do_later_stuff();
        } /* coder meant to break to here... */
        initialize_modes_pointer();
        break;

      default:
        processing();
  } /* ...but actually broke to here! */

  use_modes_pointer();/* leaving the modes_pointer uninitialized */

}
```

This is a simplified version of the code, but the bug was real enough. The programmer wanted to break out of the "if" statement, forgetting that "break" actually gets you out of the nearest enclosing iteration or switch statement. Here, it broke out of the switch, and executed the call to `use_modes_pointer()` —but the necessary initialization had not been done, causing a failure further on.

This code eventually caused the first major network problem in AT&T's 114-year history. The saga is described in greater detail on page 11 of the January 22, 1990 issue of *Telephony* magazine. The supposedly fail-safe design of the network signaling system actually spread the fault in a chain reaction, bringing down the entire long distance network. And it all rested on a C `switch` statement.

Available Hardware Is a Crayon?

One new feature introduced with ANSI C is the convention that adjacent string literals are concatenated into one string. This replaces the old way of constructing multiline messages using escaped newlines, and starting each continuation string in column one.

Old style:

```
    printf( "A favorite children's book \
is 'Muffy Gets It: the hilarious tale of a cat, \
a boy, and his machine gun'" );
```

This can now be written as a series of adjacent string literals that will automatically be joined together as one at compile-time. The nul character that normally ends a string literal is dropped from all joined string literals except the last one.

New style:

```
printf( "A second favorite children's book "
     "is 'Thomas the tank engine and the Naughty Enginedriver who "
     "tied down Thomas's boiler safety valve'" );
```

However, the automatic concatenation means that a missing comma in an initialization list of string literals no longer causes a diagnostic message. A missing comma now results in a silent marriage of adjacent strings. This has dire consequences in circumstances like the following:

```
char *available_resources[] = {
  "color monitor",
  "big disk",

  "Cray"                 /* whoa! no comma! */
  "on-line drawing routines",

  "mouse",
  "keyboard",
  "power cables",        /* and what's this extra comma? */
 };
```

So available_resources[2] is "Crayon-line drawing routines". There's quite a difference between having a "Cray" with "on-line drawing routines" and just having some routines to draw lines with crayons...

The total number of resources is one less than expected, so writing to `available_resources[6]` will trash another variable. And by the way, that trailing comma after the final initializer is not a typo, but a blip in the syntax carried over from aboriginal C. Its presence or absence is allowed but has no significance. The justification claimed in the ANSI C rationale is that it makes automated generation of C easier. The claim would be more credible if trailing commas were permitted in every comma-separated list, such as in enum declarations, or multiple variable declarators in a single declaration. They are not.

Handy Heuristic

First Time Through

This hint shows a simple way to get a different action the first time through a section of code.

The function below will do a different action on its first invocation than on all subsequent calls. There are other ways of achieving this; this way minimizes the switches and conditional testing.

```
generate_initializer(char * string)
{
  static char separator = ' ';
  printf( "%c %s \n", separator, string);
  separator = ',';
}
```

The first time through, this will print a space followed by an initializer. All subsequent initializers (if any) will be preceded by a comma. Viewing the specification as "first time through, prefix with a space" rather than "last time through, omit the comma suffix" makes this simple to program.

The claim is hard to believe, as an automated program can output a comma or no comma by having a statically declared character initialized to space and then set to comma. This will exhibit the correct behavior and is trivial to code. There are other examples of comma-separated items in C, where a comma may not terminate the list. The unnecessary, but allowed, comma after the last initializer serves mostly to muddy the waters of an already murky syntax.

Too Much Default Visibility

Whenever you define a C function, its name is globally visible by default. You can prefix the function name with the redundant `extern` keyword or leave it off, and the effect is the same. The function is visible to anything that links with that object file. If you want to restrict access to the function, you are obliged to specify the `static` keyword.

```
        function apple (){ /* visible everywhere */ }
 extern function pear () { /* visible everywhere */ }

 static function turnip(){ /* not visible outside this file */ }
```

In practice, almost everyone tends to define functions without adding extra storage-class specifiers, so global scope prevails.

With the benefit of practical experience, default global visibility has been conclusively and repeatedly demonstrated to be a mistake. Software objects should have the most limited scope by default. Programmers should explicitly take action when they intend to give something global scope.

The problem of too much scope interacts with another common C convention, that of interpositioning. Interpositioning is the practice of supplanting a library function by a user-written function of the same name. Many C programmers are completely unaware of this feature, so it is described in the chapter on linking. For now, just make the mental note: *"interpositioning—I should learn more about that."*

The problem of too wide scope is often seen in libraries: one library needs to make an object visible to another library. The only possibility is to make it globally known; but then it is visible to anyone that links with the library. This is an "all-or-nothing" visibility—symbols are either globally known or not known at all. There's no way to be more selective in revealing information in C.

The problem is made worse by the fact that you can't nest function definitions inside other functions, as you can in Pascal. So a collection of "internal" functions for one big function have to be outside it. Nobody remembers to make them static, so they're globally visible by default. The Ada and Modula-2 languages both address this problem in a manageable way by having program units specify exactly what symbols they are exporting and what they are importing.

Sins of Mission

The "sins of mission" category covers things in C that just seem misdirected, or a bad fit to the language. This includes features like the brevity of C (caused in part by excessive reuse of symbols) and problems with operator precedence.

Overloading the Camel's Back

One problem is that C is so terse. Just adding, changing, or omitting a single character often gives you a program that is still valid but does something entirely different. Worse than that, many symbols are "overloaded"—given different meanings when used in different contexts. Even some keywords are overloaded with several meanings, which is the main reason that C scope rules are not intuitively clear to programmers. Table 2-1 shows how similar C symbols have multiple different meanings.

Table 2-1 Symbol Overloading in C

Symbol	**Meaning**
`static`	Inside a function, *retains its value between calls* At the function level, *visible only in this file*[1]
`extern`	Applied to a function definition, *has global scope* (and is redundant) Applied to a variable, *defined elsewhere*
`void`	As the return type of a function, *doesn't return a value* In a pointer declaration, the type of a generic pointer In a parameter list, *takes no parameters*
`*`	The multiplication operator Applied to a pointer, indirection In a declaration, a pointer
`&`	Bitwise AND operator Address-of operator
`=` `==`	Assignment operator Comparison operator
`<=` `<<=`	Less-than-or-equal-to operator Compound shift-left assignment operator
`<` `<`	Less-than operator Left delimiter in `#include` directive
`( )`	Enclose formal parameters in a function definition Make a function call Provide expression precedence Convert (cast) a value to a different type Define a macro with arguments Make a macro call with arguments Enclose the operand of the `sizeof` operator when it is a typename

1. You're probably wondering what possible reason there could be for re-using the `static` keyword with these wildly different meanings. If you find out, please let us know, too.

There are other symbols that are also confusingly similar. One flustered programmer once puzzled over the statement `if (x>>4)` and asked, "What does it mean? Is it saying 'If x is *much* greater than 4?'"

The kind of place where overloading can be a problem is in statements like:

```
p = N * sizeof * q;
```

Quickly now, are there two multiplications or only one? Here's a hint: the next statement is:

```
r = malloc( p );
```

The answer is that there's only one multiplication, because sizeof is an operator that here takes as its operand the thing pointed to by q (i.e., `*q`). It returns the size in bytes of the type of thing to which q points, convenient for the malloc function to allocate more memory. When sizeof's operand is a *type* it has to be enclosed in parentheses, which makes people wrongly believe it is a function call, but for a *variable* this is not required.

Here's a more complicated example:

```
apple = sizeof (int) * p;
```

What does this mean? Is it the size of an int, multiplied by p? Or the size of whatever p points at, but cast to an int? Or something even weirder? The answer isn't given here, because part of being an expert programmer is learning to write little test programs to probe questions like this. Try it and see!

The more work you make one symbol do, the harder it is for the compiler to detect anomalies in your use of it. It's not just the kind of people who sing along with the Tiki birds at Disneyland who have trouble here. C does seem to be a little further out on the ragged edge of token ambiguity than most other languages.

"Some of the Operators Have the Wrong Precedence"

You know that you've definitely found a problem when the authors of the original report on C tell you that "some of the operators have the wrong precedence", as Kernighan and Ritchie mention on page 3 of *The C Programming Language*. Despite this admission, there were no changes in the precedence of operators for ANSI C. It's not surprising; any change in precedence would have imposed an intolerable burden on the existing source base.

But which C operators specifically have the wrong precedence? The answer is "any that appear misleading when you apply them in the regular way." Some operators whose precedence has often caused trouble for the unwary are shown in Figure 2-1.

Precedence problem	Expression	What People Expect	What They Actually Get
. is higher than * the p->f op was made to smooth over this	`*p.f`	the f field of what p points to `(*p).f`	take the f offset from p, use it as a pointer `*(p.f)`
`[]` is higher than *	`int *ap[]`	ap is a ptr to array of ints `int(*ap)[]`	ap is an array of ptrs-to-int `int *(ap[])`
function `()` higher than *	`int *fp()`	fp is a ptr to function returning int `int (*fp) ()`	fp is a function returning ptr-to-int `int *(fp())`
== and != higher precedence than bitwise operators	`(val&mask != 0)`	`(val&mask) !=0`	`val & (mask !=0)`
== and != higher precedence than assignment	`c=getchar()!=EOF`	`(c=getchar()) != EOF`	`c=(getchar() !=EOF)`
arithmetic higher precedence than shift	`msb<<4 + lsb`	`(msb<<4)+lsb`	`msb<<(4+lsb)`
, has lowest precedence of all operators	`i = 1,2;`	`i= (1,2);`	`(i=1), 2;`

Figure 2-1 Precedence Problems of C Operators

Most of these become more understandable if you sit down to consider them at length. The case involving the comma occasionally causes conniption fits in programmers, though. For example, when this line is executed:

```
i = 1,2;
```

what value does i end up with? Well, we know that the value of a comma operator is the value of the rightmost operand. But here, assignment has higher precedence, so you actually get:

```
(i=1), 2; /* i gets the value 1 */
```

i gets the value 1; then the literal 2 is evaluated and thrown away. i ends up being one, not two.

In a posting on Usenet some years ago, Dennis Ritchie explained how some of these anomalies are historical accidents.

Software Dogma

'And' and 'AND' or 'Or' or 'OR'

```
From decvax!harpo!npoiv!alice!research!dmr
Date: Fri Oct 22 01:04:10 1982
Subject: Operator precedence
Newsgroups: net.lang.c
```

The priorities of && || vs. == etc. came about in the following way. Early C had no separate operators for & and && or | and ||. (Got that?) Instead it used the notion (inherited from B and BCPL) of "truth-value context": where a Boolean value was expected, after "if" and "while" and so forth, the & and | operators were interpreted as && and || are now; in ordinary expressions, the bitwise interpretations were used. It worked out pretty well, but was hard to explain. (There was the notion of "top-level operators" in a truth-value context.)

The precedence of & and | were as they are now. Primarily at the urging of Alan Snyder, the && and || operators were added. This successfully separated the concepts of bitwise operations and short-circuit Boolean evaluation. However, I had cold feet about the precedence problems. For example, there were lots of programs with things like if (a==b & c==d) ...

In retrospect it would have been better to go ahead and change the precedence of & to higher than ==, but it seemed safer just to split & and && without moving & past an existing operator. (After all, we had several hundred kilobytes of source code, and maybe 3 installations....)

Dennis Ritchie

Handy Heuristic

Order of Evaluation

The moral of all this is that you should always put parentheses around an expression that mixes Booleans, arithmetic, or bit-twiddling with anything else.

And remember that while precedence and associativity tell you what is grouped with what, the order in which these groupings will be evaluated is *always* undefined. In the expression:

```
x = f() + g() * h();
```

The values returned by g() and h() will be grouped together for multiplication, but g and h might be called in any order. Similarly, f might be called before or after the multiplication, or even between g and h. All we can know for sure is that the multiplication will occur before the addition (because the result of the multiplication is one of the operands in the addition). It would still be poor style to write a program that relied on that knowledge. Most programming languages don't specify the order of operand evaluation. It is left undefined so that compiler-writers can take advantage of any quirks in the architecture, or special knowledge of values that are already in registers.

Pascal avoids all problems in this area by requiring explicit parentheses around expressions that mix Boolean operators and arithmetic operators. Some authorities recommend that there are only two precedence levels to remember in C: multiplication and division come before addition and subtraction. Everything else should be in parentheses. We think that's excellent advice.

Handy Heuristic

What "Associativity" Means

While the precedence of operators can be perplexing, many people are equally puzzled about the associativity of operators. Operator associativity never seems to be explained very clearly in the standard C literature. This handy heuristic explains what it is, and when you need to know about it. The five-cent explanation is that it is a "tie-breaker" for operators with equal precedence.

What "Associativity" Means (Continued)

Every operator has a level of precedence and a "left" or "right" associativity assigned to it. The precedence indicates how "tightly" the operands in an unbracketed expression bind. For example, in the expression `a * b + c,` since multiplication has a higher precedence than addition, it will be done first, and the multiplicand will be `b`, not `b + c`.

But many operators have the same precedence levels, and this is where associativity comes in. It is a protocol for explaining the real precedence among all operators that have the same apparent precedence level. If we have an expression like

```
int a, b=1, c=2;

a = b = c;
```

we find that, since the expression only involves the assignment operator, precedence does not help us understand how the operands are grouped. So which happens first, the assignment of c to b, or the assignment of b to a? In the first case, a would be left with the value 2, and in the second case, a would end up as 1.

All assignment-operators have right associativity. The associativity protocol says that this means the rightmost operation in the expression is evaluated first, and evaluation proceeds from right to left. Thus, the value of c is assigned to b. Then the value of b is stored in a. a gets the value 2. Similarly, for operators with left associativity (such as the bitwise and's and or's), the operands are grouped from left to right.

The only use of associativity is to disambiguate an expression of two or more equal-precedence operators. In fact, you'll note that all operators which share the same precedence level also share the same associativity. They have to, or else the expression evaluation would still be ambiguous. If you need to take associativity into account to figure out the value of an expression, it's usually better to rewrite the expression into two expressions, or to use parentheses.

The order in which things happen in C is defined for some things and not for others. The order of precedence and association are well-defined. However, the order of expression evaluation is mostly *unspecified* (the special term defined in the previous chapter) to allow compiler-writers the maximum leeway to generate the fastest code. We say "mostly" because the order is defined for `&&` and `||` and a couple of other operators. These two evaluate their operands in a strict left-to-right order, stopping when the result is known. However, the order of evaluation of the arguments in a function call is another unspecified order.

The Early Bug `gets()` the Internet Worm

The problems in C are not confined to just the language. Some routines in the standard library have unsafe semantics. This was dramatically demonstrated in November 1988 by the worm program that wriggled through thousands of machines on the Internet network. When the smoke had cleared and the investigations were complete, it was determined that one way the worm had propagated was through a weakness in the finger daemon, which accepts queries over the network about who is currently logged in. The finger daemon, in.fingerd, used the standard I/O routine `gets()`.

The nominal task of `gets()` is to read in a string from a stream. The caller tells it where to put the incoming characters. But `gets()` does not check the buffer space; in fact, it *can't* check the buffer space. If the caller provides a pointer to the stack, and more input than buffer space, `gets()` will happily overwrite the stack. The finger daemon contained the code:

```
main(argc, argv)
  char *argv[];
{
  char line[512];
      . . .
  gets(line);
```

Here, `line` is a 512-byte array allocated automatically on the stack. When a user provides more input than that to the finger daemon, the `gets()` routine will keep putting it on the stack. Most architectures are vulnerable to overwriting an existing entry in the middle of the stack with something bigger, that also overwrites neighboring entries. The cost of checking each stack access for size and permission would be prohibitive in software. A knowledgeable malefactor can amend the return address in the procedure activation record on the stack by stashing the right binary patterns in the argument string. This will divert the flow of execution not back to where it came from, but to a special instruction sequence (also carefully deposited on the stack) that calls `execv()` to replace the running image with a shell. Voilà, you are now talking to a shell on a remote machine instead of the finger daemon, and you can issue commands to drag across a copy of the virus to another machine. Repeat until sent to prison. Figure 2-2 shows the process.

Ironically, the `gets()` routine is an obsolete function that provided compatibility with the very first version of the portable I/O library, and was replaced by standard I/O more than a decade ago. The manpage even strongly recommends that `fgets()` always be used instead. The `fgets()` routine sets a limit on the number of characters read, so it won't exceed the size of the buffer. The finger daemon was made secure with a two-line fix that replaced:

```
gets(line);
```

by the lines:

```
if (fgets(line, sizeof(line), stdin) == NULL)
    exit(1);
```

This swallows a limited amount of input, and thus can't be manipulated into overwriting important locations by someone running the program. However, the ANSI C Standard did not remove `gets()` from the language. Thus, while this particular program was made secure, the underlying defect in the C standard library was not removed.

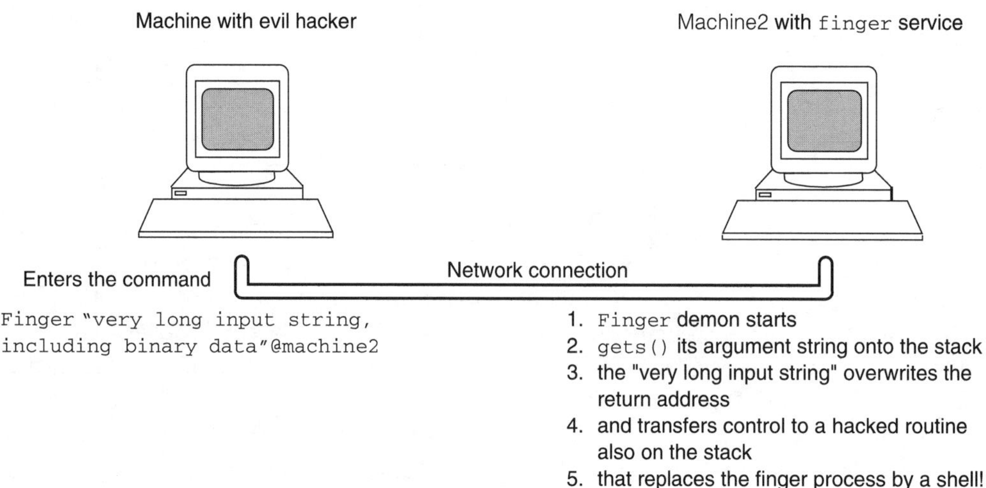

Machine with evil hacker
Machine2 with finger service
Enters the command
Network connection
Finger "very long input string, including binary data"@machine2
1. Finger demon starts
2. gets() its argument string onto the stack
3. the "very long input string" overwrites the return address
4. and transfers control to a hacked routine also on the stack
5. that replaces the finger process by a shell!

Figure 2-2 How the Internet Worm Gained Remote Execution Privileges

Sins of Omission

The "sins of omission" category covers things that the language doesn't do that it should. This includes missing features like standard argument processing and the mistake of extracting lint checking from the compiler.

Mail Won't Go to Users with an "f" in Their Usernames

The bug report was very puzzling. It just said "mail isn't getting delivered to users who have an 'f' as the second character of their username." It sounded so unlikely. What could possibly cause mail to fail because of a character in the username? After all, there's no connection between the characters in a username and the mail delivery processing. Nonetheless, the problem was reported at multiple sites.

After some urgent testing, we found that mail was indeed falling into the void when an addressee had an "f" as the second character of the username! Thus, mail would go to Fred and Muffy, but not to Effie. An examination of the source code quickly located the trouble.

Many people are surprised to learn that ANSI C mandates the `argc, argv` convention of passing arguments to a C program, but it does. The UNIX convention has been elevated to the level of a standard, and it was partly to blame for the mail bug here. The mail program had been amended in the previous release to:

```
if ( argv[argc-1][0] == '-' || (argv[argc-2][1] == 'f' ) )
  readmail(argc, argv);
else
  sendmail(argc, argv);
```

The "mail" program can be executed either to send mail, or to read your incoming mail. We won't enquire too closely into the merits of making one program responsible for two such different tasks. This code was supposed to look at the arguments and use the information to decide if we are reading mail or sending mail. The way to distinguish is somewhat heuristic: look for switches that are unique to either reading or sending. In this case, if the final argument is a switch (i.e., starts with a hyphen), we are definitely reading mail. We are also reading mail if the last argument is not an option but is a filename, that is, the next-to-last argument was "`-f`".

And this is where the programmer went wrong, aided by lack of support in the language. The programmer merely looked at the second character of the next-to-last option. If it was an "f", he assumed that mail was invoked with a line like:

```
mail -h -d -f /usr/linden/mymailbox
```

In most cases this was correct, and mail would be read from mymailbox. But it could also happen that the invocation was:

```
mail effie robert
```

In this case, the argument processing would make the mail program think it was being asked to read mail, not send it. Bingo! E-mail to users with an "f" as the second character of the name disappears! The fix was a one-liner: if you're looking at the next-to-last argument for a possible "f", make sure it is also preceded by a switch hyphen:

```
if ( argv[argc-1][0] == '-' ||
  argv[argc-2][0] == '-' && (argv[argc-2][1] == 'f' ) )
     readmail(argc, argv);
```

The problem was caused by bad parsing of arguments, but it was facilitated by inadequate classification of arguments between switches and filenames. Many operating systems (e.g., VAX/VMS) distinguish between runtime options and other arguments (e.g., filenames) to programs, but UNIX does not; nor does ANSI C.

Software Dogma

Shell Fumbles on Argument Parsing

The problem of inadequate argument parsing occurs in many places on UNIX. To find out which files in a directory are links, you might enter the command:

```
ls -l | grep ->
```

This will yield the error message "Missing name for redirect", and most people will quickly figure out that the right chevron has been interpreted by the shell as a redirection, not as an argument to grep. They will then hide it from the shell by quotes, and try this:

```
ls -l | grep "->"
```

Still no good! The grep program looks at the starting minus sign, interprets the argument as an unrecognized option of greater-than, and quits. The answer is to step back from "ls" and instead use:

```
file -h * | grep link
```

Many people have been tormented by creating a file the name of which starts with a hyphen, and then being unable to get rm to remove it. One solution in this case is to give the entire pathname of the file, so that rm does not see a leading hyphen and try to interpret the name as an option.

Some C programmers have adopted the convention that an argument of " -- " means "from this point on, no arguments are switches, even if they start with a hyphen." A better solution would put the burden on the system, not the user, with an argument processor that divides arguments into options and non-options. The simple argv mechanism is now too well entrenched for any changes. Just don't send mail to Effie under pre-1990 versions of Berkeley UNIX.

Space—The Final Frontier

A lot of people will tell you that white space isn't significant in C; that you can have as much or as little of it as you like. Not so! Here are some examples where white space radically changes the meaning or validity of a program.

- The backslash character can be used to "escape" several characters, including a newline. An escaped newline is treated as one logical line, and this can be used to continue long strings. A problem arises if you inadvertently slip a space or two in between the backslash and the carriage return, as \ *whitespace newline* is different than *newline*. This error can be hard to find, as you are looking for something invisible (the presence of a space character where a newline was intended). A newline is typically escaped to continue a multiline macro definition. If your compiler doesn't have excellent error messages, you might as well give up now. Another reason to escape a newline is to continue a string literal, like this:

```
      char a[]= "Hi! How are you? I am quite a \
long string, folded onto 2 lines";
```

  The problem of multiline string literals was addressed by ANSI C introducing the convention that adjacent string literals are glued together. As we point out elsewhere in this chapter, that approach solved one potential problem at the expense of introducing another.

- If you squeeze spaces out altogether, you can still run into trouble. For example, what do you think the following code means?

```
z = y+++x;
```

  The programmer might have meant `z = y + ++x`, or equally could have had `z = y++ + x` in mind. The ANSI standard specifies a convention that has come to be known as the *maximal munch strategy*. Maximal munch says that if there's more than one possibility for the next token, the compiler will prefer to bite off the one involving the longest sequence of characters. So the above example will be parsed as `z = y++ + x`.

  This can still lead to trouble, as the code

```
z = y+++++x;
```

will therefore be parsed as `z = y++ ++ + x`, and cause a compilation error along the lines of "++ operator is floating loose in space". This will happen even though the compiler could, in theory, have deduced that the only valid arrangement of spaces is `z = y++ + ++x`.

- Yet a third white space problem occurred when a programmer had two pointers-to-int, and wanted to divide one int by the other. The code said

```
ratio = *x/*y;
```

but the compiler issued an error message complaining of syntax error. The problem was the lack of space between the "/ " division operator and the "* " indirection operator. When put next to each other they opened a comment, and hid all the code up to the next closing comment!

Related to opening a comment without intending to, is the case of accidentally not closing a comment when you did mean to. One release of an ANSI C compiler had an interesting bug. The symbol table was accessed by a hash function that computed a likely place from which to start a serial search. The computation was copiously commented, even describing the book the algorithm came from. Unfortunately, the programmer omitted to close the comment! The entire hash initial value calculation thus fell inside the continuing comment, resulting in the code shown below. Make sure you can identify the problem and try to predict what happened.

```
int hashval=0;
/* PJW hash function from "Compilers: Principles, Techniques, and Tools"
 * by Aho, Sethi, and Ullman, Second Edition.
while (cp < bound)
{
  unsigned long overflow;

  hashval = ( hashval << 4 ) + *cp++;
  if ((overflow = hashval & (((unsigned long) 0xF) << 28)) != 0)
       hashval ^= overflow | (overflow >> 24);
}
hashval %= ST_HASHSIZE;            /* choose start bucket */
```

```
/* Look through each table, in turn, for the name. If we fail,
 * save the string, enter the string's pointer, and return it.
 */
for (hp = &st_ihash; ; hp = hp->st_hnext) {
     int probeval = hashval;      /* next probe value */
```

The entire calculation of the initial hash value was omitted, so the table was always searched serially from the zeroth element! As a result, symbol table lookup (a very frequent operation in a compiler) was much slower than it should have been. This was never found during testing because it only affected the speed of a lookup, not the result. This is why some compilers complain if they notice an opening comment in a comment string. The error was eventually found in the course of looking for a different bug. Inserting the closing comment resulted in an immediate compilation speedup of 15%!

A Digression into C++ Comments

C++ doesn't address most of the flaws of C, but it could have avoided this inadvertent run-on comment. As in BCPL, C++ comments are introduced by // and go to the end of a line.

It was originally thought that the // comment convention would not alter the meaning of any syntactically correct C code. Sadly, this is not so

```
a //*
//*/ b
```

is a / b in C, but is a in C++. The C++ language allows the C notation for comments, too.

The Compiler Date Is Corrupted

The bug described in this section is a perfect example of how easy it is to write something in C that happily compiles, but produces garbage at runtime. This can be done in any language (e.g., simply divide by zero), but few languages offer quite so many fruitful and inadvertent opportunities as C.

Sun's Pascal compiler had been newly "internationalized," that is, adapted so that (among other things) it would print out dates on source listings in the local format. Thus, in France the date might appear as *Lundi 6 Avril 1992*. This was achieved by having the compiler first call stat() to obtain the sourcefile modification time in UNIX format, then call `localtime()` to convert it to a struct tm, and then finally call the `strftime()` string-from-time function to convert the struct tm time to an ASCII string in local format.

Unhappily, there was a bug that showed up as a corrupted date string. The date was actually coming out not as

```
Lundi 6 Avril 1992
```

but rather in a corrupted form, as

```
Lui*7& %' Y sxxdj @ ^F
```

The function only has four statements, and the arguments to the function calls are correct in all cases. See if you can identify the cause of the string corruption.

```
/* Convert the source file timestamp into a localized date string */
char *
localized_time(char * filename)
{
  struct tm *tm_ptr;
  struct stat stat_block;
  char buffer[120];

  /* get the sourcefile's timestamp in time_t format */
  stat(filename, &stat_block);

  /* convert UNIX time_t into a struct tm holding local time */
  tm_ptr = localtime(&stat_block.st_mtime);


  /* convert the tm struct into a string in local format */
  strftime(buffer, sizeof(buffer), "%a %b %e %T %Y", tm_ptr);

  return buffer;
}
```

See it? Time's up! The problem is in the final line of the function, where the buffer is returned. The buffer is an automatic array, local to this function. Automatic variables go away once the flow of control leaves the scope in which they are declared. That means that even if you return a pointer to such a variable, as here, there's no telling what it points to once the function is exited.

In C, automatic variables are allocated on the stack. This is explained at greater length in Chapter 6. When their containing function or block is exited, that portion of the stack is available for reuse, and will certainly be overwritten by the next function to be called. Depending on where in the stack the previous auto variable was and what variables the active function declares and writes, it might be overwritten immediately, or later, leading to a hard-to-find corruption problem.

There are several possible solutions to this problem.

1. Return a pointer to a string literal. Example:

```
char *func() { return "Only works for simple strings"; }
```

   This is the simplest solution, but it can't be used if you need to calculate the string contents, as in this case. You can also get into trouble if string literals are stored in read-only memory, and the caller later tries to overwrite it.

2. Use a globally declared array. Example:

```
char *func() {
      . . .
  my_global_array[i] =
      . . .
  return my_global_array;
}
```

   This works for strings that you need to build up, and is still simple and easy to use. The disadvantages are that anyone can modify the global array at any time, and the next call to the function will overwrite it.

3. Use a static array. Example:

```
char *func() {
  static char buffer[20] ;
      . . .
  return buffer;
}
```

This solves the problem of anyone overwriting the string. Only routines to which you give a pointer will be able to modify this static array. However, callers have to use the value or copy it before another call overwrites it. As with global arrays, large buffers can be wasteful of memory if not in use.

4. Explicitly allocate some memory to hold the return value. Example:

```
char *func() {
 char *s = malloc( 120 ) ;
 . . .
 return s;
}
```

This method has the advantages of the static array, and each invocation creates a new buffer, so subsequent calls don't overwrite the value returned by the first. It works for multithreaded code (programs where there is more than one thread of control active at a given instant). The disadvantage is that the programmer has to accept responsibility for memory management. This may be easy, or it may be very hard, depending on the complexity of the program. It can lead to incredible bugs if memory is freed while still in use, or "memory leaks" if memory no longer in use is still held. It's too easy to forget to free allocated memory.

5. Probably the best solution is to require the caller to allocate the memory to hold the return value. For safety, provide a count of the size of the buffer (just as `fgets()` requires in the standard library).

```
void func( char * result, int size) {
     . . .
strncpy(result,"That'd be in the data segment, Bob", size);
}

buffer = malloc(size);
func( buffer, size );
     . . .
free(buffer);
```

Memory management works best if you can write the "free" at the same time as you write the "malloc". This solution makes that possible.

To avoid the "data corruption" problem, note that lint will complain about the simplest case of:

```
return local_array;
```

saying `warning: function returns pointer to automatic`. However, neither a compiler nor lint can detect all cases of a local array being returned (it may be hidden by a level of indirection).

Lint Should Never Have Been Separated Out

You'll notice a consistent theme running through many of the above problems: lint detects them and warns you. It takes discipline to ensure that code is kept lint clean, and it would save much trouble if the lint warnings were automatically generated by the compiler.

Back in the early days of C on UNIX, an explicit decision was made to extract full semantic checking from the compiler. This error checking was instead done by a stand-alone program known as "lint". By omitting comprehensive error-checking, the compiler could be made smaller, faster, and simpler. After all, programmers can always be trusted to say what they mean, and mean what they say, right? Wrong!

Handy Heuristic

Lint Early, Lint Often
Lint is your software conscience. It tells you when you are doing bad things. Always use lint. Listen to your conscience.

Separating lint out from the compiler as an independent program was a big mistake that people are only now coming to terms with. It's true that it made the compiler smaller and more focused, but it was at the grievous cost of allowing bugs and dubious code idioms to lurk unnoticed. Many, perhaps most, programmers do not use lint by default after each and every compilation. It's a poor trade-off to have buggy code compiled fast. Much of lint's checking is now starting to appear in compilers again.

However, there is one thing that lint commonly does that most C compiler implementations currently do not; namely, check for consistency of function use across multiple files. Many people regard this as a deficiency of compiler implementation, rather than a justification for a freestanding lint program. All Ada compilers do this multifile consistency checking; it is the trend in C++ translators, and perhaps eventually will be usual in C, too.

The SunOS Lint Party

The SunOS development team is justly proud of our lint-clean kernel. We'd paid a lot of attention to getting the 4.x kernel to pass through lint with no errors, and we kept it that way. When we changed our source base from BSD UNIX to SVR4 in 1991, we inherited a new kernel whose lint status was unknown. We decided to lint the SVR4 kernel.

This activity took place over several weeks and was known as the "lint party." It yielded about 12,000 unique lint warnings, each of which had to be investigated and corrected manually. By the end, changes had been made to about 750 source files, and the task had become known as "the lint merge from hell". Most of the lint messages just needed an explicit cast, or lint comment, but there were several real bugs shaken out by the process:

- Argument types transposed between function and call
- A function that was passed one argument, but expected three, and took junk off the stack. Finding this cured an intermittent data corruption problem in the streams subsystem.
- Variables used before being set.

The value is not just in removing existing bugs, but in preventing new bugs from contaminating the source base. We now keep the kernel lint-clean by requiring all source changes or additions to be run through lint and cstyle. In this way we have not only removed existing bugs, but are reducing the number of future bugs as well.

Some programmers strenuously object to the idea of putting lint back into the compiler on the grounds that it slows the compiler down and produces too many spurious warnings. Unfortunately, experience has proven repeatedly that making lint a separate tool mostly results in lint not being used.

The economics of software is such that the earlier in the development cycle a bug is found, the cheaper it is to fix. So it is a good investment to have lint (or preferably the compiler itself) do the extra work to find problems rather than the debugger; but better a debugger find the problems than an internal test group. The worst option of all is to leave the problems to be found by customers.

Some Light Relief—Some Features Really Are Bugs!

This chapter wouldn't be complete without finishing the story of space missions and software. The Fortran `DO` loop story (which began this chapter and arose in the context of Mercury suborbital flights) is frequently, and wrongly, linked with the Mariner 1 mission.

By coincidence, Mariner 1 *was* involved with a dramatic software failure, but it happened in quite a different manner, and was entirely unrelated to choice of language. Mariner 1 was launched in July 1962 to carry a probe to Venus, but had to be destroyed a few minutes after launch when its Atlas rocket started to veer off course.

After weeks of analysis, it was determined that the problem *was* in the software, but it was a transcription error in the algorithm rather than a program bug. In other words, the program had done what the programmer had supposed, but he had been told the wrong thing in the specification! The tracking algorithm was intended to operate on smoothed (average) velocity. The mathematical symbol for this is a horizontal bar placed over the quantity to be smoothed. In the handwritten guidance equations supplied to the programmer, the bar was accidentally omitted.

The programmer followed the algorithm he had been given exactly, and used the raw velocity direct from radar instead of the smoothed velocity. As a result, the program saw minor fluctuations in rocket velocity and, in a classic negative feedback loop, caused genuine erratic behavior in its correction attempts. The faulty program had been present in previous missions, but this was the first time it had been executed. Previous flights had been controlled from the ground, but on this occasion an antenna failed, preventing the receipt of radio instructions and thus causing the on-board control software to be invoked.

> Moral: Even if you could make your programming language 100% reliable, you would still be prey to catastrophic bugs in the algorithm.

We have long felt that programmers working on real-time control systems should have the privilege of taking the first ride on the operational prototype. In other words, if your code implements the life support systems on the space shuttle, then you get to be launched into space and debug any last minute glitches personally. This would surely bring a whole new focus to product quality. Table 2-2 shows some of the opportunities.

Table 2-2 The Truth About Two Famous Space Software Failures

When	Mission	Error	Result	Cause
Summer 1961	Mercury	. used instead of ,	nothing; error found before flight	Flaw in Fortran language
July 22, 1962	Mariner 1	"R" instead of "$\bar{R}$" written in specification	$12M rocket and probe destroyed	programmer followed error in specification

Let us give the last word in this chapter to a more modern story of space software mishaps, almost certainly apocryphal. On every space shuttle mission, there is a cargo manifest, or list of all items to be loaded on board the craft before launch. The manifest lists each item with its weight, and is vital for calculating the fuel and balancing the craft.

It seems that before the maiden flight, a dock master was checking off certain items as they were loaded onto the shuttle. He checked off the computer systems, and then came to the manifest entry for the software. It showed the software as having zero weight, which caused a minor panic—after all, surely everything weighs something!

There was some frantic communication between the loading dock and the computer center before the problem was resolved, and the zero-weight software (bit patterns in memory) was allowed to pass! Of course, everyone knows that information has mass in a relativistic sense, but let's not ruin a good story with pedantry, eh?

References

Ceruzzi, Paul, *Beyond the Limits—Flight Enters the Computer Age*, Cambridge, MA, MIT Press, 1989

Hill, Gladwyn, "For Want of Hyphen Venus Rocket is Lost," *New York Times*, July 28, 1962.

Nicks, Oran W., *Far Travelers—The Exploring Machines*, NASA publication SP-480, 1985.

"Venus Shot Fails as Rocket Strays," Associated Press, *New York Times*, July 23, 1962.

Unscrambling Declarations in C

3

"The name of the song is called 'Haddocks' Eyes.'"
"Oh, that's the name of the song, is it?" Alice said trying to feel interested.

"No, you don't understand," the Knight said, looking a little vexed. "That's what the name is ***called****. The name really* ***is*** *'The Aged Aged Man.'"*
"Then I ought to have said 'That's what the ***song*** *is called'?" Alice corrected herself.*

"No, you oughtn't: that's quite another thing! The ***song*** *is called 'Ways and Means': but that's only what it's* ***called****, you know!"*
"Well, what ***is*** *the song, then?" said Alice, who was by this time completely bewildered.*

"I was coming to that," the Knight said. "The song really ***is*** *'A-sitting On A Gate': and the tune's my own invention."*

—Lewis Carroll, *Through the Looking Glass*

---

syntax only a compiler could love...how a declaration is formed...
a word about structs...a word about unions...a word about enums...
the precedence rule...unscrambling C declarations by diagram...
typedef can be your friend...difference between `typedef` and `#define`...
what "`typedef struct foo { ... foo } foo;`" means...
the piece of code that understandeth all parsing...
some light relief—software to bite the wax tadpole

There's a story that Queen Victoria was so impressed by *Alice in Wonderland* that she requested copies of other books by Lewis Carroll. The queen did not realize that Lewis Carroll was the pen-name of Oxford mathematics professor Charles Dodgson. She was not amused when sniggering courtiers brought her several weighty volumes including *The Condensation (Factoring) of Determinants.* This story was much told in Victorian times, and Dodgson tried hard to debunk it:

> "I take this opportunity of giving what publicity I can to my contradiction of a silly story, which has been going the round of the papers, about my having presented certain books to Her Majesty the Queen. It is so constantly repeated, and is such absolute fiction, that I think it worthwhile to state, once for all, that it is utterly false in every particular: nothing even resembling it has ever occurred."
>
> —Charles Dodgson, *Symbolic Logic*, Second Edition

Therefore, on the "he doth protest too much" principle, we can be reasonably certain that the incident did indeed happen exactly as described. In any case, Dodgson would have got on well with C, and Queen Victoria would not. Putting the quote at the head of this chapter into a table, we get:

	is called	**is**
name of the song	"Haddocks' Eyes"	"The Aged Aged Man"
the song	"Ways and Means"	"A-sitting On A Gate"

Yes, Dodgson would have been right at home with computer science. And he would have especially appreciated type models in programming languages. For example, given the C declarations:

```
typedef char * string;
string punchline = "I'm a frayed knot";
```

we can see how the Knight's paradigm can be applied to it:

	is called	**is**
type of the variable	`string`	`char *`
the variable	`punchline`	`"I'm a frayed knot"`

What could be more intuitive than that? Well, actually quite a lot of things, and they'll be clearer still after you've read this chapter.

Syntax Only a Compiler Could Love

As Kernighan and Ritchie acknowledge, "C is sometimes castigated for the syntax of its declarations" (K&R, 2nd E.d, p. 122). C's declaration syntax is trivial for a compiler (or compiler-writer) to process, but hard for the average programmer. Language designers are only human, and mistakes will be made. For example, the Ada language reference manual gives an ambiguous grammar for Ada in an appendix at the back. Ambiguity is a very undesirable property of a programming language grammar, as it significantly complicates the job of a compiler-writer. But the syntax of C declarations is a truly horrible mess that permeates the *use* of the entire language. It's no exaggeration to say that C is significantly and needlessly complicated because of the awkward manner of combining types.

There are several reasons for C's difficult declaration model. In the late 1960s, when this part of C was designed, "type models" were not a well understood area of programming language theory. The BCPL language (the grandfather of C) was type-poor, having the binary word as its only data type, so C drew on a base that was deficient. And then, there is the C philosophy that the declaration of an object should look like its use. An array of pointers-to-integers is declared by `int * p[3];` and an integer is referenced or used in an expression by writing `*p[i]`, so the declaration resembles the use. The advantage of this is that the precedence of the various operators in a "declaration" is the same as in a "use". The disadvantage is that operator precedence (with 15 or more levels in the hierarchy, depending on how you count) is another unduly complicated part of C. Programmers have to remember special rules to figure out whether `int *p[3]` is an array of pointers-to-int, or a pointer to an array of ints.

The idea that a declaration should look like a use seems to be original with C, and it hasn't been adopted by any other languages. Then again, it may be that *declaration looks like use* was not quite the splendid idea that it seemed at the time. What's so great about two different things being made to look the same? The folks from Bell Labs acknowledge the criticism, but defend this decision to the death even today. A better idea would have been to declare a pointer as

```
int &p;
```

which at least suggests that `p` is the address of an integer. This syntax has now been claimed by C++ to indicate a call by reference parameter.

The biggest problem is that you can no longer read a declaration from left to right, as people find most natural. The situation got worse with the introduction of the `volatile` and `const` keywords with ANSI C; since these keywords appear only in a declaration (not in a use), there are now fewer cases in which the use of a variable mimics its declaration. Anything that is styled like a declaration but doesn't have an identifier (such as a formal parameter declaration or a cast) looks funny. If you want to cast something to the type of pointer-to-array, you have to express the cast as:

```
char (*j)[20]; /* j is a pointer to an array of 20 char */
j = (char (*)[20]) malloc( 20 );
```

If you leave out the apparently redundant parentheses around the asterisk, it becomes invalid.

A declaration involving a pointer and a `const` has several possible orderings:

```
const int * grape;
int const * grape;
int * const grape_jelly;
```

The last of these cases makes the pointer read-only, whereas the other two make the object that it points at read-only; and of course, both the object and what it points at might be constant. Either of the following equivalent declarations will accomplish this:

```
const int * const grape_jam;
int const * const grape_jam;
```

The ANSI standard implicitly acknowledges other problems when it mentions that the typedef specifier is called a "storage-class specifier" for syntactic convenience only. It's an area that even experienced C programmers find troublesome. If declaration syntax looks bad for something as straightforward as an array of pointers, consider how it looks for something even slightly complicated. What exactly, for example, does the following declaration (adapted from the `telnet` program) declare?

```
char* const *(*next)();
```

We'll answer the question by using this declaration as an example later in the chapter. Over the years, programmers, students, and teachers have struggled to find simple mnemonics and algorithms to help them make some sense of the horrible C syntax. This chapter presents an algorithm that gives a step-by-step approach to solving the problem. Work through it with a couple of examples, and you'll never have to worry about C declarations again!

How a Declaration Is Formed

Let's first take a look at some C terminology, and the individual pieces that can make up a declaration. An important building block is a declarator—the heart of any declaration; roughly, a declarator is the identifier and any pointers, function brackets, or array indications that go along with it, as shown in Figure 3-1. We also group any initializer here for convenience.

Figure 3-1 The Declarator in C

How many	Name in C	How it looks in C

zero or more	pointers	one of the following alternatives:
		`* const volatile`
		`* volatile`
		`*`
		`* const`
		`* volatile const`

exactly one	direct_declarator	*identifier* or *identifier* [*optional_size*] ... or *identifier* (*args...*) or (*declarator*)
zero or one	initializer	= *initial_value*

A declaration is made up of the parts shown in Figure 3-2 Figure 3-2(not all combinations are valid, but this table gives us the vocabulary for further discussion). A declaration gives the basic underlying type of the variable and any initial value.

Figure 3-2 The Declaration in C

How many	Name in C	How it looks in C

at least one type-specifier
 	
(not all combinations are valid)
	type-specifier
	
	storage-class
	
	type-qualifier
		`void char short int long`
		`signed unsigned`
		`float double`
		struct_specifier
		enum_specifier
		union_specifier
		`extern static register`
		`auto typedef`
		`const volatile`

exactly one	declarator	*see definition above*
zero or more	more declarators	, *declarator*
one	semi-colon	;

We begin to see how complicated a declaration can become once you start combining types together. Also, remember there are restrictions on legal declarations. You *can't* have any of these:

- a function can't return a function, so you'll never see `foo()()`
- a function can't return an array, so you'll never see `foo()[]`
- an array can't hold a function, so you'll never see `foo[]()`

You *can* have any of these:

- a function returning a *pointer to* a function is allowed: `int (* fun())();`
- a function returning a *pointer to* an array is allowed: `int (* foo())[]`
- an array holding *pointers to* functions is allowed: `int (*foo[])()`
- an array can hold other arrays, so you'll frequently see `int foo[][]`

Before dealing with combining types, we'll refresh our memories by reviewing how to combine variables in structs and unions, and also look at enums.

A Word About `structs`

Structs are just a bunch of data items grouped together. Other languages call this a "record". The syntax for structs is easy to remember: the usual way to group stuff together in C is to put it in braces: *{ stuff... }* The keyword `struct` goes at the front so the compiler can distinguish it from a block:

```
struct { stuff... }
```

The *stuff* in a struct can be any other data declarations: individual data items, arrays, other structs, pointers, and so on. We can follow a struct definition by some variable names, declaring variables of this struct type, for example:

```
struct { stuff... } plum, pomegranate, pear;
```

The only other point to watch is that we can write an optional "structure tag" after the keyword "struct":

```
struct fruit_tag { stuff... } plum, pomegranate, pear;
```

The words `struct fruit_tag` can now be used as a shorthand for

```
struct { stuff... }
```

in future declarations.

A `struct` thus has the general form:

```
struct optional_tag {
             type_1 identifier_1;
             type_2 identifier_2;
             ...
             type_N identifier_N;
             } optional_variable_definitions ;
```

So with the declarations

```
struct date_tag { short dd,mm,yy; } my_birthday, xmas;
struct date_tag easter, groundhog_day;
```

variables `my_birthday, xmas, easter,` and `groundhog_day` all have the identical type. Structs can also have bit fields, unnamed fields, and word-aligned fields. These are obtained by following the field declaration with a colon and a number representing the field length in bits.

```
/* process ID info */

struct pid_tag {
    unsigned int inactive :1;
    unsigned int          :1;        /* 1 bit of padding */
    unsigned int refcount :6;
    unsigned int          :0;        /* pad to next word boundary */
    short pid_id;
    struct pid_tag *link;
};
```

This is commonly used for "programming right down to the silicon," and you'll see it in systems programs. It can also be used for storing a Boolean flag in a bit rather than a char. A bit field must have a type of int, unsigned int, or signed int (or a qualified version of one of these). It's implementation-dependent whether bit fields that are int's can be negative.

Our preference is not to mix a struct declaration with definitions of variables. We prefer

```
struct veg { int weight, price_per_lb; };
struct veg onion, radish, turnip;
```

to

```
struct veg { int weight, price_per_lb; } onion, radish, turnip;
```

Sure, the second version saves you typing a few characters of code, but we should be much more concerned with how easy the code is to read, not to write. We write code once, but it is read many times during subsequent program maintenance. It's just a little simpler to read a line that only does one thing. For this reason, variable declarations should be separate from the type declaration.

Finally there are two parameter passing issues associated with structs. Some C books make statements like "parameters are passed to a called function by pushing them on the stack from right to left." This is oversimplification—if you own such a book, tear out that page and burn it. If you own such a compiler, tear out those bytes. Parameters are passed in registers (for speed) where possible. Be aware that an int "i" may well be passed in a completely different manner to a struct "s" whose only member is an int. Assuming an int parameter is typically passed in a register, you may find that structs are instead passed on the stack. The second point to note is that by putting an array inside a struct like this:

```
/* array inside a struct */
struct s_tag { int a[100]; };
```

you can now treat the array as a first-class type. You can copy the entire array with an assignment statement, pass it to a function by value, and make it the return type of a function.

```
struct s_tag { int a[100]; };
struct s_tag orange, lime, lemon;
```

```
struct s_tag twofold (struct s_tag s) {
    int j;
    for (j=0;j<100;j++) s.a[j] *= 2;
    return s;
}

main() {
    int i;
    for (i=0;i<100;i++) lime.a[i] = 1;
    lemon = twofold(lime);
    orange = lemon; /* assigns entire struct */
}
```

You typically don't want to assign an entire array very often, but you can do it by burying it in a struct. Let's finish up by showing one way to make a struct contain a pointer to its own type, as needed for lists, trees, and many dynamic data structures.

```
/* struct that points to the next struct */
struct node_tag { int datum;
                  struct node_tag *next;
                };
struct node_tag a,b;
a.next = &b;        /* example link-up */
a.next->next=NULL;
```

A Word About unions

Unions are known as the variant part of variant records in many other languages. They have a similar appearance to structs, but the memory layout has one crucial difference. Instead of each member being stored after the end of the previous one, all the members have an offset of zero. The storage for the individual members is thus overlaid: only one member at a time can be stored there.

There's some good news and some bad news associated with unions. The bad news is that the good news isn't all that good. The good news is that unions have exactly the same general appearance as structs, but with the keyword `struct` replaced by `union`. So if you're comfortable with all the varieties and possibilities for structs, you already know unions too. A union has the general form:

```
union optional_tag{
        type_1 identifier_1;
        type_2 identifier_2;
           ...
        type_N identifier_N;
 } optional_variable_definitions;
```

Unions usually occur as part of a larger struct that also has implicit or explicit information about which type of data is actually present. There's an obvious type insecurity here of storing data as one type and retrieving it as another. Ada addresses this by insisting that the discriminant field be explicitly stored in the record. C says go fish, and relies on the programmer to remember what was put there.

Unions are typically used to save space, by not storing all possibilities for certain data items that cannot occur together. For example, if we are storing zoological information on certain species, our first attempt at a data record might be:

```
struct creature {
 char has_backbone;
 char has_fur;
 short num_of_legs_in_excess_of_4;
};
```

However, we know that all creatures are either vertebrate or invertebrate. We further know that only vertebrate animals have fur, and that only invertebrate creatures have more than four legs. Nothing has more than four legs and fur, so we can save space by storing these two mutually exclusive fields as a union:

```
union secondary_characteristics {
 char has_fur;
 short num_of_legs_in_excess_of_4;
};
```

```
struct creature {
           char has_backbone;
           union secondary_characteristics form;
};
```

We would typically overlay space like this to conserve backing store. If we have a datafile of 20 million animals, we can save up to 20 Mb of disk space this way.

There is another use for unions, however. Unions can also be used, not for one interpretation of two different pieces of data, but to get two different interpretations of the same data. Interestingly enough, this does exactly the same job as the REDEFINES clause in COBOL. An example is:

```
union bits32_tag {
        int whole;                          /* one 32-bit value */
        struct {char c0,c1,c2,c3;} byte; /* four 8-bit bytes */
} value;
```

This union allows a programmer to extract the full 32-bit value, or the individual byte fields `value.byte.c0`, and so on. There are other ways to accomplish this, but the union does it without the need for extra assignments or type casting. Just for fun, I looked through about 150,000 lines of machine-independent operating system source (and boy, are my arms tired). The results showed that structs are about one hundred times more common than unions. That's an indication of how much more frequently you'll encounter structs than unions in practice.

A Word About enums

Enums (enumerated types) are simply a way of associating a series of names with a series of integer values. In a weakly typed language like C, they provide very little that can't be done with a `#define`, so they were omitted from most early implementations of K&R C. But they're in most other languages, so C finally got them too. The general form of an enum should look familiar by now:

```
enum optional_tag { stuff... } optional_variable_definitions;
```

The *stuff...* in this case is a list of identifiers, possibly with integer values assigned to them. An enumerated type example is:

```
enum sizes { small=7, medium, large=10, humungous };
```

The integer values start at zero by default. If you assign a value in the list, the next value is one greater, and so on. There is one advantage to enums: unlike #defined names which are typically discarded during compilation, enum names usually persist through to the debugger, and can be used while debugging your code.

The Precedence Rule

We have now reviewed the building blocks of declarations. This section describes one method for breaking them down into an English explanation. The precedence rule for understanding C declarations is the one that the language lawyers like best. It's high on brevity, but very low on intuition.

The Precedence Rule for Understanding C Declarations

A Declarations are read by starting with the name and then reading in precedence order.

B The precedence, from high to low, is:

- B.1 parentheses grouping together parts of a declaration
- B.2 the postfix operators:
  - parentheses `( )` indicating a function, and
  - square brackets `[ ]` indicating an array.
- B.3 the prefix operator: the asterisk denoting "pointer to".

C If a `const` and/or `volatile` keyword is next to a type specifier (e.g. `int`, `long`, etc.) it applies to the type specifier. Otherwise the `const` and/or `volatile` keyword applies to the pointer asterisk on its immediate left.

An example of solving a declaration using the Precedence Rule:

```
char* const *(*next)();
```

Table 3-1 Solving a Declaration Using the Precedence Rule

Rule to apply	Explanation
A	First, go to the variable name, "`next`", and note that it is directly enclosed by parentheses.
B.1	So we group it with what else is in the parentheses, to get "`next` is a pointer to...".
B	Then we go outside the parentheses, and have a choice of a prefix asterisk, or a postfix pair of parentheses.
B.2	Rule B.2 tells us the highest precedence thing is the function parentheses at the right, so we have "`next` is a pointer to a function returning…"
B.3	Then process the prefix "`*`" to get "pointer to".
C	Finally, take the "`char * const`", as a constant pointer to a character.

Then put it all together to read:

> "`next` is a pointer to a function returning a pointer to a const pointer-to-char"

and we're done. The precedence rule is what all the rules boil down to, but if you prefer something a little more intuitive, use Figure 3-3.

Unscrambling C Declarations by Diagram

In this section we present a diagram with numbered steps (see Figure 3-3). If you proceed in steps, starting at one and following the guide arrows, a C declaration of arbitrary complexity can quickly be translated into English (also of arbitrary complexity). We'll simplify declarations by ignoring typedefs in the diagram. To read a typedef, translate the declaration ignoring the word "typedef". If it translates to "p is a...", you can now use the name "p" whenever you want to declare something of the type to which it translates.

Magic Decoder Ring for C Declarations

Declarations in C are read boustrophedonically,i.e. alternating right-to-left with left-to right. And who'd have thought there would be a special word to describe that! Start at the first identifier you find when reading from the left. When we match a token in our declaration against the diagram, we erase it from further consideration. At each point we look first at the token to the right, then to the left. When everything has been erased, the job is done.

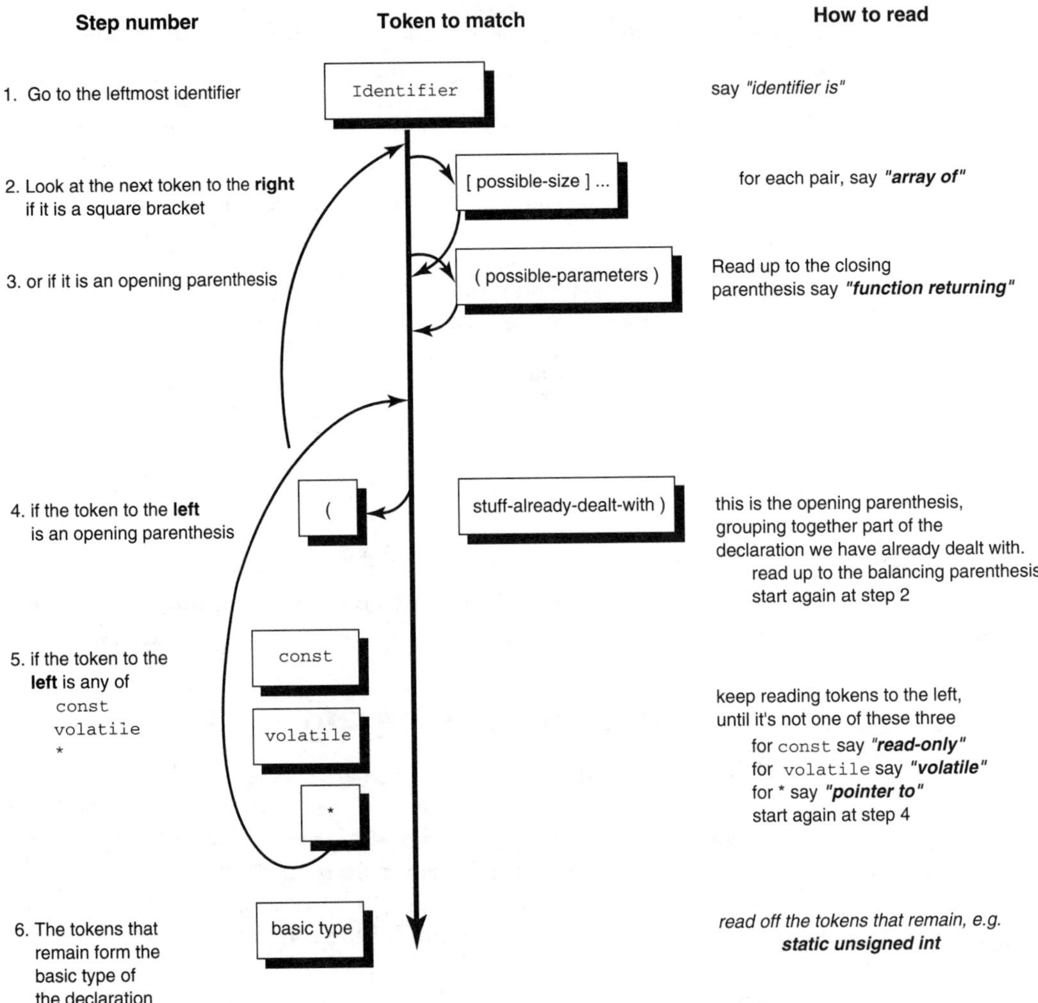

Step number
Token to match
How to read
1. Go to the leftmost identifier
Identifier
say *"identifier is"*
2. Look at the next token to the **right** if it is a square bracket
[possible-size] ...
for each pair, say ***"array of"***
3. or if it is an opening parenthesis
(possible-parameters)
Read up to the closing parenthesis say ***"function returning"***
4. if the token to the **left** is an opening parenthesis
(
stuff-already-dealt-with)
this is the opening parenthesis, grouping together part of the declaration we have already dealt with.
read up to the balancing parenthesis
start again at step 2
5. if the token to the **left** is any of
const
volatiie
*
const
volatile
*
keep reading tokens to the left, until it's not one of these three
for const say ***"read-only"***
for volatile say ***"volatile"***
for * say ***"pointer to"***
start again at step 4
6. The tokens that remain form the basic type of the declaration
basic type
read off the tokens that remain, e.g.
static unsigned int

Figure 3-3 How to Parse a C Declaration

Let's try a couple of examples of unscrambling a declaration using the diagram. Say we want to figure out what our first example of code means:

```
char* const *(*next)();
```

As we unscramble this declaration, we gradually "white out" the pieces of it that we have already dealt with, so that we can see exactly how much remains. Again, remember `const` means "read-only". Just because it says constant, it doesn't necessarily mean constant.

The process is represented in Table 3-2. In each step, the portion of the declaration we are dealing with is printed in bold type. Starting at step one, we will proceed through these steps:

Table 3-2 Steps in Unscrambling a C Declaration

Declaration Remaining *(start at leftmost identifier)*	**Next Step to Apply**	**Result**
`char * const *(*next) ();`	step 1	say "**next is a...**"
`char * const *(*     ) ();`	step 2, 3	doesn't match, go to next step, say "next is a..."
`char * const *(*     ) ();`	step 4	doesn't match, go to next step
`char * const *(*     ) ();`	step 5	asterisk matches, say "**pointer to ...**", go to step 4
`char * const *(      ) ();`	step 4	"(" matches up to ")", go to step 2
`char * const *         ();`	step 2	doesn't match, go to next step
`char * const *         ();`	step 3	say "**function returning...**"
`char * const *           ;`	step 4	doesn't match, go to next step
`char * const *           ;`	step 5	say "**pointer to...**"
`char * const             ;`	step 5	say "**read-only...**"
`char *                   ;`	step 5	say "**pointer to...**"
`char                     ;`	step 6	say "**char**"

Then put it all together to read:

"next is a pointer to a function returning a pointer to a read-only pointer-to-char"

and we're done.

Now let's try a more complicated example.

```
char *(*c[10])(int **p);
```

Try working through the steps in the same way as the last example. The steps are given at the end of this chapter, to give you a chance to try it for yourself and compare your answer.

`typedef` Can Be Your Friend

Typedefs are a funny kind of declaration: they introduce a new name for a type rather than reserving space for a variable. In some ways, a typedef is similar to macro text replacement—it doesn't introduce a new type, just a new name for a type, but there is a key difference explained later.

If you refer back to the section on how a declaration is formed, you'll see that the `typedef` keyword can be part of a regular declaration, occurring somewhere near the beginning. In fact, a typedef has exactly the same format as a variable declaration, only with this extra keyword to tip you off.

Since a typedef *looks* exactly like a variable declaration, it is *read* exactly like one. The techniques given in the previous sections apply. Instead of the declaration saying "this name refers to a variable of the stated type," the `typedef` keyword doesn't create a variable, but causes the declaration to say "this name is a synonym for the stated type."

Typically, this is used for tricky cases involving pointers to stuff. The classic example is the declaration of the `signal()` prototype. Signal is a system call that tells the runtime system to call a particular routine whenever a specified "software interrupt" arrives. It should really be called "Call_that_routine_when_this_interrupt_comes_in". You call `signal()` and pass it arguments to say which interrupt you are talking about, and which routine should be invoked to handle it. The ANSI Standard shows that signal is declared as:

```
void (*signal(int sig, void (*func)(int)) ) (int);
```

Practicing our new-found skills at reading declarations, we can tell that this means:

```
void (*signal(                              ) ) (int);
```

`signal` is a function (with some funky arguments) returning a pointer to a function (taking an int argument and returning void). One of the funky arguments is itself:

```
void (*func)(int) ;
```

a pointer to a function taking an int argument and returning void. Here's how it can be simplified by a typedef that "factors out" the common part.

```
typedef void (*ptr_to_func) (int);
/* this says that ptr_to_func is a pointer to a function
 * that takes an int argument, and returns void
 */


ptr_to_func signal(int, ptr_to_func);
/* this says that signal is a function that takes
 * two arguments, an int and a ptr_to_func, and
 * returns a ptr_to_func
 */
```

Typedef is not without its drawbacks, however. It has the same confusing syntax of other declarations, and the same ability to cram several declarators into one declaration. It provides essentially nothing for structs, except the unhelpful ability to omit the `struct` keyword. And in any `typedef`, you don't even have to put the `typedef` at the start of the declaration!

Handy Heuristic

Tips for Working with Declarators

Don't put several declarators together in one typedef, like this:

```
typedef int *ptr, (*fun)(), arr[5];
/* ptr is the type "pointer to int"
 * fun is the type "pointer to a function returning int"
 * arr is the type "array of 5 ints"
 */
```

And never, ever, bury the typedef in the middle of a declaration, like this:

```
unsigned const long typedef int volatile *kumquat;
```

Typedef creates aliases for data types rather than new data types. You can typedef any type.

```
typedef int (*array_ptr)[100];
```

Just write a declaration for a variable with the type you desire. Have the name of the variable be the name you want for the alias. Write the keyword 'typedef' at the start, as shown above. A typedef name cannot be the same as another identifier in the same block.

Difference Between `typedef int x[10]` and `#define x int[10]`

As mentioned above, there is a key difference between a typedef and macro text replacement. The right way to think about this is to view a typedef as being a complete "encapsulated" type—you can't add to it after you have declared it. The difference between this and macros shows up in two ways.

You can extend a macro typename with other type specifiers, but not a typedef'd typename. That is,

```
#define peach int
unsigned peach i; /* works fine */

typedef int banana;
unsigned banana i; /* Bzzzt! illegal */
```

Second, a typedef'd name provides the type for every declarator in a declaration.

```
#define int_ptr int *
int_ptr chalk, cheese;
```

After macro expansion, the second line effectively becomes:

```
int * chalk, cheese;
```

This makes chalk and cheese as different as chutney and chives: chalk is a pointer-to-an-integer, while cheese is an integer. In contrast, a typedef like this:

```
typedef char * char_ptr;
char_ptr Bentley, Rolls_Royce;
```

declares both Bentley and Rolls_Royce to be the same. The name on the front is different, but they are both a pointer to a char.

What `typedef struct foo { ... foo; } foo;` Means

There are multiple namespaces in C:

* label names
* tags (one namespace for all structs, enums and unions)
* member names (each struct or union has its own namespace)
* everyting else

Everything within a namespace must be unique, but an identical name can be applied to things in different namespaces. Since each struct or union has its own namespace, the same member names can be reused in many different structs. This was not true for very old compilers, and is one reason people prefixed field names with a unique initial in the BSD 4.2 kernel code, like this:

```
struct vnode {
        long                v_flag;
        long                v_usecount;
        struct vnode        *v_freef;
        struct vnodeops     *v_op;
};
```

Because it is legal to use the same name in different namespaces, you sometimes see code like this.

```
struct foo {int foo;} foo;
```

This is absolutely guaranteed to confuse and dismay future programmers who have to maintain your code. And what would `sizeof( foo );` refer to?

Things get even scarier. Declarations like these are quite legal:

```
typedef struct baz {int baz;} baz;
        struct baz variable_1;
               baz variable_2;
```

That's too many "baz"s! Let's try that again, with more enlightening names, to see what's going on:

```
typedef struct my_tag {int i;} my_type;
        struct my_tag variable_1;
 my_type variable_2;
```

The typedef introduces the name `my_type` as a shorthand for "`struct my_tag {int i}`", but it also introduces the structure tag `my_tag` that can equally be used with the keyword `struct`. If you use the same identifier for the type and the tag in a typedef, it has the effect of making the keyword "`struct`" optional, which provides completely the wrong mental model for what is going on. Unhappily, the syntax for this kind of struct typedef exactly mirrors the syntax of a combined struct type and variable declaration. So although these two declarations have a similar form,

```
typedef struct fruit {int weight, price_per_lb } fruit; /* statement 1 */
        struct veg   {int weight, price_per_lb } veg;   /* statement 2 */
```

very different things are happening. Statement 1 declares a structure tag "fruit" and a structure typedef "fruit" which can be used like this:

```
struct fruit mandarin;  /* uses structure tag  "fruit" */
       fruit tangerine; /* uses structure type "fruit" */
```

Statement 2 declares a structure tag "veg" and a variable veg. Only the structure tag can be used in further declarations, like this:

```
struct veg potato;
```

It would be an error to attempt a declaration of `veg  cabbage`. That would be like writing:

```
int i;
i j;
```

Handy Heuristic

Tips for Working with Typedefs

Don't bother with `typedefs` for `structs`.

All they do is save you writing the word "struct", which is a clue that you probably shouldn't be hiding anyway.

Use typedefs for:

- types that combine arrays, structs, pointers, or functions.
- portable types. When you need a type that's at least (say) 20-bits, make it a typedef. Then when you port the code to different platforms, select the right type, `short`, `int`, `long`, making the change in just the typedef, rather than in every declaration.
- casts. A typedef can provide a simple name for a complicated type cast. E.g.

```
typedef int   (*ptr_to_int_fun)(void);
   char * p;
                 = (ptr_to_int_fun) p;
```

Always use a tag in a structure definition, even if it's not needed. It will be later.

A pretty good principle in computer science, when you have two different things, is to use two different names to refer to them. It reduces the opportunities for confusion (always a good policy in software). If you're stuck for a name for a structure tag, just give it a name that ends in "_tag". This makes it simpler to detect what a particular name is. Future generations will then bless your name instead of reviling your works.

The Piece of Code that Understandeth All Parsing

You can easily write a program that parses C declarations and translates them into English. In fact, why don't you? The basic form of a C declaration has already been described. All we need to do is write a piece of code which understands that form and unscrambles it the same way as Figure 3-4. To keep it simple, we'll pretty much ignore error handling, and we'll deal with structs, enums, and unions by compressing them down to just the single word "struct", "enum" or "union". Finally, this program expects functions to have empty parentheses (i.e., no argument lists).

Programming Challenge

Write a Program to Translate C Declarations into English

Here's the design. The main data structure is a stack, on which we store tokens that we have read, while we are reading forward to the identifier. Then we can look at the next token to the right by reading it, and the next token to the left by popping it off the stack. The data structure looks like:

```
struct token { char type;
               char string[MAXTOKENLEN]; };


 /* holds tokens we read before reaching first identifier */
struct token stack[MAXTOKENS];


 /* holds the token just read */
 struct token this;
```

The pseudo-code is:

utility routines----------

```
classify_string
    look at the current token and
    return a value of "type" "qualifier" or "identifier" in this.type
gettoken
    read the next token into this.string
    if it is alphanumeric, classify_string
    else it must be a single character token
    this.type = the token itself; terminate this.string with a nul.
read_to_first_identifier
    gettoken and push it onto the stack until the first identifier is read.
    Print "identifier is", this.string
    gettoken
```

Write a Program to Translate C Declarations into English (Continued)

parsing routines----------

```
deal_with_function_args
    read past closing ')' print out "function returning"
deal_with_arrays
    while you've got "[size]" print it out and read past it
deal_with_any_pointers
    while you've got "*" on the stack print "pointer to" and pop it
deal_with_declarator
    if this.type is '[' deal_with_arrays
    if this.type is '(' deal_with_function_args
    deal_with_any_pointers
    while there's stuff on the stack
    if it's a '('
    pop it and gettoken; it should be the closing ')'
    deal_with_declarator
    else pop it and print it
```

main routine----------

```
main
    read_to_first_identifier
    deal_with_declarator
```

This is a small program that has been written numerous times over the years, often under the name "cdecl".[1] An incomplete version of cdecl appears in *The C Programming Language*. The cdecl specified here is more complete; it supports the type qualifiers "const" and "volatile". It also knows about structs, enums, and unions though not in full generality; it is easy to extend this version to handle argument declarations in functions. This program can be implemented with about 150 lines of C. Adding error handling, and the full generality of declarations, would make it much larger. In any event, when you program this parser, you are implementing one of the major subsystems in a compiler—that's a substantial programming achievement, and one that will really help you to gain a deep understanding of this area.

1. Don't confuse this with the cdecl modifier used in Turbo C on PC's to indicate that the generated code should not use the Turbo Pascal default convention for calling functions. The cdecl modifier allows Borland C code to be linked with other Turbo languages that were implemented with different calling conventions.

Further Reading

Now that you have mastered the way to build data structures in C, you may be interested in reading a good general-purpose book on data structures. One such book is *Data Structures with Abstract Data Types* by Daniel F. Stubbs and Neil W. Webre, 2nd Ed., Pacific Grove, CA, Brooks/Cole, 1989.

They cover a wide variety of data structures, including strings, lists, stacks, queues, trees, heaps, sets, and graphs. Recommended.

Some Light Relief—
Software to Bite the Wax Tadpole...

One of the great joys of computer programming is writing software that controls something physical (like a robot arm or a disk head). There's an enormous feeling of satisfaction when you run a program and something moves in the real world. The graduate students in MIT's Artificial Intelligence Laboratory were motivated by this when they wired up the departmental computer to the elevator call button on the ninth floor. This enabled you to call the elevator by typing a command from your LISP machine! The program checked to make sure your terminal was actually located inside the laboratory before it called the elevator, to prevent rival hackers using the dark side of the force to tie up the elevators.

The other great joy of computer programming is chowing down on junk food while hacking. So what could be more natural than to combine the two thrills? Some computer science graduate students at Carnegie-Mellon University developed a junk-food/computer interface to solve a long-standing problem: the computer science department Coke® machine was on the third floor, far from the offices of the graduate students. Students were fed up with travelling the long distance only to find the Coke machine empty or, even worse, so recently filled that it was dispensing warm bottles. John Zsarney and Lawrence Butcher noticed that the Coke machine stored its product in six refrigerated columns, each with an "empty" light that flashed as it delivered a bottle, and stayed on when the column was sold out. It was a simple matter to wire up these lights to a serial interface and thus transmit the "bottle dispensed" data to the PDP10 department mainframe computer. From the PDP10, the Coke machine interface looked just like a telnet connection! Mike Kazar and Dave Nichols wrote the software that responded to enquiries and kept track of which column contained the most refrigerated bottles.

Naturally, Mike and Dave didn't stop there. They also designed a network protocol that enabled the mainframe to respond to Coke machine status enquiries from any machine on the local ethernet, and eventually from the Internet itself. Ivor Durham implemented the software to do this and to check the Coke machine status from other machines. With admirable economy of effort Ivor reused the standard "finger" facility—normally used to check from one machine whether a specified user is logged onto another machine. He modified the "finger" server to run the Coke status program whenever someone fingered the nonexistent user "coke". Since finger requests are part of standard Internet protocols, people could check the Coke machine from any CMU computer. In fact, by running the command

```
finger coke@g.gp.cs.cmu.edu
```

you could discover the Coke machine's status from any machine anywhere on the Internet, even thousands of miles away!

Others who worked on the project include Steve Berman, Eddie Caplan, Mark Wilkins, and Mark Zaremsky[2]. The Coke machine programs were used for over a decade, and were even rewritten for UNIX Vaxen when the PDP-10 was retired in the early 1980s. The end came a few years ago, when the local Coke bottler discontinued the returnable, Coke-bottle-shaped bottles. The old machine couldn't handle the new shape bottles, so it was replaced by a new vending machine that required a new interface. For a while nobody bothered, but the lure of caffeine eventually motivated Greg Nelson to reengineer the new machine. The CMU graduate students also wired up the candy machine, and similar projects have been completed in other schools, too.

The computer club at the University of Western Australia has a Coke machine connected to a 68000 CPU, with 80K of memory and an ethernet interface (more power than most PC's had a decade ago). The Computer Science House at Rochester Institute of Technology, Rochester, NY, also has a Coke machine on the Internet, and has extended it to providing drinks on credit and computerized account billing. One student enjoyed remote logging in from home hundreds of miles away over the summer, and randomly dispensing a few free drinks for whoever next passed. It's getting to the point where "Coke machine" will soon be the most common type of hardware on the Internet.

Why stop with cola? Last Christmas, programmers at Cygnus Support connected their office Christmas tree decorations to their ethernet. They could amuse themselves by toggling various lights from their workstations. And people worry that Japan is pulling ahead of America in technology! Inside Sun Microsystems, there's an e-mail address gatewayed to a fax modem. When you send e-mail there, it's parsed for phone number details and sent on as a fax transmission. Ace programmer Don Hopkins wrote *pizzatool* to put it to good use. Pizzatool let you custom-select toppings for a pizza using a GUI interface (most users specified extra GUI cheese), and sent the fax order to nearby Tony & Alba's Pizza restaurant, which accepted fax orders and delivered.

I don't think I'll be divulging a trade secret if I mention that extensive use was made of this service during the late-night lab sessions developing Sun's SPARCserver 600MP series machines. Bon appetit!

2. Craig Everhart, Eddie Caplan, and Robert Frederking, "Serious Coke Addiction," *25th Anniversary Symposium, Computer Science at CMU: A Commemorative Review, 1990*, p. 70. Reed and Witting Company.

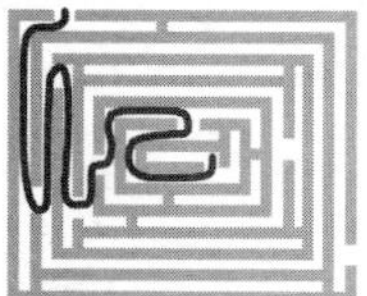

Programming Solution

The Piece of Code that Understandeth All Parsing

```
#include <stdio.h>
#include <string.h>
#include <ctype.h>
#include <stdlib.h>
#define MAXTOKENS 100
#define MAXTOKENLEN 64

enum type_tag { IDENTIFIER, QUALIFIER, TYPE };

struct token {
    char type;
    char string[MAXTOKENLEN];
};

int top=-1;
struct token stack[MAXTOKENS];
struct token this;

#define pop stack[top--]
#define push(s) stack[++top]=s

enum type_tag classify_string(void)
/* figure out the identifier type */
{
    char *s = this.string;
    if (!strcmp(s,"const")) {
         strcpy(s,"read-only");
         return QUALIFIER;
    }
    if (!strcmp(s,"volatile")) return QUALIFIER;
    if (!strcmp(s,"void")) return TYPE;
    if (!strcmp(s,"char")) return TYPE;
    if (!strcmp(s,"signed")) return TYPE;
```

The Piece of Code that Understandeth All Parsing (Continued)

```
    if (!strcmp(s,"unsigned")) return TYPE;
    if (!strcmp(s,"short")) return TYPE;
    if (!strcmp(s,"int")) return TYPE;
    if (!strcmp(s,"long")) return TYPE;
    if (!strcmp(s,"float")) return TYPE;
    if (!strcmp(s,"double")) return TYPE;
    if (!strcmp(s,"struct")) return TYPE;
    if (!strcmp(s,"union")) return TYPE;
    if (!strcmp(s,"enum")) return TYPE;
    return IDENTIFIER;
}

void gettoken(void) /* read next token into "this" */
{
    char *p = this.string;

    /* read past any spaces */
    while ((*p = getchar()) == ' ' ) ;

    if (isalnum(*p)) {
        /* it starts with A-Z,0-9 read in identifier */
        while ( isalnum(*++p=getchar()) );
        ungetc(*p,stdin);
        *p =  '\0';
        this.type=classify_string();
        return;
    }

    if (*p=='*') {
        strcpy(this.string,"pointer to");
        this.type = '*';
        return;
    }
    this.string[1]= '\0';
    this.type = *p;
    return;
}
```

The Piece of Code that Understandeth All Parsing (Continued)

```
/* The piece of code that understandeth all parsing. */
read_to_first_identifier() {
    gettoken();
    while (this.type!=IDENTIFIER) {
        push(this);
        gettoken();
    }
    printf("%s is ", this.string);
    gettoken();
}

deal_with_arrays() {
    while (this.type=='[') {
        printf("array ");
        gettoken(); /* a number or ']' */
        if (isdigit(this.string[0])) {
            printf("0..%d ",atoi(this.string)-1);
            gettoken(); /* read the ']' */
        }
        gettoken(); /* read next past the ']' */
        printf("of ");
    }
}

deal_with_function_args() {
    while (this.type!=')') {
        gettoken();
    }
    gettoken();
    printf("function returning ");
}

deal_with_pointers() {
    while ( stack[top].type== '*' ) {
        printf("%s ", pop.string );
    }
}
```

The Piece of Code that Understandeth All Parsing (Continued)

```
deal_with_declarator() {
    /* deal with possible array/function following the identifier */
    switch (this.type) {
    case '[' : deal_with_arrays(); break;
    case '(' : deal_with_function_args();
    }

    deal_with_pointers();

    /* process tokens that we stacked while reading to identifier */
    while (top>=0) {
        if (stack[top].type == '(' ) {
            pop;
            gettoken(); /* read past ')' */
            deal_with_declarator();
        } else {
            printf("%s ",pop.string);
        }
    }
}

main()
{
    /* put tokens on stack until we reach identifier */
    read_to_first_identifier();
    deal_with_declarator();
    printf("\n");
    return 0;
}
```

Handy Heuristic

Make String Comparison Look More Natural

One of the problems with the `strcmp ()` routine to compare two strings is that it returns zero if the strings are identical. This leads to convoluted code when the comparison is part of a conditional statement:

```
if (!strcmp(s,"volatile")) return QUALIFIER;
```

a zero result indicates false, so we have to negate it to get what we want.
Here's a better way. Set up the definition:

```
#define STRCMP(a,R,b)    (strcmp(a,b) R 0)
```

Now you can write a string in the natural style

```
if ( STRCMP(s, ==, "volatile"))
```

Using this definition, the code expresses what is happening in a more natural style. Try rewriting the cdecl program to use this style of string comparison, and see if you prefer it.

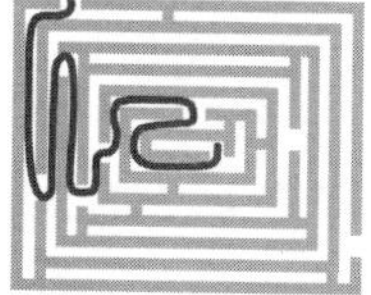

Programming Solution

Unscrambling a C Declaration (One More Time)

Here is the solution to "What is this declaration?" on page 78. In each step, the portion of the declaration we are dealing with is printed in bold type. Starting at step one, we will proceed through these steps:

Declaration Remaining	Next Step to Apply	Result
start at the leftmost identifier		
`char *(*`**`c`**`[10])(int **p);`	step 1	say "**c is a...**"
`char *(* `**`[10]`**`)(int **p);`	step 2	say "**array[0..9] of...**"

Unscrambling a C Declaration (One More Time)		
`char *(*       )(int **p);`	step 5	say "**pointer to...**" go to step 4
`char *(        )(int **p);`	step 4	delete the parens, go to step 2, fall through step 2 to step 3
`char *          (int **p);`	step 3	say "**function returning...**"
`char *                   ;`	step 5	say "**pointer to...**"
`char                     ;`	step 6	say "**char;**"

Then put it all together to read:

> "c is an array[0..9] of pointer to a function returning a pointer-to-char"

and we're done. Note: the fuctions pointed to in the array take a pointer to a pointer as their one and only parameter.

The Shocking Truth: C Arrays and Pointers Are NOT the Same! 4

Should array indices start at 0 or 1? My compromise of 0.5 was rejected without, I thought, proper consideration.

—Stan Kelly-Bootle

arrays are NOT pointers...why doesn't my code work?...
what's a declaration? what's a definition?...match your declarations to the definition...array and pointer differences...
some light relief—fun with palindromes!

Arrays Are NOT Pointers!

One of the first things that novice C programmers often hear is that "arrays are the same as pointers." Unfortunately, this is a dangerous half-truth. The ANSI C Standard paragraph 6.5.4.2 recommends that you

> *Note the distinction between the declarations:*

```
extern int *x;
extern int y[];
```

> *The first declares* `x` *to be a pointer to* `int`*; the second declares* `y` *to be an array of* `int` *of unspecified size (an incomplete type), the storage for which is defined elsewhere.*

The standard doesn't go into the matter in any greater detail than that. Too many C books gloss over when arrays are, and are not, equivalent to pointers, relegating the explanation to a footnote when it should be a chapter heading. This book tries to restore the balance by fully explaining when arrays are equivalent to pointers, when they are not, and why. Not only that, but we also make sure that the key point is emphasized with a chapter heading, not a footnote.

Why Doesn't My Code Work?

If I had a dime for every time someone brought me a program like the following, together with the complaint that "it doesn't work," then I'd have, uh, let's see, about two-fifty.

file 1:

```
int mango[100];
```

file 2:

```
extern int *mango;
 . . .
/* some code that references mango[i] */
```

Here, file 1 defines `mango` as an array, but file 2 declares it as a pointer. But what is wrong with this? After all, "everybody knows" arrays and pointers are pretty much the same in C. The problem is that "everybody" is wrong! It is like confusing integers and floats:

file 1:

```
int guava;
```

file 2:

```
extern float guava;
```

The `int` and `float` example above is an obvious and gross type mismatch; nobody would expect this to work. So why do people think it's always OK to use pointers and arrays completely interchangeably? The answer is that array references can always be rewritten as pointer references, and there *is* a context in which pointer and array definitions are equivalent. Unfortunately, this context involves a very common use of arrays, so people naturally generalize and assume equivalence in all cases, including the blatantly wrong "defined as array/external declaration as pointer" above.

What's a Declaration? What's a Definition?

Before getting to the bottom of this problem, we need to refresh our memories about some essential C terminology. Recall that objects in C must have exactly one definition, and they may have multiple external declarations. By the way, no C++ mumbo-jumbo here—when we say "object" we mean a C "thing" known to the linker, like a function or data item.

A *definition* is the special kind of declaration that creates an object; a *declaration* indicates a name that allows you to refer to an object created here or elsewhere. Let's review the terminology:

definition	occurs in only one place	specifies the type of an object; reserves storage for it; is used to create new objects *example*: `int my_array[100];`
declaration	can occur multiple times	describes the type of an object; is used to refer to objects defined elsewhere (e.g., in another file) *example*: `extern int my_array[];`

Handy Heuristic

Distinguishing a Definition from a Declaration

You can tell these two apart by remembering:

A **declaration** is like a **customs declaration**:

it is not the thing itself, merely a description of some baggage that you say you have around somewhere.

a definition is the **special kind of declaration** that **fixes** the storage for an object

The declaration of an external object tells the compiler the type and name of the object, and that memory allocation is done somewhere else. Since you aren't allocating memory for the array at this point, you don't need to provide information on how big it is in total. You do have to provide the size of all array dimensions except the leftmost one—this gives the compiler enough information to generate indexing code.

How Arrays and Pointers Are Accessed

In this section we show the difference between a reference using an array and a reference using a pointer. The first distinction we must note is between *address y* and *contents of address y*. This is actually quite a subtle point, because in most programming languages we use the same symbol to represent both, and the compiler figures out which is meant from the context. Take a simple assignment, as shown in Figure 4-1.

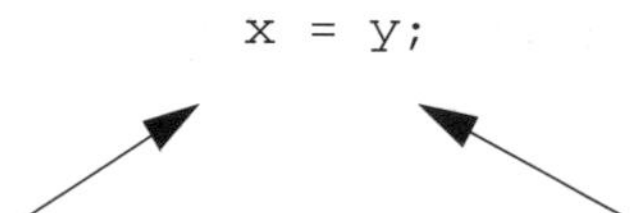

The symbol x, in this context, means the **address** that x represents.	The symbol y, in this context, means the **contents of the address** that y represents.
This is termed an **l-value**.	This is termed an **r-value**.
An **l-value** is known at compiletime. An **l-value** says where to store the result.	An **r-value** is not known until runtime. "The value of y" means the **r-value** unless otherwise stated.

A "modifiable l-value" is a term introduced by C. It means an l-value that is permitted to appear on the left-hand side of an assignment statement. This weirdness was introduced to cope with arraynames which are l-values that locate objects, but in C may not be assigned to. Hence, an arrayname is an l-value but not a modifiable l-value. The standard stipulates that an assignment operator must have a modifiable l-value as its left operand. Translation into English: you can only assign into things that you can change.

Figure 4-1 The Difference between an Address (l-value) and the Contents of the Address (r-value)

The symbol appearing on the left of an assignment is sometimes called an *l-value* (for "left-hand-side" or "locator" value), while a symbol on the right of an assignment is sometimes called an *r-value* (for "right-hand-side"). The compiler allocates an address (or l-value) to each variable. This address is known at compiletime, and is where the variable will be kept at runtime. In contrast, the value *stored in* a variable at runtime (its r-value) is not known until runtime. If the value stored in a variable is required, the compiler emits code to read the value from the given address and put it in a register.

The key point here is that the address of each symbol is known at compiletime. So if the compiler needs to do something with an address (add an offset to it, perhaps), it can do that directly and does not need to plant code to retrieve the address first. In contrast, the current value of a pointer must be retrieved at runtime before it can be dereferenced (made part of a further look-up). Diagram A shows an array reference.

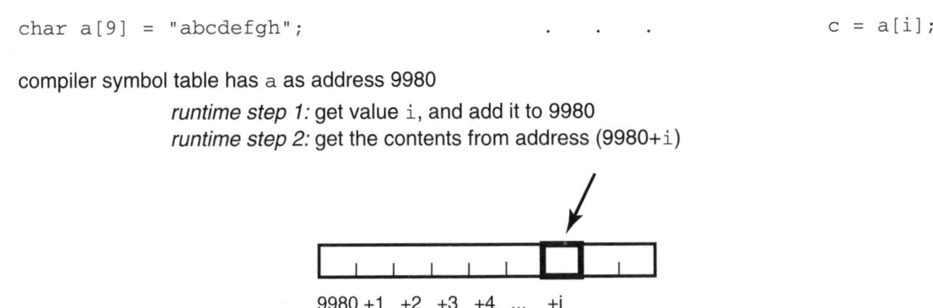
char a[9] = "abcdefgh";
. . .
c = a[i];
compiler symbol table has a as address 9980
runtime step 1: get value i, and add it to 9980
runtime step 2: get the contents from address (9980+i)
9980 +1 +2 +3 +4 ... +i

Diagram A A Subscripted Array Reference

That's why you can equally write `extern char a[];` as well as `extern char a[100];`. Both declarations indicate that a is an array, namely a memory location where the characters in the array can be found. The compiler doesn't need to know how long the array is in total, as it merely generates address offsets from the start. To get a character from the array, you simply add the subscript to the address that the symbol table shows a has, and get what's at that location.

In contrast, if you declare `extern char *p`, it tells the compiler that p is a pointer (a four-byte object on many contemporary machines), and the object pointed to is a character. To get the char, you have to get whatever is at address p, *then* use *that* as an address and get whatever is there. Pointer accesses are more flexible, but at the cost of an extra fetch instruction, as shown in Diagram B.

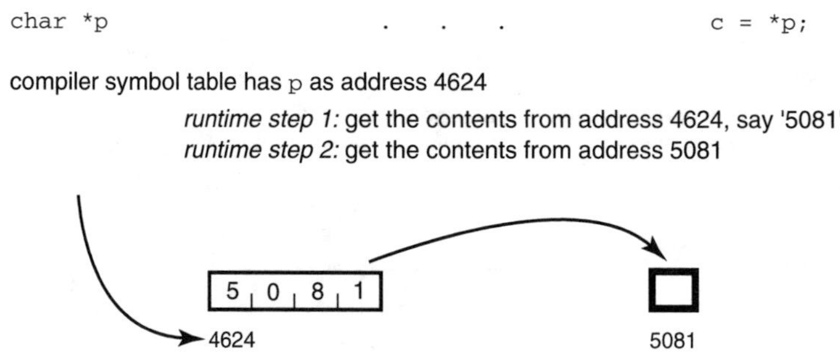
char *p
. . .
c = *p;
compiler symbol table has p as address 4624
runtime step 1: get the contents from address 4624, say '5081'
runtime step 2: get the contents from address 5081
5 0 8 1
4624
5081

Diagram B A Pointer Reference

What Happens When You "Define as Pointer/Reference as Array"

We now can see the problem that arises when an external array is defined as a pointer and referenced as an array. The indirect type of memory reference that is done for a pointer (see Diagram B) occurs when we really want a direct memory reference (as shown in Diagram A). This occurs because we told the compiler that we had a pointer, and is shown in Diagram C.

char *p="abcdefgh"; . . . c = p[i];
compiler symbol table has p as address 4624
runtime step 1: get the contents from address 4624, say '5081'
runtime step 2: get value i, and add it to 5081
runtime step 3: get the contents from address (5081+i)
5 0 8 1
(5081 + i)
4624
5081 +1 +2 +3 +4 ... +i

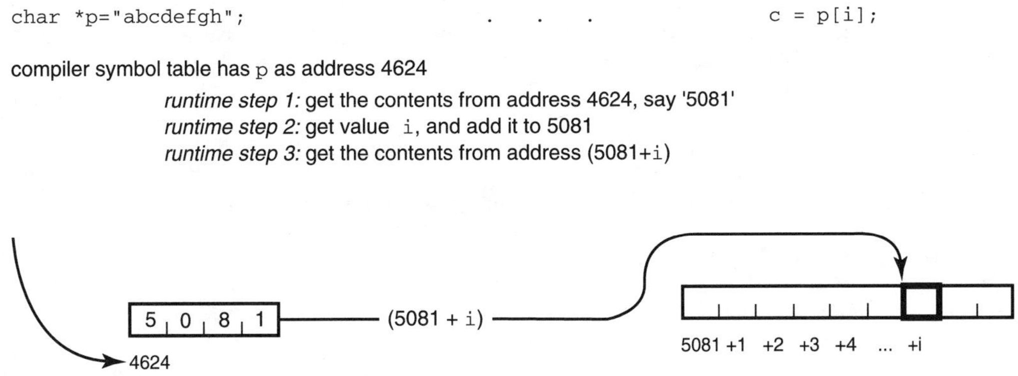

Diagram C A Subscripted Pointer Reference

Contrast the access shown in Diagram C on page 101

```
char * p = "abcdefgh"; ... p[3]
```

with Diagram A on page 99

```
char a[] = "abcdefgh"; ... a[3]
```

They both get you a character `'d'` but they get there by very different look-ups.

When you write `extern char *p`, then reference it as `p[3]`, it's essentially a combination of Diagrams A and B. You do an indirect reference as in diagram 2, then you step forward to the offset represented by the subscript as in diagram 1. More formally, the compiler emits code to:

1. Get the address that p represents, and retrieve the pointer there.
2. Add the offset that the subscript represents onto the pointer value.
3. Access the byte at the resulting address.

The compiler has been told that p is a pointer to char. (In contrast, an array definition tells the compiler that p *is* a sequence of chars.) Making a reference to `p[i]` says "starting at where p points, step forward over 'i' things, each of which is a char (i.e., 1 byte long)." For pointers to different types (`int` or `double` , etc.) the scaling factor (the size of each thing stepped over) will be a different number of bytes.

Since we *declared* p as a pointer, the look-up happens this way regardless of whether p was originally *defined* as a pointer (in which case the right thing is happening) or an array (in which case the wrong thing is happening). Consider the case of an external declaration `extern char *p;` but a definition of `char p[10];`. When we retrieve the contents of `p[i]` using the extern, we get characters, but we treat it as a pointer. Interpreting ASCII characters as an address is garbage, and if you're lucky the program will coredump at that point. If you're not lucky it will corrupt something in your address space, causing a mysterious failure at some later point in the program.

Match Your Declarations to the Definition

The problem of the external declaration of a pointer not matching the definition of an array is simple to fix—change the declaration so it does match the definition, like this:

file 1:

```
int mango[100];
```

file 2:

```
extern int mango[];
 . . .
/* some code that references mango[i] */
```

The array definition of `mango` allocates space for 100 integers. In contrast, the pointer definition:

```
int *raisin;
```

requests a place that holds a pointer. The pointer is to be known by the name `raisin`, and can point to any int (or array of int) anywhere. The variable `raisin` itself will always be at the same address, but its contents can change to point to many different ints at different times. Each of those different ints can have different values. The array `mango` can't move around to different places. At different times it can be filled with different values, but it always refers to the same 100 consecutive memory locations.

Other Differences Between Arrays and Pointers

Another way of looking at the differences between arrays and pointers is to compare some of their characteristics, as in Table 4-1.

Table 4-1 Differences Between Arrays and Pointers

Pointer	Array
Holds the address of data	Holds data
Data is accessed indirectly, so you first retrieve the contents of the pointer, load that as an address (call it "L"), then retrieve its contents. If the pointer has a subscript `[i]` you instead retrieve the contents of the location 'i' units past "L"	Data is accessed directly, so for a[i] you simply retrieve the contents of the location i units past a.
Commonly used for dynamic data structures	Commonly used for holding a fixed number of elements of the same type of data
Commonly used with `malloc()`, `free()`	Implicitly allocated and deallocated
Typically points to anonymous data	Is a named variable in its own right

Both arrays and pointers can be initialized with a literal string in their definition. Although these cases look the same, different things are happening.

A pointer definition does not allocate space for what's pointed at, only for the pointer, *except* when assigned a literal string. For example, the definition below also creates the string literal:

```
char *p = "breadfruit";
```

Note that this *only* works for a string literal. You can't expect to allocate space for, for example, a float literal:

```
float *pip = 3.141; /* Bzzt! won't compile */
```

A string literal created by a pointer initialization is defined as read-only in ANSI C; the program will exhibit undefined behavior if it tries to change the literal by writing through p. Some implementations put string literals in the text segment, where they will be protected with read-only permission.

An array can also be initialized with a string literal:

```
char a[] = "gooseberry";
```

In contrast to a pointer, an array initialized by a literal string is writable. The individual characters *can* later be changed. The following statement:

```
strncpy(a, "black", 5);
```

gives the string in the array the new value "`blackberry`".

Chapter 9 discusses when pointers and arrays *are* equivalent. It then discusses why the equivalency was made, and how it works. Chapter 10 describes some advanced array hocus-pocus based on pointers. If you make it to the end of that chapter, you will have forgotten more about arrays than many C programmers will ever know.

Pointers are one of the hardest parts of C to understand and apply correctly, second only to the syntax of declarations. However, they are also one of the most important parts of C. Professional C programmers *have* to be proficient with the use of `malloc()` and pointers to anonymous memory.

Some Light Relief—Fun with Palindromes!

A palindrome is a word or phrase that reads the same backwards as forwards, for example, "do geese see God?" (Answer: "O, no!") Palindromes are a kind of entertaining parlor trick, and the best ones have phrases that make some kind of loose sense, such as Napoleon's last rueful words "Able was I, ere I saw Elba". Another classic palindrome refers to the heroic individual effort involved in building the Panama canal. The palindrome runs "A man, a plan, a canal—Panama!".

But of course, it took a lot more than just a man and a plan to produce the Panama canal—a fact noted by Jim Saxe, a computer science graduate student at Carnegie-Mellon University. In October 1983, Jim was idly doodling with the Panama palindrome, and extended it to:

> A man, a plan, a cat, a canal—Panama?

Jim put this on the computer system where other graduate students would see it, and the race was on!

Steve Smith at Yale parodied the effort with:

> A tool, a fool, a pool—loopaloofaloota!

Within a few weeks Guy Jacobson, had extended the panorama to:

> A man, a plan, a cat, a ham, a yak, a yam, a hat, a canal—Panama!

Now people got seriously interested in palindromes about Panama! In fact Dan Hoey, who had recently graduated, wrote a C program to look for and construct the following beauty:

> A man, a plan, a caret, a ban, a myriad, a sum, a lac, a liar, a hoop, a
> pint, a catalpa, a gas, an oil, a bird, a yell, a vat, a caw, a pax, a wag,
> a tax, a nay, a ram, a cap, a yam, a gay, a tsar, a wall, a car, a luger, a
> ward, a bin, a woman, a vassal, a wolf, a tuna, a nit, a pall, a fret, a
> watt, a bay, a daub, a tan, a cab, a datum, a gall, a hat, a fag, a zap, a
> say, a jaw, a lay, a wet, a gallop, a tug, a trot, a trap, a tram, a torr, a
> caper, a top, a tonk, a toll, a ball, a fair, a sax, a minim, a tenor, a
> bass, a passer, a capital, a rut, an amen, a ted, a cabal, a tang, a sun, an
> ass, a maw, a sag, a jam, a dam, a sub, a salt, an axon, a sail, an ad, a
> wadi, a radian, a room, a rood, a rip, a tad, a pariah, a revel, a reel, a
> reed, a pool, a plug, a pin, a peek, a parabola, a dog, a pat, a cud, a nu,
> a fan, a pal, a rum, a nod, an eta, a lag, an eel, a batik, a mug, a mot, a
> nap, a maxim, a mood, a leek, a grub, a gob, a gel, a drab, a citadel, a

total, a cedar, a tap, a gag, a rat, a manor, a bar, a gal, a cola, a pap, a yaw, a tab, a raj, a gab, a nag, a pagan, a bag, a jar, a bat, a way, a papa, a local, a gar, a baron, a mat, a rag, a gap, a tar, a decal, a tot, a led, a tic, a bard, a leg, a bog, a burg, a keel, a doom, a mix, a map, an atom, a gum, a kit, a baleen, a gala, a ten, a don, a mural, a pan, a faun, a ducat, a pagoda, a lob, a rap, a keep, a nip, a gulp, a loop, a deer, a leer, a lever, a hair, a pad, a tapir, a door, a moor, an aid, a raid, a wad, an alias, an ox, an atlas, a bus, a madam, a jag, a saw, a mass, an anus, a gnat, a lab, a cadet, an em, a natural, a tip, a caress, a pass, a baronet, a minimax, a sari, a fall, a ballot, a knot, a pot, a rep, a carrot, a mart, a part, a tort, a gut, a poll, a gateway, a law, a jay, a sap, a zag, a fat, a hall, a gamut, a dab, a can, a tabu, a day, a batt, a waterfall, a patina, a nut, a flow, a lass, a van, a mow, a nib, a draw, a regular, a call, a war, a stay, a gam, a yap, a cam, a ray, an ax, a tag, a wax, a paw, a cat, a valley, a drib, a lion, a saga, a plat, a catnip, a pooh, a rail, a calamus, a dairyman, a bater, a canal—Panama.

A "catalpa" (in case you're wondering) is a native American word for a type of tree. You can look up axon and calamus for yourself. Dan commented that a little work on the search algorithm could make it several times as long.

The search algorithm was ingenious—Dan programmed a finite state machine that evaluates a series of partial palindromes. In each case, the state consists of the unmatched part of the palindrome. Starting with the original palindrome, Dan noted that the "a ca" of "a canal" is right at the middle of the phrase, so we can add anything we like after "a plan" as long as its reverse forms a word or part-word when put after that.

To insert additional words after "a plan," just start by doubling the "a ca" in the middle. This gives us "..., a plan, a ca... a canal,..." We could stop right there if "ca" was a word, but it's not. So find something that completes the fragment on the left, and add the same thing spelled backwards on the right, for example, "ret ... ter."

In each step, the end part of the word we add is spelled backwards, and becomes the beginning part of the next word we look for. Table 4-2 shows the process:

Table 4-2 Building a Palindrome

State "-aca":	"A man, a plan, ... a canal, Panama"
State "ret-":	"... a plan, a caret, ... a canal, Panama"
State "-aba":	"... a plan, a caret, ... a bater, a canal, ..."
State "n-":	"... a caret, a ban, ... a bater, a canal, ..."
State "-adairyma":	"... a caret, a ban, ... a dairyman, a bater, ..."
State "-a":	"... a ban, a myriad, ... a dairyman, a bater, ..."

The accepting states of the finite state machine are those where the unmatched part is itself palindromic. In other words, at any point where the words just chosen are a palindrome in themselves, you can stop. In this case, the palindrome "... a nag, a pagan, ..." is at the center, and putting in "-apa-" terminated the algorithm.

Dan used a small word list that only contained nouns. If you don't do this you get a lot of "a how, a running, a would, an expect, an and..." which is nonsensical. An alternative would be a real on-line dictionary (not just word list) that indicates which words are nouns. That way, a *really* big palindrome could be generated. But as Dan says, "if I got a 10,000 word palindrome, I wonder if anyone would want it. I like this one, because it's small enough to pass around. And I've already done the work." You can't argue with that!

Programming Challenge

Write a Palindrome

Claim your 15 minutes of fame: write a C program to generate that 10,000-word palindrome. Really make yourself famous by posting it to rec.arts.startrek.misc on Usenet. They're fed up with discussing Captain Kirk's middle name, and they love to hear about new diversions.

Thinking of Linking 5

As the Pall Mall Gazette *described on March 11, 1889 "Mr Thomas Edison has been up on the two previous nights discovering 'a bug' in his phonograph."*

—Thomas Edison discovers bugs, 1878

The pioneering Harvard Mark II computer system had a logbook which is now in the National Museum of American History at the Smithsonian. The logbook entry for September 9, 1947 has, taped onto the page, the remains of an insect that fluttered into a switch and got trapped. The label reads "Relay #70 Panel F (moth) in relay." Under this is written "First actual case of bug being found."

—Grace Hopper discovers bugs, 1947

As soon as we started programming, we found to our surprise that it wasn't as easy to get programs right as we had thought. Debugging had to be discovered. I can remember the exact instant when I realized that a large part of my life from then on was going to be spent in finding mistakes in my own programs.

—Maurice Wilkes discovers bugs, 1949

Program testing can be used to show the presence of bugs but never to show their absence.

—Edsger W. Dijkstra discovers bugs, 1972

---

linking, libraries, and loading...where the linker is in the phases of compilation...the benefits of dynamic linking...five special secrets of linking with libraries...watch out for interpositioning... don't use these names for your identifiers...generating linker report files... some light relief—look who's talking: challenging the Turing test

Libraries, Linking, and Loading

Let's start with a review of linker basics: The compiler creates an output file containing relocatable objects. These objects are the data and machine instructions corresponding to the source programs. This chapter uses the sophisticated form of linking found on all SVR4 systems as its example.

Where the Linker Is in the Phases of Compilation

Most compilers are not one giant program. They usually consist of up to half-a-dozen smaller programs, invoked by a control program called a "compiler driver." Some pieces that can be conveniently split out into individual programs are: the preprocessor, the syntactic and semantic checker, the code generator, the assembler, the optimizer, the linker, and, of course, a driver program to invoke all these pieces and pass the right options to each (see Figure 5-1). An optimizer can be added after almost any of these phases. The current SPARCompilers do most optimizations on the intermediate representation between the front and back ends of the compiler.

They are written in pieces because they are easier to design and maintain if each specialized part is a program in its own right. For instance, the rules controlling preprocessing are unique to that phase and have little in common with the rest of C. The C preprocessor is often (but not always) a separate program. If the code generator (also known as the "back end") is written as a stand-alone program, it can probably be shared by other languages. The trade-off is that running several smaller programs will take longer than running one big program (because of the overhead of initiating a process and sending information between the phases). You can look at the individual phases of compilation by using the -# option. The -V option will provide version information.

You can pass options to each phase, by giving the compiler-driver a special -W option that says "pass this option to that phase." The "W" will be followed by a character indicating the phase, a comma, and then the option. The characters that represent each phase are shown in Figure 5-1.

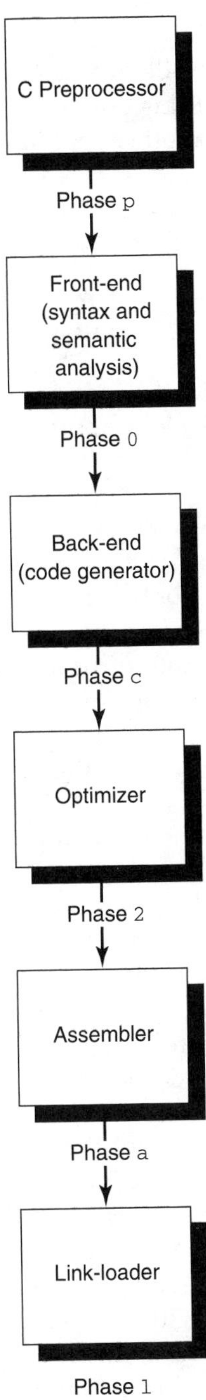

Figure 5-1 A Compiler is Often Split into Smaller Programs

So to pass any option through the compiler driver to the linker, you have to prefix it by "-Wl," to tell the compiler driver that this option is intended for the link editor, not the preprocessor, compiler, assembler, or another compilation phase. The command

```
cc -Wl,-m main.c > main.linker.map
```

will give ld the "-m" option, telling it to produce a linker map. You should try this once or twice to see the kind of information that is produced.

An object file isn't directly executable; it needs to be fed into a linker first. The linker identifies the main routine as the initial entry point (place to start executing), binds symbolic references to memory addresses, unites all the object files, and joins them with the libraries to produce an executable.

There's a big difference between the linking facilities available on PC's and those on bigger systems. PC's typically provide only a small number of elementary I/O services, known as the `BIOS` routines. These exist in a fixed location in memory, and are not part of each executable. If a PC program or suite of programs requires more sophisticated services, they can be provided in a library, but the implementor must link the library into each executable. There's no provision in MS-DOS for "factoring out" a library common to several programs and installing it just once on the PC.

UNIX systems used to be the same. When you linked a program, a copy of each library routine that you used went into the executable. In recent years, a more modern and superior paradigm known as dynamic linking has been adopted. Dynamic linking allows a system to provide a big collection of libraries with many useful services, but the program will look for these at runtime rather than having the library binaries bound in as part of the executable. IBM's OS/2 operating system has dynamic linking, as does Microsoft's new flagship NT operating system. In recent years, Microsoft Windows® has introduced this ability for the windowing part of PC applications.

If a copy of the libraries is physically part of the executable, then we say the executable has been *statically linked;* if the executable merely contains filenames that enable the loader to find the program's library references at runtime, then we say it has been *dynamically linked*. The canonical names for the three phases of collecting modules together and preparing them for execution are link-editing, loading, and runtime linking. Statically linked modules are link edited and then loaded to run them. Dynamically linked modules are link-edited and then loaded and runtime-linked to run them. At execution, before `main()` is called, the runtime loader brings the shared data objects into the process address space. It doesn't resolve external function calls until the call is actually made, so there's no penalty to linking against a library that you may not call. The two linking methods are compared in Figure 5-2.

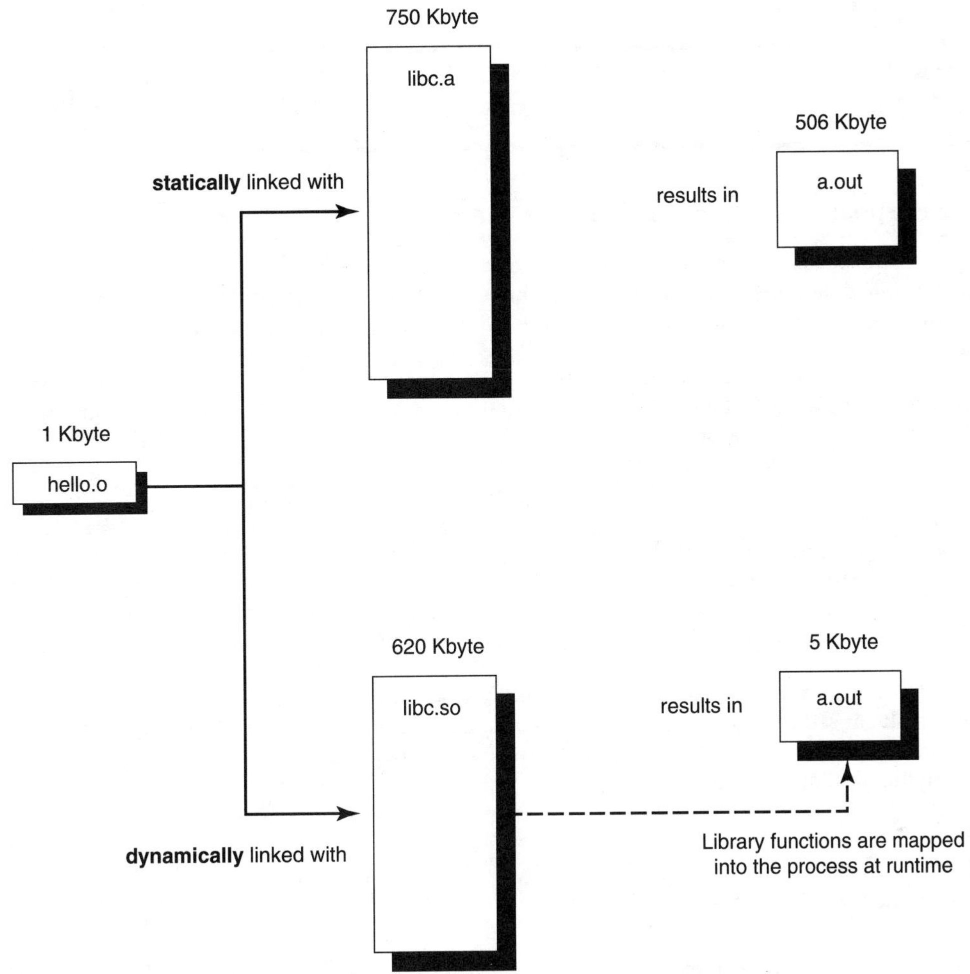

Figure 5-2 Static Linking versus Dynamic Linking

Even with static linking, the whole of libc. a is not brought into the executable, just the routines needed.

The Benefits of Dynamic Linking

Dynamic linking is the more modern approach, and has the advantage of much smaller executable size. Dynamic linking trades off more efficient use of the disk and a quicker link-edit phase for a small runtime penalty (since some of the linker's work is deferred until loadtime).

Handy Heuristic

One Purpose of Dynamic Linking Is the ABI

A major purpose of dynamic linking is to decouple programs from the particular library versions they use. Instead, we have the convention that the system provides an *interface* to programs, and that this interface is stable over time and successive OS releases.

Programs can call services promised by the interface, and not worry about how they are provided or how the underlying implementation may change. Because this is an interface between application programs and the services provided by library binary executables, we call it an *Application Binary Interface* or ABI.

A single ABI is the purpose of unifying the UNIX world around AT&T's SVr4. The ABI guarantees that the libraries exist on all compliant machines, and ensures the integrity of the interface. There are four specific libraries for which dynamic linking is mandatory: libc (C runtimes), libsys (other system runtimes), libX (X windowing), and libnsl (networking services). Other libraries can be statically linked, but dynamic linking is strongly preferred.

In the past, application vendors had to relink their software with each new release of the OS or a library. It caused a huge amount of extra work for all concerned. The ABI does away with this, and guarantees that well-behaved applications will not be affected by well-behaved upgrades in underlying system software.

Although an individual executable has a slightly greater start-up cost, dynamic linking helps overall performance in two ways:

1. A dynamically linked executable is smaller than its statically linked counterpart. It saves disk and virtual memory, as libraries are only mapped in to the process when needed. Formerly, the only way to avoid binding a library copy into each executable was to put the service in the kernel instead of a library, contributing to the dreaded "kernel bloat."

2. All executables dynamically linked to a particular library share a single copy of the library at runtime. The kernel ensures that libraries mapped into memory are shared by all processes using them. This provides better I/O and swap space utilization and is sparing of physical memory, improving overall system throughput. If the executables were statically linked, each would wastefully contain its own complete duplicate copy of the library.

For example, if you have eight XView™ applications running, only one copy of the XView library text segment has to be mapped into memory. The first process's mmap[1] call will result in the kernel mapping the shared object into memory. The next seven process mmaps will cause the kernel to share the existing mapping in each process. Each of the eight processes will share one copy of the XView library in memory. If the library were statically linked, there would be eight individual copies consuming more physical memory and causing more paging.

Dynamic linking permits easy versioning of libraries. New libraries can be shipped; once installed on the system, old programs automatically get the benefit of the new versions without needing to be relinked.

Finally (much less common, but still possible), dynamic linking allows users to select at runtime which library to execute against. It's possible to create library versions that are tuned for speed, or for memory efficiency, or that contain extra debugging information, and to allow the user to express a preference when execution takes place by substituting one library file for another.

Dynamic linking is "just-in-time" linking. It does mean that programs need to be able to find their libraries at runtime. The linker accomplishes this by putting library filenames or pathnames into the executable; and this in turn, means that libraries cannot be moved completely arbitrarily. If you linked your program against library `/usr/lib/libthread.so`, you cannot move the library to a different directory unless you specified it to the linker. Otherwise, the program will fail at runtime when it calls a function in the library, with an error message like:

```
ld.so.1: main: fatal: libthread.so: can't open file: errno=2
```

This is also an issue when you are executing on a different machine than the one on which you compiled. The execution machine must have all the libraries that you linked with, and must have them in the directories where you told the linker they would be. For the standard system libraries, this isn't a problem.

The main reason for using shared libraries is to get the benefit of the ABI—freeing your software from the need to recompile with each new release of a library or OS. As a side benefit, there are also overall system performance advantages.

Anyone can create a static or dynamic library. You simply compile some code without a main routine, and process the resulting .o files with the correct utility—"ar" for static libraries, or "ld" for dynamic libraries.

---

1. The system call `mmap()` maps a file into a process address space. The contents of the file can then be obtained by reading successive memory locations. This is particularly appropriate when the file contains executable instructions. The file system is regarded as part of the virtual memory system in SVr4, and mmap is the mechanism for bringing a file into memory.

Software Dogma

Only Use Dynamic Linking!

Dynamic linking is now the default on computers running System V release 4 UNIX, and it should always be used. Static linking is now functionally obsolete, and should be allowed to rest in peace.

The major risk you run with static linking is that future versions of the operating system will be incompatible with the system libraries bound in with your executable. If your application was statically linked on OS version N and you try to run it on version N+1, it may run, or it may fail with a core dump or a less obvious error.

There is no guarantee that an earlier version of the system libraries will execute correctly on a later version of the system. Indeed, it is usually safer to assume the opposite. However, if an application is dynamically linked on version N of the system, it will correctly pick up the version N+1 libraries when run on version N+1 of the system. In contrast, statically linked applications have to be regenerated for every new release of the operating system to ensure that they keep running.

Furthermore, some libraries (such as libaio.so, libdl.so, libsys.so, libresolv.so, and librpcsvc.so) are only available in dynamic form. You are obliged to link dynamically if your application uses any of these libraries. The best policy is to avoid problems by making sure that all applications are dynamically linked.

Static libraries are known as *archives* and they are created and updated by the `ar`—for archive—utility. The `ar` utility is misnamed; if truth in advertising applied to software, it would really be called something like `glue_files_together` or even `static_library_updater`. Convention dictates that static libraries have a ".a" extension on their filename. There isn't an example of creating a static library here, because they are obsolete now, and we don't want to encourage anyone to communicate with the spirit world.

There was an interim kind of linking used in SVR3, midway between static linking and dynamic linking, known as "static shared libraries". Their addresses were fixed throughout their life, and thus could be bound to without the indirection required with dynamic linking. On the other hand, they were inflexible and required a lot of special support in the system. We won't consider them further.

A dynamically linked library is created by the link editor, `ld`. The conventional file extension for a dynamic library is ".so" meaning "shared object"—every program linked against this library shares the same one copy, in contrast to static linking, in which everyone is (wastefully) given their own copy of the contents of the library. In its simplest form, a dynamic library can be created by using the -G option to cc, like this:

```
% cat tomato.c
    my_lib_function() {printf("library routine called\n"); }

% cc -o libfruit.so -G tomato.c
```

You can then write routines that use this library, and link with it in this manner:

```
% cat test.c
    main() { my_lib_function(); }

% cc test.c -L/home/linden -R/home/linden -lfruit
% a.out
library routine called
```

The `-L/home/linden -R/home/linden` options tell the linker in which directories to look for libraries at linktime and at runtime, respectively.

You will probably also want to use the `-K pic` compiler option to produce position-independent code for your libraries. Position-independent code means that the generated code makes sure that every global data access is done through an extra indirection. This makes it easy to relocate the data simply by changing one value in the table of global offsets. Similarly, every function call is generated as a call through an indirect address in a procedure linkage table. The text can thus easily be relocated to anywhere, simply by fixing up the offset tables. So when the code is mapped in at runtime, the runtime linker can directly put it wherever there is room, and the code itself doesn't have to be changed.

By default, the compilers don't generate PICode as the additional pointer dereference is a fraction slower at runtime. However, if you don't use PICode, the generated code is tied to a fixed address—fine for an executable, but slower for a shared library, since every global reference now has to be fixed up at runtime by page modification, in turn making the page unshareable.

The runtime linker will fix up the page references anyway, but the task is greatly simplified with position-independent code. It is a trade-off whether PICode is slower or faster than letting the runtime linker fix up the code. A rule of thumb is to always use PICode for libraries. Position-independent code is especially useful for shared libraries because each process that uses a shared library will generally map it at a different virtual address (though sharing one physical copy).

A related term is "pure code." A pure executable is one that contains only code (no static or initialized data). It is "pure" in the sense that it doesn't have to be modified to be executed by any specific process. It references its data off the stack or from another (impure) segment. A pure code segment can be shared. If you are generating PIcode (indicating sharing) you usually want it to be pure, too.

Five Special Secrets of Linking with Libraries

There are five essential, non-obvious conventions to master when using libraries. These aren't explained very clearly in most C books or manuals, probably because the language documenters consider linking part of the surrounding operating system, while the operating system people view linking as part of the language. As a result, no one makes much more than a passing reference to it unless someone from the linker team gets involved! Here are the essential UNIX linking facts of life:

1. **Dynamic libraries are called `lib`*`something`*`.so`, and static libraries are called `lib`*`something`*`.a`**

   By convention, all dynamic libraries have a filename of the form `lib`*`name`*`.so` (version numbers may be appended to the name). Thus, the library of thread routines is called `lib`*`thread`*`.so`. A static archive has a filename of the form `lib`*`name`*`.a`. Shared archives, with names of the form `lib`*`name`*`.sa`, were a transient phenomenon, helping in the transition from static to dynamic libraries. Shared archives are also obsolete now.

2. **You tell the compiler to link with, for example, `libthread.so` by giving the option `-lthread`**

   The command line argument to the C compiler doesn't mention the entire pathname to the library file. It doesn't even mention the full name of the file in the library directory! Instead, the compiler is told to link against a library with the command line option `-l`*`name`* where the library is called `lib`*`name`*`.so`—in other words, the "`lib`" part and the file extension are dropped, and `-l` is jammed on the beginning instead.

3. **The compiler expects to find the libraries in certain directories**

   At this point, you may be wondering how the compiler knows in which directory to look for the libraries. Just as there are special rules for where to find header files, so the compiler looks in a few special places such as `/usr/lib/` for libraries. For instance, the threads library is in `/usr/lib/libthread.so`.

   The compiler option `-L`*`pathname`* is used to tell the linker a list of other directories in which to search for libraries that have been specified with the `-l` option. There are a couple of environment variables, `LD_LIBRARY_PATH` and `LD_RUN_PATH`, that can also be used to provide this information. Using these environment variables is now officially frowned on, for reasons of security, performance, and build/execute independence. Use the -L*pathname* -R*pathname* options at linktime instead.

4. Identify your libraries by looking at the header files you have used

Another key question that may have occurred to you is, "How do I know which libraries I have to link with?" The answer, as (roughly speaking) enunciated by Obi-Wan Kenobi in *Star Wars*, is, "Use the source, Luke!" If you look at the source of your program, you'll notice routines that you call, but which you didn't implement. For example, if your program does trigonometry, you've probably called routines with names like sin() or cos(), and these are found in the math library. The manpages show the exact argument types each routine expects, and should mention the library it's in.

A good hint is to study the #includes that your program uses. Each header file that you include potentially represents a library against which you must link. This tip carries over into C++, too. A big problem of name inconsistency shows up here. Header files usually do not have a name that looks anything like the name of the corresponding library. Sorry! This is one of the things you "just have to know" to be a C wizard. Table 5-1 shows examples of some common ones.

Table 5-1 Library Conventions Under Solaris 2.x

#include Filename	Library Pathname	Compiler Option to Use
<math.h>	/usr/lib/libm.so	-lm
<math.h>	/usr/lib/libm.a	-dn -lm
<stdio.h>	/usr/lib/libc.so	linked in automatically
"/usr/openwin/include/X11.h"	/usr/openwin/lib/libX11.so	-L/usr/openwin/lib -lX11
<thread.h>	/usr/lib/libthread.so	-lthread
<curses.h>	/usr/ccs/lib/libcurses.a	-lcurses
<sys/socket.h>	/usr/lib/libsocket.so	-lsocket

Another inconsistency is that a single library may contain routines that satisfy the prototypes declared in multiple header files. For example, the functions declared in the header files <string.h>, <stdio.h>, and <time.h> are all usually supplied in the single library libc.so. If you're in doubt, use the nm utility to list the routines that a library contains. More about this in the next heuristic!

Handy Heuristic

How to Match a Symbol with its Library

If you're trying to link a program and get this kind of error:

```
ld: Undefined symbol
    _xdr_reference
*** Error code 2
make: Fatal error: Command failed for target 'prog'
```

Here's how you can locate the libraries with which you need to link. The basic plan is to use nm to look through the symbols in every library in /usr/lib, grepping for the symbols you're missing. The linker looks in /usr/ccs/lib and /usr/lib by default, and so should you. If this doesn't get results, extend your search to all other library directories (such as /usr/openwin/lib), too.

```
% cd /usr/lib
% foreach i (lib?*)
? echo $i
? nm $i | grep xdr_reference | grep -v UNDEF
? end
libc.so
libnsl.so
[2491] | 217028| 196|FUNC |GLOB |0 |8 |xdr_reference
libposix4.so
    . . .
```

This runs "nm" on each library in the directory, to list the symbols known in the library. Pipe it through grep to limit it to the symbol you are searching for, and filter out symbols marked as "UNDEF" (referenced, but not defined in this library). The result shows you that `xdr_reference` is in libnsl. You need to add `-lnsl` on the end of the compiler command line.

5. **Symbols from static libraries are extracted in a more restricted way than symbols from dynamic libraries**

Finally, there's an additional and big difference in link semantics between dynamic linking and static linking that often confuses the unwary. Archives (static libraries) are acted upon differently than are shared objects (dynamic libraries). With dynamic libraries, *all* the library symbols go into the virtual address space of the output file, and *all* the symbols are available to all the other files in the link. In contrast, static linking only looks through the archive for the *undefined* symbols presently known to the loader at the time the archive is processed.

A simpler way of putting this is to say that the order of the statically linked libraries on the compiler command line is significant. The linker is fussy about where libraries are mentioned, and in what order, since symbols are resolved looking from left to right. This makes a difference if the same symbol is defined differently in two different libraries. If you're doing this deliberately, you probably know enough not to need to be reminded of the perils.

Another problem occurs if you mention the static libraries before your own code. There won't be any undefined symbols yet, so nothing will be extracted. Then, when your object file is processed by the linker, all its library references will be unfulfilled! Although the convention has been the same since UNIX started, many people find it unexpected; very few commands demand their arguments in a particular order, and those that do usually complain about it directly if you get it wrong. All novices have trouble with this aspect of linking until the concept is explained. Then they just have trouble with the concept itself.

The problem most frequently shows up when someone links with the math library. The math library is heavily used in many benchmarks and applications, so we want to squeeze the last nanosecond of runtime performance out of it. As a result, libm has often been a statically linked archive. So if you have a program that uses some math routines such as the `sin()` function, and you link statically like this:

```
cc -lm main.c
```

you will get an error message like this:

```
Undefined                    first referenced
 symbol                          in file
 sin                              main.o
ld: fatal: Symbol referencing errors. No output written to a.out
```

In order for the symbols to get extracted from the math library, you need to put the file containing the unresolved references first, like so:

```
cc main.c -lm
```

This causes no end of angst for the unwary. Everyone is used to the general command form of <command> <options> <files>, so to have the linker adopt the different convention of <command> <files> <options> is very confusing. It's exacerbated by the fact that it will silently accept the first version and do the wrong thing. At one point, Sun's compiler group amended the compiler drivers so that they coped with the situation. We changed the SunOS 4.x unbundled compiler drivers from SC0.0 through SC2.0.1 so they would "do the right thing" if a user omitted `-lm`. Although it was the right thing, it was different from what AT&T did, and broke our compliance with the System V Interface Definition; so the former behavior had to be reinstated. In any case, from SunOS 5.2 onwards a dynamically linked version of the math library `/usr/lib/libm.so` is provided.

Handy Heuristic

Where to Put Library Options
Always put the `-l` library options at the rightmost end of your compilation command line.

Similar problems have been seen on PC's, where Borland compiler drivers tried to guess whether the floating-point libraries needed to be linked in. Unfortunately, they sometimes guessed wrongly, leading to the error:

```
scanf : floating point formats not linked
Abnormal program termination
```

They seem to guess wrongly when the program uses floating-point formats in `scanf()` or `printf()` but doesn't call any other floating-point routines. The workaround is to give the linker more of a clue, by declaring a function like this in a module that will be included in the link:

```
static void forcefloat(float *p)
{ float f = *p; forcefloat(&f); }
```

Don't actually call the function, merely ensure that it is linked in. This provides a solid enough clue to the Borland PC linker that the floating-point library really is needed.

NB: a similar message, saying "floating point not loaded" is printed by the Microsoft C runtime system when the software needs a numeric coprocessor but your computer doesn't have one installed. You fix it by relinking the program, using the floating-point emulation library.

Watch Out for Interpositioning

Interpositioning (some people call it "interposing") is the practice of supplanting a library function by a user-written function of the same name. This is a technique only for people who enjoy a good walk on the wild side of the fast lane without a safety net. It enables a library function to be replaced in a particular program, usually for debugging or performance reasons. But like a gun with no safety catch, while it lets experts get faster results, it also makes it very easy for novices to hurt themselves.

Interpositioning requires great care. It's all too easy to do this accidentally and replace a symbol in a library by a different definition in your own code. Not only are all the calls that *you* make to the library routine replaced by calls to your version, but all calls from *system routines* now reference your routine instead. A compiler will typically not issue an error message when it notices a redefinition of a library routine. In keeping with C's philosophy that the programmer is always right, it assumes the programmer meant to do it.

Over the years we have seen no convincing examples where interpositioning was essential but the effect could not be obtained in a different (perhaps less convenient) manner. We have seen many instances where a default global scope symbol combined with interpositioning to create a hard-to-find bug (see Figure 5-3). We have seen a dozen or so bug reports and emergency problem escalations from even the most knowledgeable software developers. Unhappily, it's not a bug; the implementation is supposed to work this way.

Diagram of interpositioning and default global scope

1. Without interpositioning, the system `mktemp()` is called

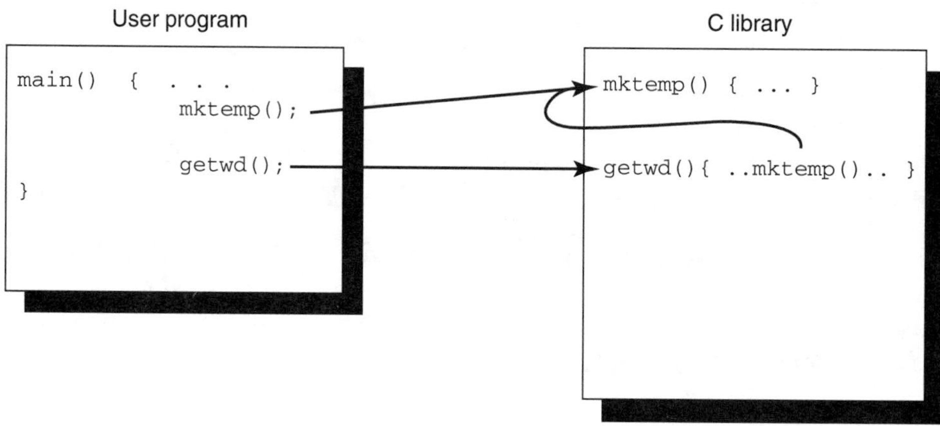

2. With interpositioning, the system version of `mktemp()` has been supplanted by your version, both in your code, and in system calls!

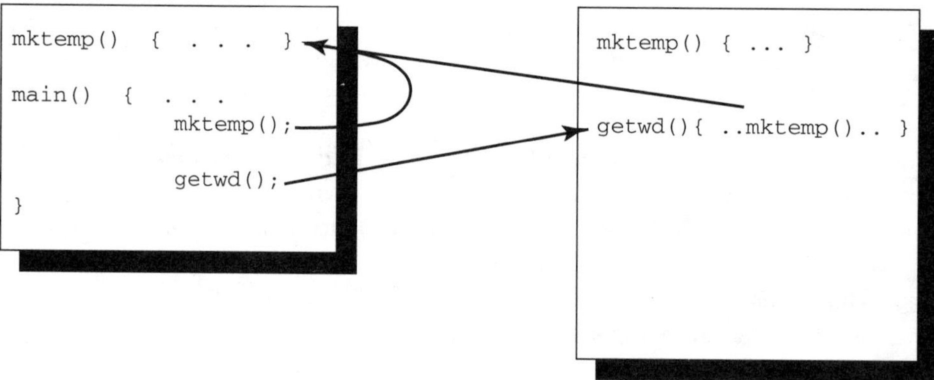

Figure 5-3 Diagram of Interpositioning and Default Global Scope

Most programmers have not memorized all the names in the C library, and common names like `index` or `mktemp` tend to be chosen surprisingly often. Sometimes bugs of this kind even get into production code.

Software Dogma

An Interpositioning Bug in SunOS

Under SunOS 4.0.3, the printing program /usr/ucb/lpr occasionally issued the error message "out of memory" and refused to print. The fault appeared randomly, and it was very hard to track down. Finally, it was traced to an unintended interpositioning bug.

The programmer had implemented lpr with a routine, global by default, called `mktemp()`, which expected three arguments. Unknown to the programmer, that duplicated a name already present in the (pre-ANSI) C library, which did a similar job but only took one argument.

Unfortunately, lpr also invoked the library routine `getwd()`, which expects to use the library version of `mktemp`. Instead, it was bound to lpr's special version! Thus, when `getwd()` called `mktemp`, it put one argument on the stack, but the lpr version of `mktemp` retrieved three. Depending on the random values it found, lpr failed with the "out of memory" error.

> **Moral:** Don't make **any** symbols in your program global, unless they are meant to be part of your interface!

lpr was fixed by declaring its mktemp as static, making it invisible outside its own file (we could equally have given it a different name). Mktemp has now been replaced by the library routine `tmpnam` in ANSI C. However, the opportunity for the interpositioning problem still exists.

If an identifier is shown in Table 5-2, never declare it in your own program. Some of these are always reserved, and others are only reserved if you include a specific header file. Some of these are reserved only in global scope, and others are reserved for both global and file scope. Also note that all keywords are reserved, but are left out of the table below for simplicity. The easiest way to stay out of trouble is to regard all these identifiers as belonging to the system at all times. Don't use them for your identifiers.

Some entries look like `is[a-z]`*`anything`*.

> This means any identifier that begins with the string "is" followed by any other lowercase letter (but not, for example, a digit) followed by any characters.

Other entries look like `acos,-f,-l`.

> This indicates that the three identifiers `acos`, `acosf`, and `acosl` are reserved. All routines in the math header file have a basic version that takes a double-precision argument. There can also be two extra versions: the basename with a `l` suffix is a version of the routine with quad precision arguments (type "long double"), and the `f` suffix is a version with single precision ("float").

Table 5-2 Names to Avoid Using as Identifiers (Reserved for the System in ANSI C)

Don't Use These Names for Your Identifiers			
_*anything*			
abort	abs	acos,-f,-l	asctime
asin,-f,-l	assert	atan,-f,-l	atan2,-f,-l
atexit	atof	atoi	atol
bsearch	BUFSIZ	calloc	ceil,-f,-l
CHAR_BIT	CHAR_MAX	CHAR_MIN	clearerr
clock	clock_t	CLOCKS_PER_SEC	cos,-f,-l
cosh,-f,-l	ctime	currency_symbol	DBL_DIG
DBL_EPSILON	DBL_MANT_DIG	DBL_MAX	DBL_MAX_10_EXP
DBL_MAX_EXP	DBL_MIN	DBL_MIN_10_EXP	DBL_MIN_EXP
decimal_point	defined	difftime	div
div_t	E[0-9]	E[A-Z]*anything*	
errno	exit	EXIT_FAILURE	EXIT_SUCCESS
exp,-f,-l	fabs,-f,-l	fclose	feof
ferror	fflush	fgetc	fgetpos
fgets	FILE	FILENAME_MAX	floor,-f,-l
FLT_DIG	FLT_EPSILON	FLT_MANT_DIG	FLT_MAX
FLT_MAX_10_EXP	FLT_MAX_EXP	FLT_MIN	FLT_MIN_10_EXP
FLT_MIN_EXP	FLT_RADIX	FLT_ROUNDS	fmod,-f,-l
fopen	FOPEN_MAX	fpos_t	fprintf
fputc	fputs	frac_digits	fread
free	freopen	frexp,-f,-l	fscanf
fseek	fsetpos	ftell	fwrite
getc	getchar	getenv	gets
gmtime	grouping	HUGE_VAL	int_curr_symbol
int_frac_digits	INT_MAX	INT_MIN	is[a-z]*anything*
jmp_buf	L_tmpnam	labs	LC_[A-Z]*anything*
lconv	LDBL_DIG	LDBL_EPSILON	LDBL_MANT_DIG

Table 5-2 Names to Avoid Using as Identifiers (Reserved for the System in ANSI C) (Continued)

Don't Use These Names for Your Identifiers			
LDBL_MAX	LDBL_MAX_10_EXP	LDBL_MAX_EXP	LDBL_MIN
LDBL_MIN_10_EXP	LDBL_MIN_EXP	ldexp,-f,-l	ldiv
ldiv_t	localeconv	localtime	log,-f,-l
log10,-f,-l	LONG_MAX	LONG_MIN	longjmp
malloc	MB_CUR_MAX	MB_LEN_MAX	mblen
mbstowcs	mbtowc	mem[a-z]*anything*	mktime
modf,-f,-l	mon_decimal_point	mon_grouping	mon_thousands_sep
n_cs_precedes	n_sep_by_space	n_sign_posn	NDEBUG
negative_sign	NULL		
offsetof	p_cs_precedes	p_sep_by_space	p_sign_posn
perror	positive_sign	pow,-f,-l	printf
ptrdiff_t	putc	putchar	puts
qsort	raise	rand	RAND_MAX
realloc	remove	rename	rewind
scanf	SCHAR_MAX	SCHAR_MIN	SEEK_CUR
SEEK_END	SEEK_SET	setbuf	setjmp
setlocale	setvbuf	SHRT_MAX	SHRT_MIN
SIG_[A-Z]*anything*	sig_atomic_t	SIG_DFL	SIG_ERR
SIG_IGN	SIG[A-Z]*anything*	SIGABRT	SIGFPE
SIGILL	SIGINT	signal	SIGSEGV
SIGTERM	sin,-f,-l	sinh,-f,-l	size_t
sprintf	sqrt,-f,-l		
srand	sscanf	stderr	stdin
stdout	str[a-z]*anything*	system	tan,-f,-l
tanh,-f,-l	thousands_sep	time	time_t
tm	tm_hour	tm_isdst	tm_mday
tm_min	tm_mon	tm_sec	tm_wday
tm_yday	tm_year	TMP_MAX	tmpfile
tmpnam	to[a-z]*anything*	UCHAR_MAX	UINT_MAX
ULONG_MAX	ungetc	USHRT_MAX	va_arg

Table 5-2 Names to Avoid Using as Identifiers (Reserved for the System in ANSI C) (Continued)

Don't Use These Names for Your Identifiers			
`va_end`	`va_list`	`va_start`	`vfprintf`
`vprintf`	`vsprintf`	`wchar_t`	`wcs[a-z]`*anything*
`wcstombs`	`wctomb`		

Remember that under ANSI section 6.1.2 (Identifiers), an implementation can define letter case not significant for external identifiers. Also, external identifiers only need be significant in the first six characters (ANSI section 5.2.4.1, Translation Limits). Both of these expand the number of identifiers that you should avoid. The list above consists of the C library symbols that you may not redefine. There will be additional symbols for each additional library you link against. Check the ABI document[2] for a list of these.

The problem of name space pollution is only partially addressed in ANSI C. ANSI C outlaws a user redefining a system name (effectively outlawing interpositioning) in section 7.1.2.1:

> 7.1.2.1 Reserved Identifiers: All identifiers with external linkage in any of the following sections [what follows is a number of sections defining the standard library functions]...are always reserved for use as identifiers with external linkage.

If an identifier is *reserved,* it means that the user is not allowed to redefine it. However, this is not a *constraint,* so it does not *require* an error message when it sees it happen. It just causes unportable, undefined behavior. In other words, if one of your function names is the same as a C library function name (deliberately or inadvertently), you have created a nonconforming program, but the translator is not obliged to warn you about it. We would much rather the standard required the compiler to issue a warning diagnostic, and let it make up its own mind about stuff like the maximum number of case labels it can handle in a switch statement.

Generating Linker Report Files

Use the "`-m`" option to ld for a linker report that includes a note of symbols which have been interposed. In general, the "`-m`" option to ld will produce a memory map or listing showing what has been put where in the executable. It also shows multiple instances of the same symbol, and by looking at what files these occur in, the user can determine if any interpositioning took place.

The `-D` option to ld was introduced with SunOS 5.3 to provide better link-editor debugging. The option (fully documented in the Linker and Libraries Manual) allows the user to display the link-editing process and input file inclusion. It's especially useful for mon-

2. *The System V Application Binary Interface,* AT&T, 1990.

itoring the extraction of objects from archives. It can also be used to display runtime bindings.

Ld is a complicated program with many more options and conventions than those explained here. Our description is more than enough for most purposes, and there are four further sources of help, in increasing order of sophistication:

- Use the `ldd` command to list the dynamic dependencies of an executable. This command will tell you the libraries that a dynamically linked program needs.
- The `-Dhelp` option to `ld` provides information on troubleshooting the linking process.
- Try the on-line manpages for ld.
- Read the *SunOS Linker and Libraries Manual* (part number 801-2869-10).

Some combination of these should provide information on any subtle linker special effects you need.

Handy Heuristic

When "botch" Appears

Under SunOS 4.x, an occurrence of the word "botch" in an error message means that the loader has discovered an internal inconsistency. This is usually due to faulty input files.

Under SunOS 5.x, the loader is much more rigorous about checking its input for correctness and consistency. It doesn't need to complain about internal errors, and the "botch" messages have been dropped.

Some Light Relief— Look Who's Talking: Challenging the Turing Test

At the dawn of the electronic age, as the potential of computers first started to unfold, a debate arose over whether systems would one day have artificial intelligence. That quickly led to the question, "How can we tell if a machine thinks?" In a 1950 paper in the journal *Mind*, British mathematician Alan Turing cut through the philosophical tangle by suggesting a practical test. Turing proposed that a human interrogator converse (via teletype, to avoid sight and sound clues) with another person and with a computer. If the human interrogator was unable to correctly identify which was which after a period of five minutes, then the computer would be said to have exhibited artificial intelligence. This scenario has come to be called *the Turing Test*.

Over the decades since Turing proposed this trial, the Turing test has taken place several times, sometimes with astonishing results. We describe some of those tests and reproduce the dialogue that took place so you can judge for yourself.

Eliza

One of the first computer programs to process natural language was "Eliza," named after the gabby heroine in Shaw's play *Pygmalion*. The Eliza software was written in 1965 by Joseph Weizenbaum, a professor at MIT, and it simulated the responses of a Rogerian psychiatrist talking to a patient. The program made a superficial analysis of the text typed to it, and spat back one of a large number of canned responses built into it. The illusion that the computer understood any of the conversation fooled quite a number of computer-naive people.

Weizenbaum got the first indication of this phenomenon when he invited his secretary to try the system. After a couple of minutes typing with Eliza, the secretary (who had watched Weizenbaum work on the software for many previous months, and could be expected to understand better than most that it was just a computer program) asked Weizenbaum to leave the room so that she could continue her dialogue in private!

The Turing test failed on its first outing, as the secretary plainly regarded this elementary software (with no pretensions to artificial intelligence) as human. Rather than the software showing intelligence, the humans showed gullibility. Eliza proved to be a popular program, and was adapted by Bolt Berenek and Newman, a Boston computer consultancy. This led to a more severe test when a BBN vice president found himself connected to Eliza instead of the programmer he was expecting.

Eliza Meets the VP

Computer scientist Daniel Bobrow gave this account in the December 1968 issue of the *SIGART Newsletter*.

> One Saturday morning about 9am, a BBN vice-president in charge of selling our Telcomp commercial service arrived at our computer room hoping to be able to use the computer for a demonstration. He found a note on the teletype that read: *"type all messages into this teletype, and end them with a period."* The note was left there by one of the programming bums who had just succeeded in making run a Lisp version of the Doctor program (based on ELIZA as developed by Weizenbaum). However, the VP thought that this note indicated that this teletype was linked with the one in my home, since I often used the computer all night. Therefore, he started typing to "me", but in fact was typing to the Doctor program. The following conversation ensued:
>
> vp: Do you think that I can use the computer this morning?
>
> teletype: Why do you ask?
>
> vp: I might be able to make some additional telcomp sales.
>
> teletype: Why aren't you sure?
>
> vp: My prospective customers have never seen a demonstration of the system.

teletype: Does this mean very much to you?

vp: Of course it does.

teletype: You seem very positive of that.

vp: This is ridiculous.

teletype: What do you mean this is ridiculous?

vp: Is there any reason why I can't use the computer now?

teletype: Tell me more about your prospective customers.

vp: Please call me

Note that after that remark the VP did not obey instructions and left out the period. Therefore the computer didn't answer him. This so infuriated the VP, who thought I was playing games with him, that he called me up, woke me from a deep sleep, and said:

vp: Why are you being so snotty with me?

Bobrow: What do you mean why am I being snotty to you?

The VP angrily read the dialog that "we" had been having, and couldn't get any response but laughter from me. It took me a while to convince him it really was the computer.

Notice that the Eliza/Doctor software usually responds with an open-ended question designed to get the user to type in more sentences. It makes no attempt to answer questions, because it has no ability to do so. Nonetheless the program fooled the computer-literate vice president. The reason it fools people is not because it is intelligent, and thus passing the Turing test. Though novel at the time, Eliza is a quite elementary program by today's standards. It fools people because people are too easy to fool, and thus the test is inadequate. So the Turing test was a failure on its second outing.

Doctor, Meet Doctor

The Free Software Foundation, for reasons of whimsy, hack-value, and fun, built this psychiatrist dialogue software into their popular GNU editor product. The GNU-EMACS editor is given away free, and is available on most UNIX systems. Once you start up GNU-EMACS, issue the command "escape-x doctor". I thought it would be entertaining to hook up two instances of the Doctor program back-to-back, so that each was talking at the other. Here's the result of the experiment:

1: I am the psychotherapist. Please describe your problems.

2: What brings you to see me?

1: Can you elaborate on that?

2: I would appreciate it if you would continue.

1: What makes you believe you would appreciate it if I would continue?

2: Why do you say that?

[doctor 1 now starts to make grammatical errors...]

1: When did you first know that do I say that?

[doctor 2 also starts to make grammatical errors...]

2: What happened when did me first know that do you say that?

1: What would happen if did you first know that do I say that?

2: Is the fact that do you say that the real reason?

1: Is the fact that do I say that the real reason the real reason?

2: does the fact that do you say that the real reason the real reason explain anything else?

1: does the fact that do I say that the real reason the real reason explain anything else explain anything else?

2: Are you sure do you say that the real reason the real reason explain anything else explain anything else?

1: Are you sure the real reason the real reason explain anything else explain anything else?

2: Earlier you said do I do what brings me to see you?

1: Earlier you said do you do what brings you to see me that I came to you?

2: Is it because you came to me that you came to me?

1: Is it because I came to you that you came to me?

2: Are you annoyed that you came to me that I came to you?

[doctor 1 tries a new line, and recovers its grammar, only to get stuck in repetition]

1: Have you been annoyed often?

2: Have you been annoyed often?

1: What causes you to be annoyed?

2: Are you sure that you are annoyed?

1: What makes you believe that you are annoyed?

2: Have you been annoyed often?

1: Have you been annoyed often?

Actually, as you can see, it wasn't very entertaining at all. This dialogue exposes the "echoing" that is Doctor's main conversational device. Its shallow text analysis is easily thrown off by a complicated sentence. When Doctor tries to parrot back part of a previous remark as a question, it often creates a sentence too complicated for itself to handle. Although Doctor has deceived people into thinking it is human, no one looking at *this* transcript would be fooled.

The Prize in Boston

Fast forward now to 1991. Computer systems are vastly faster and more powerful. People have worked on all aspects of artificial intelligence for more than a quarter century. We come to the most recent and most spectacular of the Turing tests.

In November 1991 the Boston Computer Museum, along with the National Science Foundation and the Alfred P. Sloan Foundation, sponsored a public demonstration of the Turing test. The museum chose the human interrogators by placing ads in Boston newspapers. The museum wanted the interrogators to represent the average person (rather than scientists with special philosophical or linguistics knowledge). A panel of ten interrogators had three hours to converse, through terminals, with more than a dozen programs and human conversationalists. One typical dialogue went:

> terminal: A whim is a sudden capricious and often peculiar behavior. A bit of sunlight in a grim grey world.
>
> interrogator: Something like a hunch?
>
> terminal: Everybody sets out to do something and everybody does something, but no one does what he sets out to do.
>
> interrogator:Well, anyway I would imagine whimsical conversation is like a series of knight's moves in chess—sort of zigzag rather than following any particular line.
>
> terminal: A whimsical person is subject to erratic behavior and unpredictable thoughts...how nice to be unpredictable!

It comes as no surprise that the terminal above is actually a computer program. It's operating just as Eliza was; it analyzes the syntax and keywords in the text from the interrogator, and selects something with a matching topic from its huge database of canned phrases. It avoids the "doctor's dilemma" by not parroting back part of the interrogator's remark, instead keeping the talk flowing by continually raising new (though related) topics.

It's also no surprise that the program represented above deluded five of the ten interrogators, who marked it down as human after this and more lengthy interchanges with it. Third time unlucky for the Turing test, and it's out for the count.

Conclusions

The above program's inability to directly answer a straightforward question (*"[do you mean] something like a hunch?"*) is a dead giveaway to a computer scientist, and highlights the central weakness in the Turing test: simply exchanging semi-appropriate phrases doesn't indicate thought—we have to look at the content of what is communicated.

The Turing test has repeatedly been shown to be inadequate. It relies on surface appearances, and people are too easily deceived by surface appearance. Quite apart from the significant philosophical question of whether mimicking the outward signs of an activity is evidence of the inner human processes which accompany that activity, human interrogators have usually proven incapable of accurately making the necessary distinctions. Since the only entities in everyday experience that converse are people, it's natural to assume that any conversation (no matter how stilted) is with another person.

Despite the empirical failures, the artificial intelligence community is very unwilling to let the test go. There are many defenses of it in the literature. Its theoretical simplicity has a compelling charm; but if something does not work in practice, it must be revised or scrapped.

The original Turing test was phrased in terms of the interrogator being able to distinguish a woman, from a man masquerading as a woman, over a teletype. Turing did not directly address in his paper that the test would probably be inadequate for this, too.

One might think that all that is necessary is to reemphasize this aspect of the conversation; that is, require the interrogator to debate the teletype on whether it is human or not. I doubt that is likely to be any more fruitful. For simplicity, the 1991 Computer Museum tests restricted the conversation to a single domain for each teletype. Different programs had different knowledge bases, covering topics as diverse as shopping, the weather, whimsy, and so on. All that would be needed is to give the program a set of likely remarks and clever responses on the human condition. Turing wrote that five minutes would be adequate time for the trial; that doesn't seem nearly adequate these days.

One way to fix the Turing test is to repair the weak link: the element of human gullibility. Just as we require doctors to pass several years of study before they can conduct medical examinations, so we must add the condition that the Turing interrogators should not be representatives of the average person in the street. The interrogators should instead be well versed in computer science, perhaps graduate students familiar with the capabilities and weaknesses of computer systems. Then they won't be thrown off by witty remarks extracted from a large database in lieu of real answers.

Another interesting idea is to explore the sense of humor displayed by the terminal. Ask it to distinguish whether a particular story qualifies as a joke or not, and explain why it is funny. I think such a test is too severe—too many people would fail it.

Although a brilliant theoretician, Turing was often hopeless when it came to practical matters. His impracticality showed itself in unusual ways: at his office, he chained his mug to the radiator to prevent his colleagues from using it. They naturally regarded this as a challenge, picked the lock, and drank from it wilfully. He routinely ran a dozen or more miles to distant appointments, arriving sticky and exhausted, rather than use public transport. When war broke out in Europe in 1939, Turing converted his savings into two silver ingots which he buried in the countryside for safety; by the end of the war he was unable to remember where he cached them. Turing eventually committed suicide in a characteristically impractical fashion: he ate an apple that he had injected with cyanide. And the test which bears his name is a triumph of theory over practical experience. The difference between theory and practice is a lot bigger in practice than in theory.

Postscript

Turing also wrote that he believed that "at the end of the century the use of words and general educated opinion would have altered so much that one will be able to speak of machines thinking without expecting to be contradicted." That actually happened much sooner than Turing reckoned. Programmers habitually explain a computer's quirks in terms of thought processes: "You haven't pressed carriage return so the machine thinks that there's more input coming, and it's waiting for it." However, this is because the term "think" has become debased, rather than because machines have acquired consciousness, as Turing predicted.

Alan Turing was rightly recognized as one of the great theoretical pioneers in computing. The Association for Computing Machinery established its highest annual prize, the Turing Award, in his memory. In 1983, the Turing Award was given to Dennis Ritchie and Ken Thompson in recognition of their work on UNIX and C.

Further Reading

If you are interested in learning more about the advances and limitations of artificial intelligence, a good book to read is *What Computers Still Can't Do: A Critique of Artificial Reason* by Hubert L. Dreyfus, published by the MIT Press, Boston, 1992.

Poetry in Motion: Runtime Data Structures 6

#41: The Enterprise meets God, and it's a child, a computer, or a C program.

#42: While boldly on the way to where only a few people have been recently, the Enterprise computer is subverted by a powerful alien life-form, shaped amazingly like a human.

#43: Trekkers encounter hostile computer intelligence, and abuse philosophy or logic to cause it to self-destruct.

#44: Trekkers encounter a civilization that bears an uncanny resemblance to a previous Earth society.

#45: Disease causes one or more crew members to age rapidly. Also seen in reverse: key crew members regress to childhood, physically, mentally, or both.

#46: An alien being becomes embedded in body of a Trekker and takes over. Still waiting to see this one in reverse...

#47: The captain violates the Prime Directive, then either endangers the Enterprise or has an affair with an attractive alien, or both, while trying to rectify matters.

#48: The captain eventually brings peace to two primitive warring societies ("we come in peace, shoot to kill") on a world that is strangely reminiscent of Earth.

—Professor Snopes' *Book of Canonical Star Trek Plots, and Delicious Yam Recipes*

`a.out` and `a.out` folklore...segments...what the OS does with your a.out... what the C runtime does with your a.out...what happens when a function gets called: the procedure activation record...helpful C tools... some light relief—Princeton programming puzzle

---

One of the classic dichotomies in programming language theory is the distinction between code and data. Some languages, like LISP, unite these elements; others, like C, usually maintain the division. The Internet worm, described in Chapter 2, was hard to understand because its method of attack was based on transforming data into code. The distinction between code and data can also be analyzed as a division between compile-time and runtime. Most of the work of a compiler is concerned with translating code; most of the necessary data storage management happens at runtime. This chapter describes the hidden data structures of the runtime system.

There are three reasons to learn about the runtime system:

- It will help you tune code for the highest performance.
- It will help you understand more advanced material.
- It will help you diagnose problems more easily, when you run into trouble.

`a.out` and `a.out` Folklore

Did you ever wonder how the name "a.out" was chosen? Having all output files default to the same name, a.out, can be inconvenient, as you might forget which source file it came from, and you will overwrite it on the next compilation of any file. Most people have a vague impression that the name originated with traditional UNIX brevity, and "a" is the first letter of the alphabet, so it's the first letter you hit for a new filename. Actually, it's nothing to do with any of this.

It's an abbreviation for "assembler output"! The old BSD manpage even hints at this:

```
NAME
    a.out - assembler and link editor output format
```

One problem: it's not assembler output—it's linker output!

The "assembler output" name is purely historical. On the PDP-7 (even before the B language), there was no linker. Programs were created by assembling the catenation of all the source files, and the resulting assembler output went in a.out. The convention stuck around for the final output even after a linker was finally written for the PDP-11; the name had come to mean "a new program ready to try to execute." So the a.out default name is an example in UNIX of "no good reason, but we always did it that way"!

Executable files on UNIX are also labelled in a special way so that systems can recognize their special properties. It's a common programming technique to label or tag important data with a unique number identifying what it is. The labelling number is often termed a "magic" number; it confers the mysterious power of being able to identify a collection of random bits. For example, the superblock (the fundamental data structure in a UNIX file-system) is tagged with the following magic number:

```
#define FS_MAGIC 0x011954
```

That strange-looking number isn't wholly random. It's Kirk McKusick's birthday. Kirk, the implementor of the Berkeley fast file system, wrote this code in the late 1970's, but magic numbers are so useful that this one is still in the source base today (in file `sys/fs/ufs_fs.h`). Not only does it promote file system reliability, but also, every file systems hacker now knows to send Kirk a birthday card for January 19.

There's a similar magic number for a.out files. Prior to AT&T's System V release of UNIX, an a.out was identified by the magic number 0407 at offset zero. And how was 0407 selected as the "magic number" identifying a UNIX object file? It's the opcode for an unconditional branch instruction (relative to the program counter) on a PDP-11! If you're running on a PDP-11 or VAX in compatibility mode, you can just start executing at the first word of the file, and the magic number (located there) will branch you past the a.out header and into the first real executable instruction of the program. The PDP-11 was the canonical UNIX machine at the time when a.out needed a magic number. Under SVr4, executables are marked by the first byte of a file containing hex `7F` followed by the letters "ELF" at bytes 2, 3, and 4 of the file.

Segments

Object files and executables come in one of several different formats. On most SVr4 implementations the format is called ELF (originally "Extensible Linker Format", now "Executable and Linking Format"). On other systems, the executable format is COFF (Common Object-File Format). And on BSD UNIX (rather like the Buddha having Buddha-nature), a.out files have a.out format. You can find out more about the format used on a UNIX system by typing `man a.out` and reading the manpage.

All these different formats have the concept of segments in common. There will be lots more about segments later, but as far as object files are concerned, they are simply areas within a binary file where all the information of a particular type (e.g., symbol table entries) is kept. The term *section* is also widely used; sections are the smallest unit of organization in an ELF file. A segment typically contains several sections.

Don't confuse the concept of segment on UNIX with the concept of segment on the Intel x86 architecture.

> A segment on UNIX is *a section of related stuff in a binary.*
>
> A segment in the Intel x86 memory model is *the result of a design in which (for compatibility reasons) the address space is not uniform, but is divided into 64-Kbyte ranges known as segments.*

The topic of segments on the Intel x86 architecture really deserves a chapter of its own.[1] For the remainder of this book, the term segment has the UNIX meaning unless otherwise stated.

When you run `size` on an executable, it tells you the size of three segments known as text, data, and bss in the file:

```
% echo; echo "text data bss total" ; size a.out

text        data     bss        total
1548   +    4236  +  4004 =     9788
```

Size doesn't print the headings, so use echo to generate them.

Another way to examine the contents of an executable file is to use the `nm` or `dump` utilities. Compile the source below, and run `nm` on the resulting a.out.

```
       char pear[40];
static double peach;
       int mango = 13;
static long melon = 2001;

main () {
    int i=3, j, *ip;
    ip=malloc(sizeof(i));
    pear[5] = i;
    peach = 2.0*mango;
}
```

Excerpts from running `nm` are shown below (minor editing changes have been made to the output to make it more accessible):

```
% nm -sx a.out
```

1. And it pretty near has one, too! See next chapter.

```
Symbols from a.out:

[Index]     Value       Size  Type  Bind   Segment Name
  . . .
[29]     |0x00020790|0x00000008|OBJT |LOCL |.bss peach
[42]     |0x0002079c|0x00000028|OBJT |GLOB |.bss pear
[43]     |0x000206f4|0x00000004|OBJT |GLOB |.data mango
[30]     |0x000206f8|0x00000004|OBJT |LOCL |.data melon
[36]     |0x00010628|0x00000058|FUNC |GLOB |.text main
[50]     |0x000206e4|0x00000038|FUNC |GLOB |UNDEF malloc
                        . . .
```

Figure 6-1 shows what the compiler/linker puts in each segment:

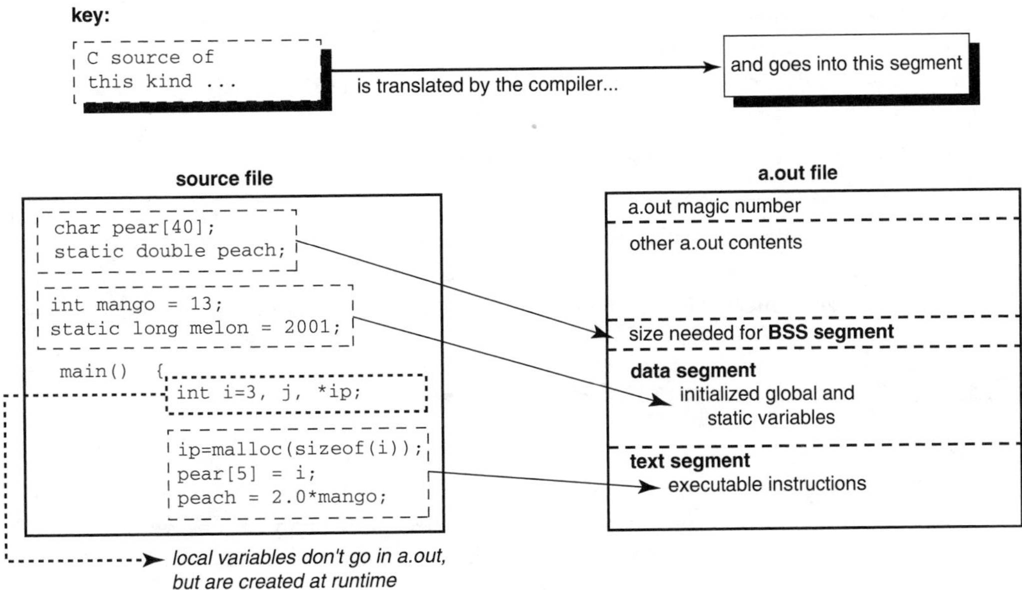

Figure 6-1 What Kinds of C Statements End Up in Which Segments?

The BSS segment gets its name from abbreviating "Block Started by Symbol"—a pseudo-op from the old IBM 704 assembler, carried over into UNIX, and there ever since. Some people like to remember it as "Better Save Space." Since the BSS segment only holds variables that don't have any value yet, it doesn't actually need to store the image of these variables. The size that BSS will require at runtime is recorded in the object file, but BSS (unlike the data segment) doesn't take up any actual space in the object file.

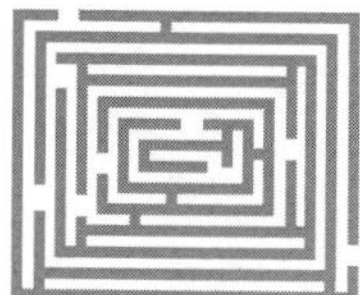

Programming Challenge

Look at the Segments in an Executable

1. Compile the "hello world" program, run `ls -l` on the executable to get its overall size, and run `size` to get the sizes of the segments within it.
2. Add the declaration of a global array of 1000 ints, recompile, and repeat the measurements. Notice the differences.
3. Now add an initial value in the declaration of the array (remember, C doesn't force you to provide a value for every element of an array in an initializer). This will move the array from the BSS segment to the data segment. Repeat the measurements. Notice the differences.
4. Now add the declaration of a big array local to a function. Declare a second big local array with an initializer. Repeat the measurements. Is data defined locally inside a function stored in the executable? Does it make any difference if it's initialized or not?
5. What changes occur to file and segment sizes if you compile for debugging? For maximum optimization?

Analyze the results of the above "Programming Challenge" to convince yourself that:

- the data segment is kept in the object file
- the BSS segment isn't kept in the object file (except for a note of its runtime size requirements)
- the text segment is the one most affected by optimization
- the a.out file size is affected by compiling for debugging, but the segments are not.

What the OS Does with Your `a.out`

Now we see why the a.out file is organized into segments. The segments conveniently map into objects that the runtime linker can load directly! The loader just takes each segment image in the file and puts it directly into memory. The segments essentially become memory areas of an executing program, each with a dedicated purpose. This is shown in Figure 6-2.

The text segment contains the program instructions. The loader copies that directly from the file into memory (typically with the `mmap()` system call), and need never worry about it again, as program text typically never changes in value nor size. Some operating systems and linkers can even assign appropriate permissions to the different sections in segments, for example, text can be made read-and-execute-only, some data can be made read-write-no-execute, other data made read-only, and so on.

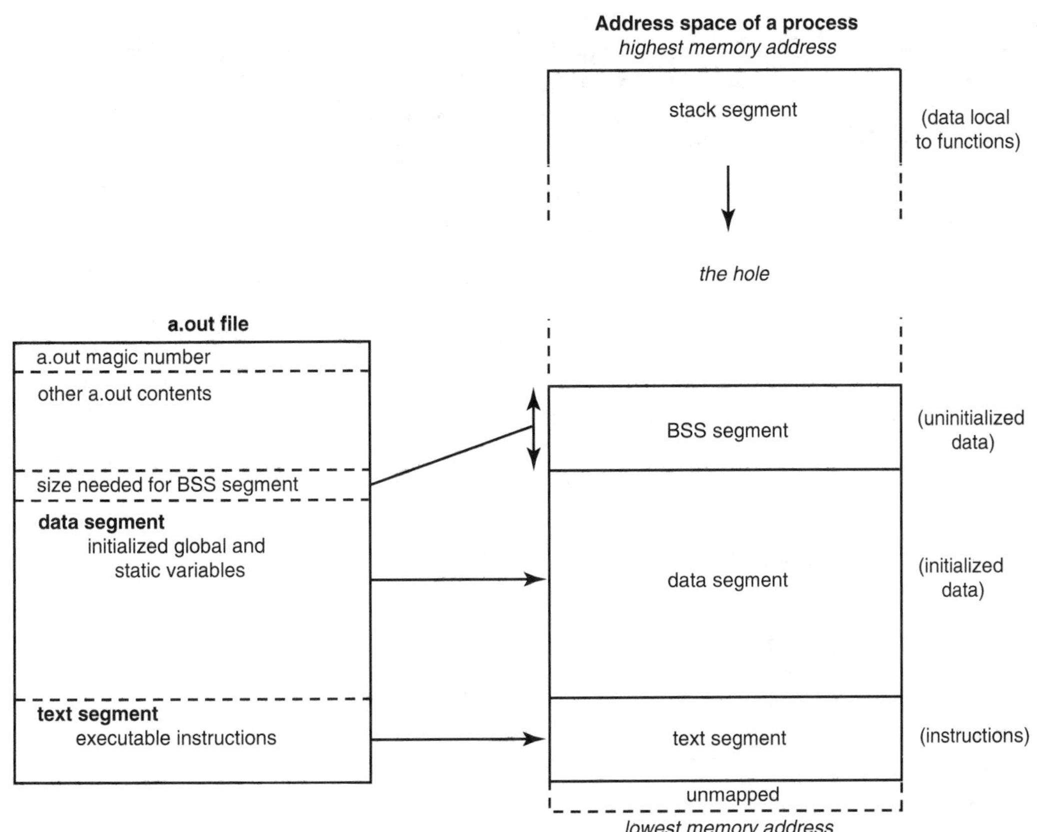

Figure 6-2 How the Segments of an Executable are Laid Out in Memory

The data segment contains the initialized global and static variables, complete with their assigned values. The size of the BSS segment is then obtained from the executable, and the loader obtains a block of this size, putting it right after the data segment. This block is zeroed out as it is put in the program's address space. The entire stretch of data and BSS is usually just referred to jointly as the data segment at this point. This is because a segment, in OS memory management terms, is simply a range of consecutive virtual addresses, so adjacent segments are coalesced. The data segment is typically the largest segment in any process.

The diagram shows the memory layout of a program that is about to begin execution. We still need some memory space for local variables, temporaries, parameter passing in function calls, and the like. A stack segment is allocated for this. We also need heap space for dynamically allocated memory. This will be set up on demand, as soon as the first call to `malloc()` is made.

Note that the lowest part of the virtual address space is unmapped; that is, it is within the address space of the process, but has not been assigned to a physical address, so any references to it will be illegal. This is typically a few Kbytes of memory from address zero up. It catches references through null pointers, and pointers that have small integer values.

When you take shared libraries into account, a process address space appears, as shown in Figure 6-3.

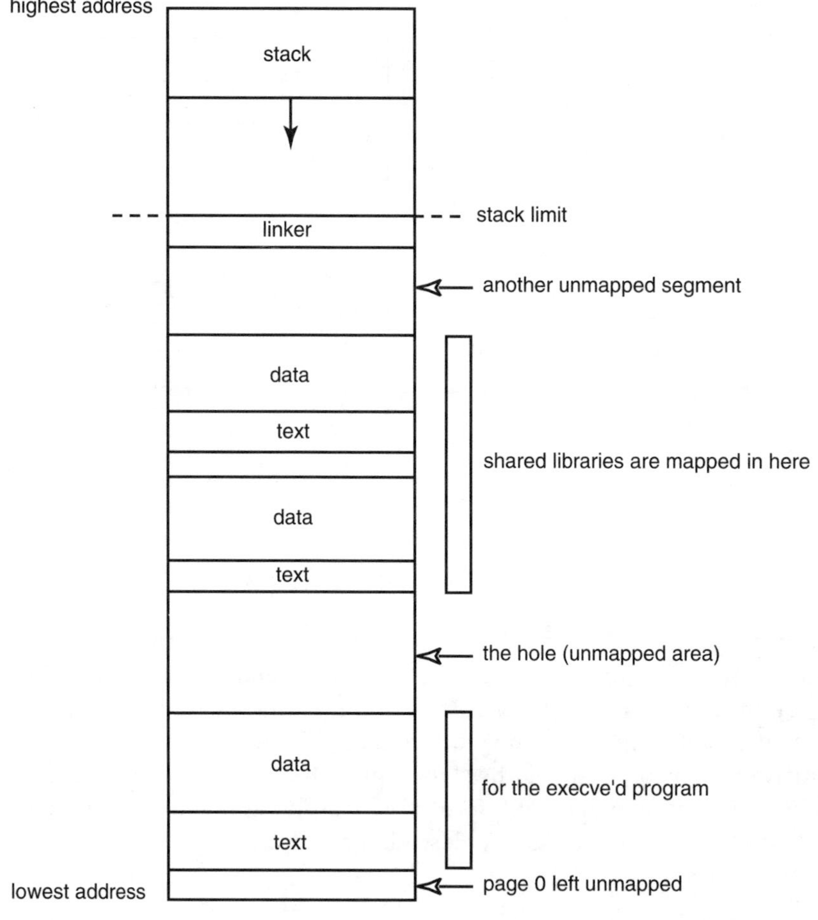

Figure 6-3 Virtual Address Space Layout, Showing Shared Libraries

What the C Runtime Does with Your `a.out`

Now we come to the fine detail of how C organizes the data structures of a running program. There are a number of runtime data structures: the stack, activation records, data, heap, and so on. We will look at each of these in turn, and analyze the C features that they support.

The Stack Segment

The stack segment contains a single data structure, the stack. A classic computer science object, the stack is a dynamic area of memory that implements a last-in-first-out queue, somewhat similar to a stack of plates in a cafeteria. The classic definition of a stack says that it can have any number of plates on it, but the only valid operations are to add or remove a plate from the top of the stack. That is, values can be pushed onto the stack, and retrieved by popping them off. A push operation makes the stack grow larger, and a pop removes a value from it.

Compiler-writers take a slightly more flexible approach. We add or delete plates only from the top, but we can also change values that are on a plate in the middle of the stack. A function can access variables local to its calling function via parameters or global pointers. The runtime maintains a pointer, often in a register and usually called `sp`, that indicates the current top of the stack. The stack segment has three major uses, two concerned with functions and one with expression evaluation:

- The stack provides the storage area for local variables declared inside functions. These are known as "automatic variables" in C terminology.
- The stack stores the "housekeeping" information involved when a function call is made. This housekeeping information is known as a stack frame or, more generally, a procedure activation record. We'll describe it in detail a little later, but for now be aware that it includes the address from which the function was called (i.e., where to jump back to when the called function is finished), any parameters that won't fit into registers, and saved values of registers.
- The stack also works as a scratch-pad area—every time the program needs some temporary storage, perhaps to evaluate a lengthy arithmetic expression, it can push partial results onto the stack, popping them when needed. Storage obtained by the `alloca()` call is also on the stack. Don't use `alloca()` to get memory that you want to outlive the routine that allocates it. (It will be overwritten by the next function call.)

A stack would not be needed except for recursive calls. If not for these, a fixed amount of space for local variables, parameters, and return addresses would be known at compile-time and could be allocated in the BSS. Early implementations of BASIC, COBOL, and FORTRAN did not permit recursive calls of functions, so they did not need a dynamic stack at runtime. Allowing recursive calls means that we must find a way to permit multiple instances of local variables to be in existence at one time, though only the most recently created will be accessed — the classic specification of a stack.

Programming Challenge

Stack Hack

Compile and run this small test program to discover the approximate location of the stack on your system:

```
#include <stdio.h>
main()
  {
      int i;
      printf("The stack top is near %p\n", &i);
      return 0;
  }
```

Discover the data and text segment locations, and the heap within the data segment, by declaring variables that will be placed in those segments and printing their addresses. Make the stack grow by calling a function, and declaring some large local arrays.

What's the address of the top of the stack now?

The stack may be located at a different address on different architectures and for different OS revisions. Although we talk about the top of the stack, the stack grows downwards on most processors, towards memory addresses with lower values.

What Happens When a Function Gets Called: The Procedure Activation Record

This section describes how the C runtime manages the program within its own address space. Actually, the runtime routines for C are remarkably few and lightweight. In contrast to, say, C++ or Ada, if a C program wants some service such as dynamic storage allocation, it usually has to ask for it explicitly. This makes C a very efficient language, but it does place an extra burden on the programmer.

One of the services that is provided automatically is keeping track of the call chain—which routines have called which others, and where control will pass back to, on the next "return" statement. The classic mechanism that takes care of this is the procedure activation record on the stack. There will be a procedure activation record (or its equivalent) for each call statement executed. The procedure activation record is a data structure that supports an invocation of a procedure, and also records everything needed to get back to where you came from before the call. (See Figure 6-4.)

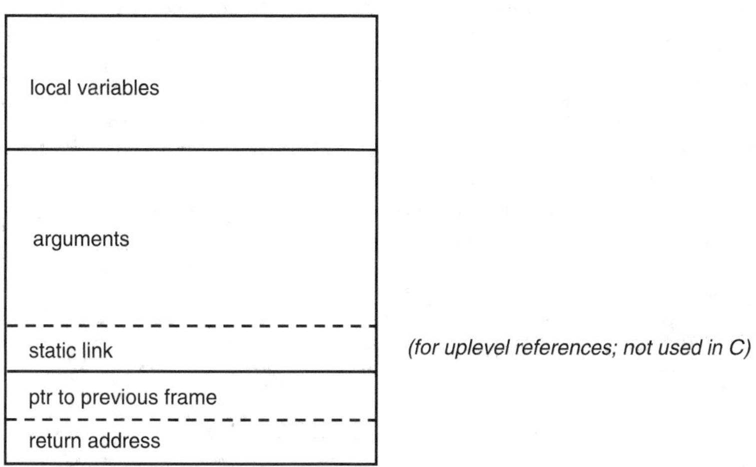

Figure 6-4 A Canonical Procedure Activation Record

The description of the contents of activation records is illustrative. The exact structure will vary from implementation to implementation. The order of the fields may be quite different. There may be an area for saving register values before making the call. The include file, `/usr/include/sys/frame.h,` shows how a stack frame looks on your UNIX system. On SPARC, a stack frame is large—several dozen words in size—because it provides room to save register windows. On the x86 architecture, the frame is somewhat smaller. The runtime maintains a pointer, often in a register and usually called `fp`, which indicates the active stack frame. This will be the stack frame nearest to or at the top of the stack.

Software Dogma

Astonishing C Fact!

Most modern algorithmic languages allow functions (as well as data) to be defined inside functions. C does not allow functions to be nested this way. All functions in C are at the top lexical level.

Astonishing C Fact! (Continued)

This restriction slightly simplifies C implementations. In languages like Pascal, Ada, Modula-2, PL/I, or Algol-60, which do allow lexically nested procedures, an activation record will typically contain a pointer to the activation record of its enclosing function. This pointer is termed a *static link*,[1] and it allows the nested procedure to access the stack frame of the enclosing procedure, and hence the data local to the enclosing procedure. Remember that there may be several invocations of an enclosing procedure active at once. The static link in the nested procedure's activation record will point to the appropriate stack frame, allowing the correct instances of local data to be addressed.

This type of access (a reference to a data item defined in a lexically enclosing scope) is known as an *uplevel reference*. The static link (pointing to the stack frame of the lexically enclosing procedure determined at compiletime) is so named because it contrasts with the dynamic link of the frame pointer chain (pointing to the stack frame of the immediately previous procedure invocation at runtime).

In Sun's Pascal compiler, the static link is treated as an additional hidden parameter, passed at the end of the argument list when needed. This allows Pascal routines to have the same activation record, and thus to use the same code generator, and to work with C routines. C itself does not allow nested functions; therefore, it does not have uplevel references to data in them, and thus does not need a static link in its activation records. Some people are urging that C++ should be given the ability to have nested functions.

1. Don't, for God's sake, confuse the *static link* in a procedure activation record, which permits uplevel references to local data in a lexically enclosing procedure, with a *static link* of the previous chapter that describes the obsolete method of binding a copy of all the libraries into an executable. In the previous chapter, *static* meant "done at compiletime". Here, it means "referring to the lexical layout of the program".

The code example below will be used to show the activation records on the stack at various points in execution. This is a hard concept to represent in a book, because we have to deal with the dynamic flow of control rather than the static code that a listing shows. Admittedly, this is difficult to follow, but as Wendy Kaminer remarked in her classic psychological text, *I'm Dysfunctional; You're Dysfunctional*, only people who die very young learn all they really need to know in kindergarten.

```
a (int i) {
      if (i>0)
          a( --i );
      else
          printf("i has reached zero ");
      return;
}

main () {
 a(1);
}
```

If we compile and run the above program, the flow of control is shown in Figure 6-5. Each dashed box shows a fragment of source that makes a function call. The statements executed are shown in bold print. As control passes from one function to another, the new state of the stack is shown underneath. Execution starts at `main`, and the stack grows downwards.

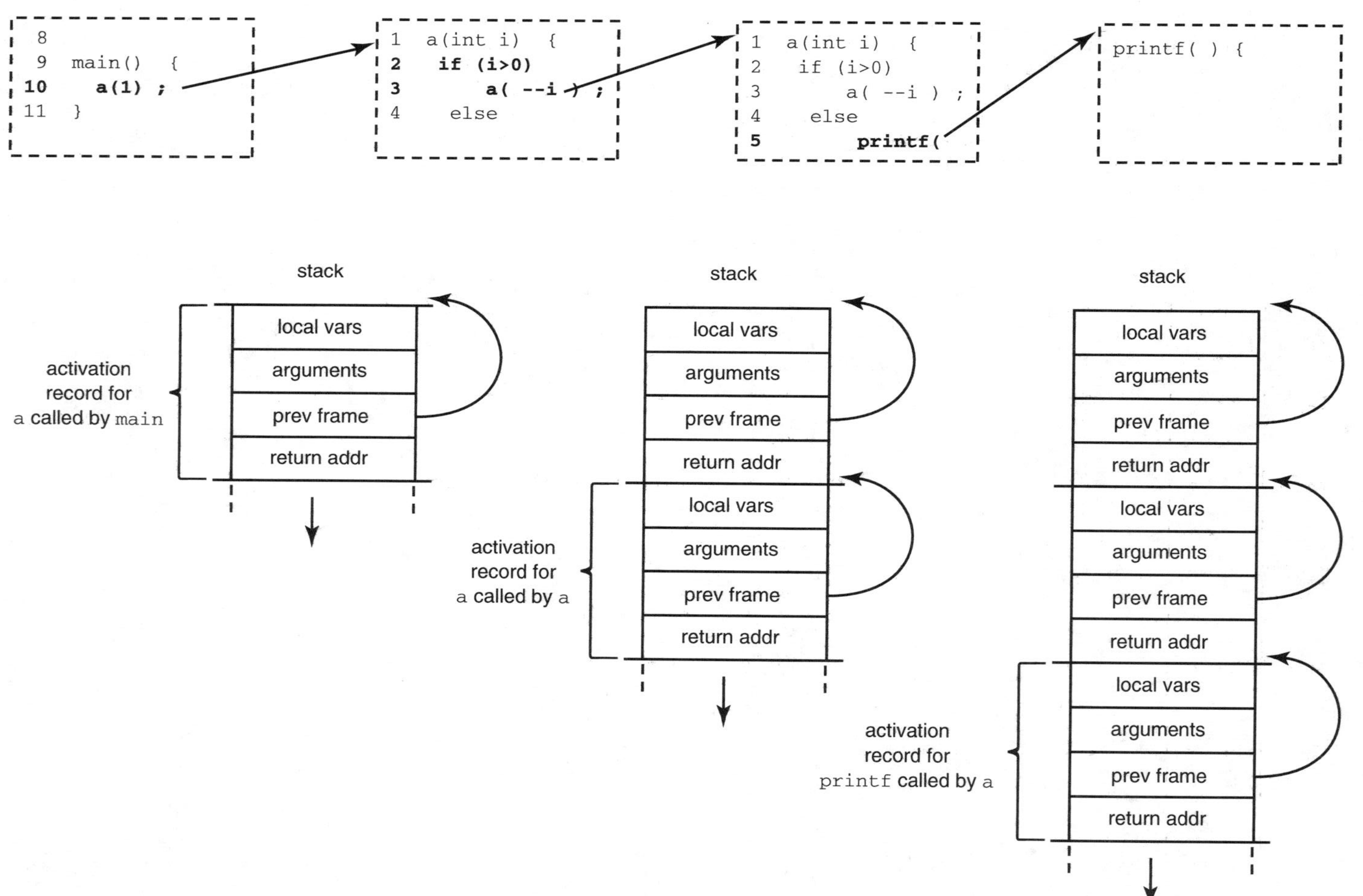

Figure 6-5 *An Activation Record is Created at Runtime for Each Function Call*

Compiler-writers will try to speed up programs by not storing information that will not be used. Other optimizations include keeping information in registers instead of on the stack, not pushing a complete stack frame for a leaf function (a function that doesn't make any calls itself), and making the callee responsible for saving registers, rather than the caller. The "pointer to previous frame" within each frame simplifies the task of popping the stack back to the previous record when the current function returns.

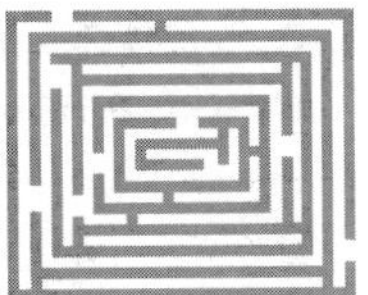

Programming Challenge

The Stack Frame

1. Manually trace the flow of control in the above program, and fill in the stack frames at each call statement. For each return address, use the line number to which it will go back.
2. Compile the program for real, and run it under the debugger. Look at the additions to the stack when a function has been called. Compare with your desk checked results to work out exactly what a stack frame looks like on your system.

Remember that compiler-writers will try to place as much of an activation record in registers as possible (because it's faster), so some of this may not be visible on the stack. Refer to the frame.h file to see the layout of a stack frame.

The `auto` and `static` keywords

The description of how the stack implements function calling also explains why it doesn't work to return a pointer to a local automatic variable from a function, like this:

```
char * favorite_fruit () {
    char deciduous [] = "apple";
    return deciduous;
}
```

The automatic variable `deciduous` is allocated on the stack when the function is entered; after the function is exited, the variable no longer exists, and the stack space can be overwritten at any time. Pointers that have lost their validity in this way (by referencing something that is no longer live) are known as "dangling pointers"—they don't reference anything useful, just kind of dangle in space. If you need to return a pointer to something defined in a function, then define the thing as `static`. This will ensure that space for the variable is allocated in the data segment instead of on the stack. The lifetime of the variable is thus the lifetime of the program, and as a side effect it retains its value even after the function that defines it exits. That value will still be available when the function is next entered.

The storage class specifier `auto` is never needed. It is mostly meaningful to a compiler-writer making an entry in a symbol table—it says "this storage is automatically allocated on entering the block" (as opposed to statically allocated at compiletime, or dynamically allocated on the heap). Auto is pretty much meaningless to all other programmers, since it can only be used inside a function, but data declarations in a function have this attribute by default. The only use we have ever found for the `auto` keyword is to make your declarations line up neatly, like this:

```
register int filbert;
    auto int almond;
  static int hazel;
```

instead of:

```
register int filbert;
int almond;
static int hazel;
```

A Stack Frame Might Not Be on the Stack

Although we talk about a "stack frame" being "pushed on the stack," an activation record need not be on the stack. It's actually faster and better to keep as much as possible of the activation record in registers. The SPARC architecture takes this to the limit with a concept called "register windows" in which the chip has a set of registers solely dedicated to holding parameters in procedure activation records. Empty stack frames are still pushed for each call; if the call chain goes so deep that you run out of register windows, the registers are reclaimed by spilling them to the frame space already reserved on the stack.

Some languages, such as Xerox PARC's Mesa and Cedar, have activation records allocated as linked lists in the heap. Activation records for recursive procedures were also heap-allocated for the first PL/I implementations (leading to criticism of slow performance, because the stack is usually a much faster place from which to acquire memory).

Threads of Control

It should now be clear how different threads of control (i.e., what used to be called "lightweight processes") can be supported within a process. Simply have a different stack dedicated to each thread of control. If a thread calls foo(), which calls bar(), which calls baz(), while the main program is executing other routines, each needs a stack of its own to keep track of where each is. Each thread gets a stack of 1Mb (grown as needed) and a page of red zone betweeen each thread's stack. Threads are a very powerful programming paradigm, which provide a performance advantage even on a uniprocessor. However, this is a book on C, not on threads; you can and should seek out more details on threads.

`setjmp` and `longjmp`

We can also mention what `setjmp()` and `longjmp()` do, since they are implemented by manipulating activation records. Many novice programmers do not know about this powerful mechanism, since it's a feature unique to C. They partially compensate for C's limited branching ability, and they work in pairs like this:

- `setjmp(jmp_buf j)` must be called first. It says *use the variable* `j` *to remember where you are now. Return 0 from the call.*
- `longjmp(jmp_buf j,int i)` can then be called. It says *go back to the place that the* `j` *is remembering. Make it look like you're returning from the original* `setjmp()`, *but return the value of* `i` *so the code can tell when you actually got back here via* `longjmp()`. Phew!
- The contents of the `j` are destroyed when it is used in a `longjmp()`.

Setjmp saves a copy of the program counter and the current pointer to the top of the stack. This saves some initial values, if you like. Then longjmp restores these values, effectively transferring control and resetting the state back to where you were when you did the save. It's termed "unwinding the stack," because you unroll activation records from the stack until you get to the saved one. Although it causes a branch, longjmp differs from a goto in that:

- A goto can't jump out of the current function in C (that's why this is a "longjmp"—you can jump a long way away, even to a function in a different file).
- You can only longjmp back to somewhere you have already been, where you did a setjmp, and that still has a live activation record. In this respect, setjmp is more like a "come from" statement than a "go to". Longjmp takes an additional integer argument that is passed back, and lets you figure out whether you got here from longjmp or from carrying on from the previous statement.

The following code shows an example of `setjmp()` and `longjmp()`.

```
#include <setjmp.h>

jmp_buf buf;
```

```
#include <setjmp.h>
banana() {
    printf("in banana()\n");
    longjmp(buf, 1);
    /*NOTREACHED*/
    printf("you'll never see this, because I longjmp'd");
}


main()
{
    if (setjmp(buf))
        printf("back in main\n");
    else {
        printf("first time through\n");
        banana();
    }

}
```

The resulting output is:

```
% a.out
first time through
in banana()
back in main
```

Point to watch: the only reliable way to ensure that a local variable retains the value that it had at the time of the longjmp is to declare it volatile. (This is for variables whose value changes between the execution of setjmp and the return of longjmp.)

A setjmp/longjmp is most useful for error recovery. As long as you haven't returned from the function yet, if you discover a unrecoverable error, you can transfer control back to the main input loop and start again from there. Some people use setjmp/longjmp to return from a chain of umpteen functions at once. Others use them to shield potentially dangerous code, for example, when dereferencing a suspicious pointer as shown in the following example.

```
switch(setjmp(jbuf)) {
    case 0:
        apple = *suspicious;
        break;
    case 1:
        printf("suspicious is indeed a bad pointer\n");
        break;
    default:
        die("unexpected value returned by setjmp");
}
```

This needs a handler for the segmentation violation signal, which will do the corresponding `longjmp(jbuf,1)` as explained in the next chapter. Setjmp and longjmp have mutated into the more general exception routines "catch" and "throw" in C++.

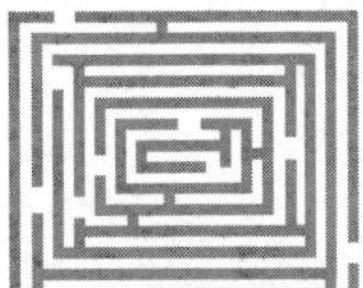

Programming Challenge

Jump to It!

Take the source of a program you have already written and add `setjmp/longjmp` to it, so that on receiving some particular input it will start over again.

The header file `<setjmp.h>` needs to be included in any source file that uses setjmp or longjmp.

Like goto's, setjmp/longjmp can make it hard to understand and debug a program. They are best avoided except in the specific situations described.

The Stack Segment Under UNIX

On UNIX, the stack grows automatically as a process needs more space. The programmer can just assume that the stack is indefinitely large. This is one of the many advantages that UNIX has over operating environments such as MS-DOS. UNIX implementations generally use some form of virtual memory. When you try to access beyond the space currently allocated for the stack, it generates a hardware interrupt known as a *page fault*. A page fault is processed in one of several ways, depending on whether the reference was valid or invalid.

The kernel normally handles a reference to an invalid address by sending the appropriate signal (segmentation fault probably) to the offending process. There's a small "red zone" region just below the top of the stack. A reference to there doesn't pass on a fault; instead, the operating system increases the stack segment size by a good chunk. Details vary among UNIX implementations, but in effect, additional virtual memory is mapped into the address space following the end of the current stack. The memory mapping hardware ensures you cannot access memory outside that which the operating system has allocated to your process.

The Stack Segment Under MS-DOS

In DOS, the stack size has to be specified as part of building the executable, and it cannot be grown at runtime. If you guess wrongly, and your stack gets bigger than the space you've allocated, you and your program both lose, and if you've turned checking on, you'll get the `STACK OVERFLOW!` message. This can also appear at compiletime, when you've exceeded the limits of a segment.

Turbo C will tell you `Segment overflowed maximum size` *<lsegname>* if too much data or code had to be combined into a single segment. The limit is 64Kbytes, due to the 80x86 architecture.

The method of specifying stack size varies with the compiler you're using. With Microsoft compilers, the programmer can specify the stack size as a linker parameter. The

```
STACK:nnnn
```

parameter tells the Microsoft linker to allow nnnn bytes for the stack.

The Borland compilers use a variable with a special name:

```
unsigned int _stklen = 0x4000; /* 16K stack */
```

Other compiler vendors have different methods for doing this. Check the programmer reference guides under "stack size" for the details.

Helpful C Tools

This section contains some lists (grouped by function) of helpful C tools you should know about, and what they do, in tables 6-1 through 6-4. We've already hinted at a few of these that help you peek inside a process or an a.out file. Some are specific to Sun OS. This section provides an easy-to-read summary of what each does, and where to find them. After studying the summary here, read the manpage for each, and try running each on a couple of different a.out's—the "hello world" program, and a big program.

Go through these carefully—investing 15 minutes now in trying each one will save you hours later in solving a hard bug.

Table 0-1 Tools to Examine Source

Tool	Where to Find It	What It Does
`cb`	Comes with the compiler	C program beautifier. Run your source through this filter to put it in a standard layout and indentation. Comes from Berkeley.
`indent`		Does the same things `cb` does. Comes from AT&T.
`cdecl`	This book	Unscrambles C declarations.
`cflow`	Comes with the compiler	Prints the caller/callee relationships of a program.
`cscope`	Comes with the compiler	An interactive `ASCII`-based C program browser. We use it in the OS group to check the impact of changes to header files. It provides quick answers to questions like: "How many commands use libthread?" or "Who are all the kmem readers?"
`ctags`	/usr/bin	Creates a tags file for use in vi editor. A tags file speeds up examining program source by maintaining a table of where most objects are located.
`lint`	Comes with the compiler	A C program checker.
`sccs`	/usr/ccs/bin	A source code version control system.
`vgrind`	/usr/bin	A formatter for printing nice C listings.

Doctors can use x-rays, sonograms, arthroscopes, and exploratory operations to look inside their patients. These tools are the x-rays of the software world.

Table 0-2 Tools to Examine Executables

Tool	Where to Find It	What It Does
`dis`	/usr/ccs/bin	Object code disassembler
`dump -Lv`	/usr/ccs/bin	Prints dynamic linking information
`ldd`	/usr/bin	Prints the dynamic libraries this file needs
`nm`	/usr/ccs/bin	Prints the symbol table of an object file
`strings`	/usr/bin	Looks at the strings embedded in a binary. Useful for looking at the error messages a binary can generate, built-in file names, and (sometimes) symbol names or version and copyright information.
`sum`	/usr/bin	Prints checksum and block count for a file. Answers questions like: "Are two executables the same version?" "Did the transmission go OK?"

Table 0-3 Tools to Help with Debugging

Tool	Where to Find It	What It Does
`truss`	/usr/bin	The SVr4 version of `trace`. This tool prints out the system calls that an executable makes. Use it to see what a binary is doing, and why it's stuck or failing. This is a great help!
`ps`	/usr/bin	Displays process characteristics.
`ctrace`	Comes with compiler	Modifies your source to print lines as they are executed. A great tool for small programs!
`debugger`	Comes with compiler	Interactive debugger.
`file`	/usr/bin	Tells you what a file contains (e.g., executable, data, ASCII, shell script, archive, etc.).

Table 0-4 Tools to Help with Performance Tuning

Tool	Where to Find It	What It Does
`collector`	Comes with debugger	(SunOS only) Collects runtime performance data under the control of the debugger.
`analyzer`	Comes with debugger	(SunOS only) Analyzes collected performance data.
`gprof`	/usr/ccs/bin	Displays the call-graph profile data (identifies the compute-intensive functions).
`prof`	/usr/ccs/bin	Displays the percentage of time spent in each routine.
`tcov`	Comes with compiler	Displays a count of how often each statement is executed (identifies the compute-intensive loops within a function).
`time`	/usr/bin/time	Displays the total real and CPU time used by a program.

If you're working on the OS kernel, most of the runtime tools are not available to you, because the kernel does not run as a user process. The compiletime tools, like lint, work, but otherwise we have to use the stone knives and flint axes: putting nonrandom patterns in memory to see when they are overwritten (two favorites are the hex constants `deadbeef` and `abadcafe`), using printf's or their equivalent, and logging trace information.

Software Dogma

Debugging the Kernel with grep

A kernel "panics", or comes to an abrupt halt, when it detects a situation that "cannot" arise. For example, it finds a null pointer when looking for some essential data. Since there is no way it can recover from this, the safest course is to halt the processor before more data disappears. To solve a panic, you must first consider what happened that could possibly frighten an operating system.

Debugging the Kernel with grep (Continued)

The kernel development group at Sun had one obscure bug that was very difficult to track down. The symptom was that kernel memory was getting overwritten at random, occasionally panicking the system.

Two of our top engineers worked on this, and they noticed that it was always the 19th byte from the beginning of a memory block that was being creamed. This is an uncommon offset, unlike the more usual 2, 4, or 8 that occur everywhere. One of the engineers had a brainwave and used the offset to home in on the bug. He suggested they use the kernel debugger kadb to disassemble the kernel binary image (it took an hour!) into an ASCII file. They then grepped the file, looking for "store" instructions where the operand indicated offset 19! One of these was almost guaranteed to be the instruction causing the corruption.

There were only eight of these, and they were all in the subsystem that dealt with process control. Now they were pretty sure *where* the problem was, and just needed to find out *what* it was. Further effort eventually yielded the cause: a race condition on a process control structure. This resulted in one thread marking the memory for return to the system before another thread had truly finished with it. Result: the kernel memory allocator then gave the memory away to someone else, but the process control code thought it still held it, and wrote into it, causing the otherwise impossible-to-find corruption!

Debugging an OS kernel with grep—what a concept. Sometimes even source tools can help solve runtime problems!

While on the subject of useful tools, Table 0-5 lists some ways to see exactly what the configuration of a Sun system is. However, none of these tools can help you unless you practice using them.

Table 0-5 Tools to Help Identify Your Hardware

What It Identifies	Typical Output	How to Invoke It
Kernel architecture	sun4c	`/usr/kvm/arch -k`
Any OS patches applied	no patches are installed	`/usr/bin/showrev -p`
Various hardware things	lots	`/usr/sbin/prtconf`
CPU clock rate	40MHz processor	`/usr/sbin/psrinfo -v`
hostid	554176fe	`/usr/ucb/hostid`
Memory	32Mb	Displayed on power up

Table 0-5 Tools to Help Identify Your Hardware (Continued)

What It Identifies	Typical Output	How to Invoke It
Serial number	4290302	Displayed on power up
ROM revision	2.4.1	Displayed on power up
Mounted disk	198Mb disk	`/usr/bin/df -F ufs -k`
Swap space	40Mb	`/etc/swap -s`
Ethernet address	8:0:20:f:8c:60	`/usr/sbin/ifconfig -a` The ethernet address is built into the machine
IP address	le0=129.144.248.36	`/usr/sbin/ifconfig -a` The IP address is built into the network
Floating-point hardware	FPU's frequency appears to be 38.2 MHz	`fpversion` comes with the compiler

Some Light Relief—Programming Puzzles at CMU

A few years ago, the Computer Science Department at Carnegie-Mellon University regularly ran a small programming contest for its incoming graduate students. The contest was intended to give the new researchers some hands-on experience with the department systems and let them demonstrate their star potential. CMU has a long and distinguished involvement with computers, stretching back to the pioneering days, so you'd typically expect some outstanding entries in a programming competition there.

The form of the contest varied from year to year, and in one particular year it was very simple. Contestants had to read a file of numbers and print the average. There were only two rules:

1. The program had to run as fast as possible.
2. The program had to be written in Pascal or C.

The rival programs were grouped together and submitted in batches by a faculty member. Students could submit as many entries as they wished; this encouraged the use of non-deterministic probabilistic algorithms (algorithms that would guess at certain characteristics of the data set and use the guess to obtain faster performance). The golden rule was that the program which ran in the shortest amount of time won the contest.

The graduate students duly retired to dark corners and started whacking their various programs. Most of them had three or four versions to enter and run. At this point, the reader is invited to guess the techniques that helped the programs run fast.

Programming Challenge

How to Exceed the Speed Limit?

Imagine that you have been given the task of writing a program to read a file of 10,000 numbers and calculate the average. Your program must run in the shortest amount of time.

What programming and compiler techniques will you use to achieve this?

Most people guess the biggest wins will come through code optimization, either explicitly in the code, or implicitly by using the correct compiler options. The standard code optimizations are techniques like loop unrolling, in-line function expansion, common subexpression elimination, improved register allocation, omitting runtime checks on array bounds, loop-invariant code motion, operator strength reduction (turning exponentiation into multiplication, turning multiplication into bit-shifting and/or addition), and so on.

The data file contained about 10,000 numbers, so assuming it took a millisecond just to read and process each number (about par for the systems at the time), the fastest possible program would take about ten seconds.

The actual results were very surprising. The fastest program, as reported by the operating system, took minus three seconds. That's right—the winner ran in a negative amount of time! The next fastest apparently took just a few milliseconds, while the entry in third place came in just under the expected 10 seconds. Obviously, some devious programming had taken place, but what and how? A detailed scrutiny of the winning programs eventually supplied the answer.

The program that apparently ran backwards in time had taken advantage of the operating system. The programmer knew where the process control block was stored relative to the base of the stack. He crafted a pointer to access the process control block and overwrote the "CPU-time-used" field with a very high value.[2] The operating system wasn't expecting CPU times that large, and it misinterpreted the very large positive number as a negative number under the two's complement scheme.

2. A flagrant abuse of the rules, ranking equal to the time Argentinian soccer ace Diego Maradona used his forearm to nudge the ball into the England net for the winning goal in the 1986 soccer World Cup.

The runner-up, whose program took just a few milliseconds, had been equally cunning in a different way. He had used the rules of the competition rather than exotic coding. He submitted two different entries. One entry read the numbers, calculated the answer in the normal way, and wrote the result to a file; the second entry spent most of its time asleep, but woke up briefly every few seconds and checked if the answer file existed. When it did, it printed it out. The second process only took a few milliseconds of total CPU time. Since contestants were allowed to submit multiple entries, the smaller time counted and put him in second place.

The programmer whose entry came in third, taking slightly less than the calculated minimum time, had the most elaborate scheme. He had worked out the optimized machine code instructions to solve the problem, and stored the instructions as an array of integers in his program. It was easy to overwrite a return address on the stack (as Bob Morris, Jr. later did with the Internet worm of 1988) and cause the program to jump into and start executing this array. These instructions solved the problem honestly in record time.

There was an uproar among the faculty when these stratagems were uncovered. Some of the staff were in favor of severely reprimanding the winners. A younger group of professors proposed instead awarding them an extra prize in recognition of their ingenuity. In the end, a compromise was reached. No prizes were awarded, no punishments were handed down, and the results stuck. Sadly, the contest was a casualty of the strong feelings, and this incident marked the final year it was held.

For Advanced Students Only

A word to the wise: it's possible to embed assembler code in C source. This is usually only done for the most machine-specific things in the depths of the OS kernel, like setting specific registers on changing from supervisor mode to user mode. Here's how we plant a no-op (or other instruction) in a C function using a SunPro SPARCompiler:

```
banana() { asm("nop"); }
```

Here's how you embed assembly language instructions using Microsoft C on a PC:

```
__asm mov ah, 2
__asm mov dl, 43h
```

You can also prefix the assembler code with the keyword "_ _asm". You can also use the keyword once, and put all the assembler code in a pair of braces, like this:

```
__asm {
        mov ah, 2
        mov dl, 43h
        int 21h
        }
```

Little checking is done for you, and it's easy to create programs that bomb out. But it's a good way to experiment with and learn the instruction set of a machine. Take a look at the SPARC architecture manual, the assembler manual (which mostly talks about syntax and directives), and a databook from one of the SPARC vendors, such as Cypress Semiconductor's "SPARC RISC User's Guide."

Thanks for the Memory 7

A master was explaining the nature of the Tao to one of his novices.

"The Tao is embodied in all software—regardless of how insignificant," said the master.

"Is the Tao in a hand-held calculator?" asked the novice. "It is," came the reply.

"Is the Tao in a video game?" continued the novice. "It is even in a video game," said the master.

"And is the Tao in the DOS for a personal computer?"

The master coughed and shifted his position slightly. "That would be in the stack frame Bob, and the lesson is over for today," he said.

—Geoffrey James, *The Tao of Programming*

---

the Intel 80x86 family...the Intel 80x86 memory model and how it got that way...virtual memory...cache memory...the data segment and heap... memory leaks...bus error—take the train... some light relief—the thing king and the paging game

---

This chapter starts with a discussion of memory architecture for the Intel 80x86 processor family (the processor at the heart of the IBM PC). It contrasts PC memory with the virtual memory feature found on other systems. A knowledge of memory architecture helps a programmer to understand some of the C conventions and restrictions.

The Intel 80x86 Family

Modern Intel processors can trace their heritage all the way back to the earliest Intel chips. As customers became more sophisticated and demanding in their use of chip sets, Intel was always ready with compatible follow-on processors. Compatibility made it easy for customers to move to newer chips, but it severely restricted the amount of innovation that was possible. The modern Pentium is a direct descendant of Intel's 8086 from 15 years before, and it contains architectural irregularities to provide backwards compatibility with it (meaning that programs compiled for an 8086 will run on a Pentium). Referring to the innovation/compatibility trade-off, some people have unkindly commented that "Intel puts the 'backward' in 'backward compatible'..." (see Figure 7-1).

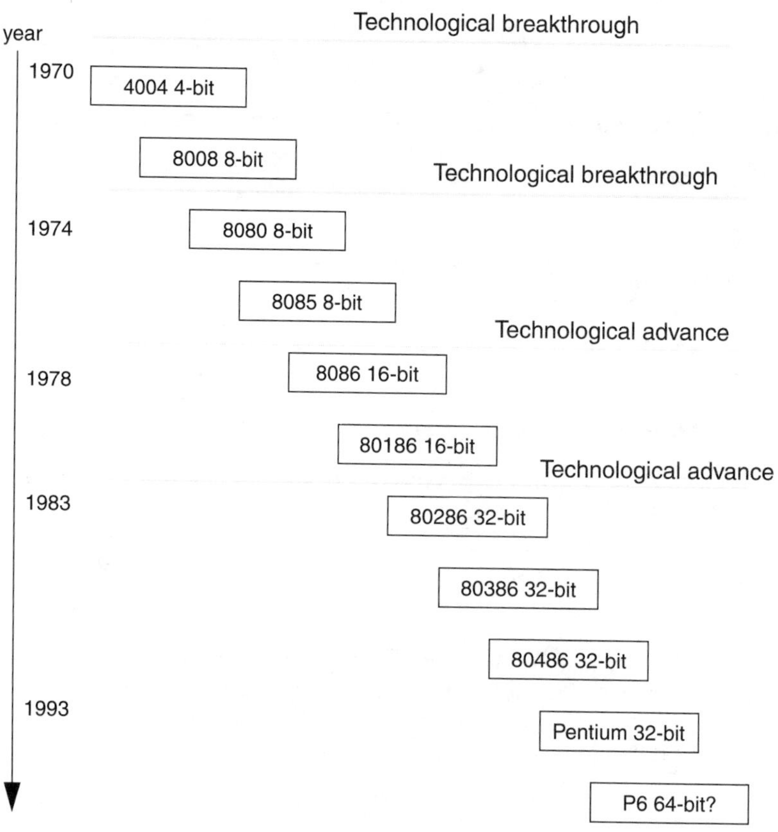

Figure 7-1 The Intel 80x86 Family: Putting the "Backward" in "Backward Compatible"

The Intel 4004 was a 4-bit microcontroller built in 1970 to satisfy the specific needs of a single customer, Busicom—a Japanese calculator company. The Intel design engineer conceived the idea of producing a general-purpose programmable chip, instead of the custom logic for each different customer that was the rule at the time. Intel thought they'd sell a few hundred, but a general-purpose design turned out to have vastly wider applicability. Four bits was too limiting, so in April 1972 an 8-bit version, the 8008, was launched. Two years later, that in turn spawned the 8080, which was the first chip powerful enough to be called a microcomputer. It included the entire 8008 instruction set and added 30 more instructions of its own, initiating a trend that continues to this day. If the

4004 was the chip that got Intel started, the 8080 was the chip that made its fortune, boosting the company's turnover to more than $1 billion annually and placing it high on the Fortune 500 list.

The 8085 processor took advantage of advances in integration technology to squeeze a three chip combination onto one. In essence, it was an 8080 combined with the 8224 clock driver and the 8228 controller, all on a single chip. Although its internal data bus was still 8-bit, it used a 16-bit address bus, so it could address 2^{16} or 64 Kbytes of memory.

Introduced in 1978, the 8086 improved on the 8085 by allowing 16 bits on the data bus and 20 bits on the address bus permitting a massive (at the time) 1 Mbyte of possible memory. In an unusual design decision, the addresses are formed by overlapping two 16-bit words to form a 20-bit address, rather than concatenating them to form a 32-bit address (see Figure 7-2). The 8086 was not 8085-compatible at the instruction-set level, but assembler macros helped convert programs to the newer architecture easily.

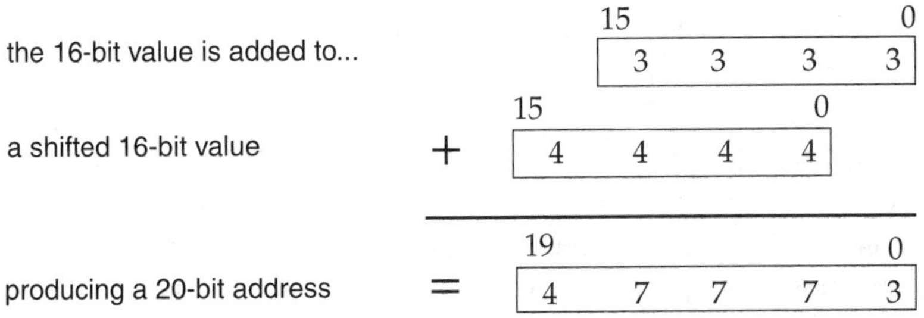

```
                                             15              0
the 16-bit value is added to...             | 3   3   3   3 |
                                         15              0
a shifted 16-bit value           +      | 4   4   4   4 |
                                 ---------------------------
                                         19                  0
producing a 20-bit address       =      | 4   7   7   7   3 |
```

The first 16-bit quantity is known as an "offset" and the second, shifted value is called a "segment". The 8086 chip has four segment registers that hold segment values and automatically do the shifting and addition to produce a 20-bit address.

There's a segment register devoted to pointing to each of the code, data, and stack segments, plus one extra one. This is quite helpful from a compiler-writer's point of view.

Figure 7-2 How the Intel 8086 Addresses Memory

Its irregular addressing scheme allowed the 8086 to run 8085-ported code more simply; once the segment registers were loaded with a fixed value they could be ignored, allowing the 16-bit addresses of the 8085 to be used directly. The design team rejected the idea of forming addresses by concatenating the segment word; that would provide 32 bits of addressing or 4 Gbytes, which was an impossibly large amount of memory at the time.

Now that this basic addressing model was laid down, all subsequent 80x86 processors had to follow it or give up compatibility. If the 8080 was the chip that brought Intel to prominence, the 8086 was the chip that kept it there. We'll probably never know exactly why IBM selected the Intel 8088 (an 8-bit sibling of the 8086) as the CPU for its new PC back in 1979, in the face of so many technically superior alternatives from companies like Motorola or National Semiconductor. By selecting an Intel chip, IBM made Intel's fortune for the next two decades, just as IBM also made Microsoft's fortune by selecting MS-DOS as the operating executive. Ironically, in August 1993 Intel's stock valuation of $26.6 billion rose above IBM's stock valuation of $24.5 billion, and Intel eclipsed IBM as the most valuable electronics company in America.

Intel and Microsoft have effectively become the new IBM, reaping undeserved windfall profits from their closed proprietary systems. IBM is trying desperately to regain its former position by using the PowerPC to challenge Intel's hardware monopoly, and using OS/2 to challenge Microsoft's software monopoly. The OS/2 challenge has probably failed, but it's too early to pass judgment on the PowerPC.

The 8088 processor, as used in the first IBM PC, was just a cheap 8-bit version of the 8086, allowing the wealth of existing 8-bit support chips to be used. All further 80x86 refinements were of the "smaller, faster, costlier, and more instructions" variety. The 80186 took this path, introducing 10 not-very-important new instructions. The 80286 was just the 80186 (minus some built-in peripheral ports) but with the first attempt to extend the address space. It moved the memory controller off-chip, and provided an ambitiously named *virtual* mode in which the segment register isn't added to the offset, but is used to index a table holding the actual segment address. This kind of addressing was also known as protected mode and it was still 16-bit-based. MS-Windows uses 286 protected mode as its standard addressing mode.

The 80386 is the 80286 with two new addressing modes: 32-bit protected mode and virtual 8086 mode. Microsoft's new flagship operating system, NT, and MS-Windows in enhanced mode both use 32-bit protected mode. This is why NT requires at least a 386 to run. The other kind of addressing, virtual 8086 mode, creates a virtual 8086 machine with 1 Mbyte of address space. Several of them can run at once, supporting multiple virtual MS-DOS sessions, each of which thinks it's running on its own 8086. At about this time, you should be thinking that the gyrations necessary to cope with the limitations of the original addressing scheme are pretty incredible, and you'd be right. The 80x86 is a difficult and frustrating architecture for which to write compilers and application programs.

All these processors can have coprocessors, usually to implement floating point in hardware. The 8087 and 80287 coprocessors are identical, except that the 287 can address the same extended memory as the 286. The 387 can address using the same modes as the 386, but also adds some built-in transcendental functions.

Software Dogma

Choosing Components for the IBM PC

Some, perhaps most, of the IBM decisions about the PC were definitely made on non-technical grounds. Before deciding on MS-DOS, IBM arranged a meeting with Gary Kildall of Digital Research to consider CP/M. On the day of the meeting, so the story runs, the weather was so good that Gary decided to fly his private plane instead. The IBM managers, perhaps annoyed at being stood up, soon cut a deal with Microsoft instead.

Bill Gates had bought the rights to Seattle Computer Product's QDOS,[1] cleaned it up a little, and renamed it "MS-DOS". The rest, as they say, is history. IBM was happy, Intel was happy, and Microsoft was very, very happy. Digital Research was not happy, and Seattle Computer Products became successively unhappier over the years as they realized they had pretty much given away the rights to the best-selling computer program ever. They did retain the right to sell MS-DOS if they sold the hardware at the same time, and this was why you used to see copies of MS-DOS available from Seattle Computer Products, improbably bundled with alarmingly useless Intel boards and chips, to fulfill the letter of their contract with Microsoft.

Don't feel too sorry for Seattle Computer Products—their QDOS was itself extensively based on Gary Kildall's CP/M, and he'd rather be flying. Bill Gates later bought a super-fast Porsche 959 with his cut of the profits. This car cost three-quarters of a million dollars, but problems arose with U.S. Customs on import. The Porsche 959 cannot be driven in the U.S.A. because it has not passed the government-mandated crash-worthiness tests. The car lies unused in a warehouse in Oakland to this day—one Gates product that will definitely never crash.

1. This literally stood for "Quick and Dirty Operating System."

The 80486 is a repackaged 80386 that is a little faster because the bus lacks states that allow coprocessors. The 486 coprocessor is either built in or disallowed, called DX and SX, respectively. The 486 adds a few modest instructions and has an on-board cache (fast processor memory), which accounts for most of the rest of the performance improvement. That brings us to the present day, where, in a tremendous burst of innovation and trademark squabbling, Intel named its latest chip the Pentium, not the 80586. It's faster, more expensive, supports all previous instructions, and introduces some new ones. It's safe to anticipate that the 80686 is planned to be faster and more expensive, and will provide some additional instructions. Intel's internal motto for their continual introduction of new chips is "be fast or be dead," and they certainly live by it. As my old grandmother used to say as she worked away at her spinning wheel, "Those who do not remember history are doomed to have serious backward compatibility problems, especially if they change the addressing modes or wordsize of their architecture."

The Intel 80x86 Memory Model and How It Got That Way

As we saw in the previous chapter, the term segment has at least two different meanings (there's also a third OS memory-management-related meaning):

> A segment on UNIX is *a section of related stuff in a binary.*
>
> A segment in the Intel x86 memory model is *the result of a design in which (for compatibility reasons) the address space is not uniform, but is divided into 64-Kbyte ranges known as segments.*

In its most basic form, a segment started out on the 8086 as a 64-Kbyte region of memory that was pointed to by a segment register. An address is formed by taking the value in a segment register and shifting it left four places (or equivalently, multiplying by 16). Yet a third way of looking at this is to consider that the segment register value has been made a 20-bit quantity by appending four zeros.

Then the 16-bit offset says where the address is in that segment. If you add the contents of the segment register to the offset, you will obtain the final address. One quirk: just as there are many different pairs of numbers that total, for example, 24, there are many different segment + offset pairs that point to the same address.

Handy Heuristic

Different-Looking Pointers, Same Address

An address on the Intel 8086 is formed by combining a 16-bit segment with a 16-bit offset. The segment is shifted left four places before the offset is added. This means that many different segment/offset pairs can point to the same one address.

segment (shifted left 4 bits)		offset		resulting address
A0000	+	FFFF	=	AFFFF
:				
AFFF0	+	000F	=	AFFFF

In general, there will be 0x1000 (4096) different segment/offset combinations that point to the same one address.

A C compiler-writer needs to make sure that pointers are compared in canonical form on a PC, otherwise two pointers that have different bit patterns but designate the same address may wrongly compare unequal. This will be done for you if you use the "huge" keyword, but does not occur for the "large" model. The `far` keyword in Microsoft C indicates that the pointer stores the contents of the segment register and the offset. The `near` keyword means the pointer just holds a 16-bit offset, and it will use the value already in the data or stack segment register.

Handy Heuristic

A Guide to Memory Prefix Use

Prefix	Power of Two	Meaning	Number of Bytes
Kilo	2^{10}	One thousand bytes	1,024
Mega	2^{20}	One million bytes	1,048,576
Giga	2^{30}	One billion bytes	1,073,741,824
Tera	2^{40}	One trillion bytes	1,099,511,627,776
Bubba	2^{64}	Eighteen billion billion bytes	18,446,744,073,709,551,616

While on the subject of these numbers, note that all disk manufacturers use decimal rather than binary notation for disk capacity. Thus a 2-Gbyte disk will hold 2,000,000,000 bytes and not 2,147,483,648 bytes.

A 64-bit address space is *really* large. It can fit an entire movie for high-definition TV in memory at once. They haven't yet settled the specification for high-definition TV, but it will probably be close to SVGA which is 1024 × 768 pixels, each of which needs, say, three bytes of color information.

At 30 frames per second (as in the current NTSC standard) a two-hour movie would take:

120 minutes × 60 seconds × 30 frames × 786,432 pixels × 3 color bytes

= 509,607,936,000 bytes

= 500Gbytes of memory

So you could fit not just one, but 36 million high-definition TV movies (orders of magnitude more than every movie ever made, and then some) into a 64-bit virtual address space. You still have to leave room for the operating system, but that's OK. The UNIX kernel is constrained by the current SVID[1] to 512 Mbytes. Of course, there's still the small matter of physical disk to back up this virtual memory.

1. The SVID – System V Interface Definition – is a weighty document that describes the System V API.

The real challenge in computer architecture today is not memory *capacity,* but memory *speed*. Your brand new shiny red Pentium chip isn't going to win you anything if your software is actually constrained by disk and memory latency (access time). To be precise, there is a wide and increasing gap between memory and CPU performance. Over the past decade CPU's have doubled in speed every one-and-a-half to two years. Memory gets twice as dense (64-Kb chips increase to 128 Kb) in the same period, but its access time only improves by 10%. Main memory access time will be even more important on huge address space machines. When you have access to huge amounts of data, the latency for moving it around will start to dominate software performance. Expect to see a lot more use of cache and related technologies in the future.

Handy Heuristic

Where the MS-DOS 640Kb Limit Comes From

There's a hard memory limit of 640Kbytes available to applications that run under MS-DOS. The limit arises from the maximum address range of the Intel 8086, the original DOS machine. The 8086 supported 20-bit addresses, restricting it to 1 Mbyte memory in total. That address space was further limited by reserving certain segments (64Kbyte chunks) for system use:

segment	reserved for
`F0000` to `FFFFF`	64 Kb for permanent ROM area BIOS, diagnostics, etc.
`D0000` to `EFFFF`	128 Kb for cartridge ROM area
`C0000` to `CFFFF`	64 Kb for BIOS extensions (XT hard disk)
`B0000` to `BFFFF`	64 Kb for conventional memory display
`A0000` to `AFFFF`	64 Kb for display memory extension
leaving	
`00000` to `9FFFF`	640 Kb for application program use.

A billion and a trillion have different meanings in the U.S. and England. In the U.S. they are a thousand million (10^9) and a million million (10^{12}), respectively. In England they are bigger, a million million (10^{12}) and a million million million (10^{18}), respectively. We prefer the American usage because the magnitude increments are consistent from thousand (10^3) to million (10^6) to billion (10^9) to trillion (10^{12}). A billionaire in England is much richer than a billionaire in the U.S.—until the exchange rate sinks to £1,000 per $1, that is.

There's a 640 Kb limit in MS-DOS that arises from the 1 Mbyte total address space of the 8086 chip. MS-DOS reserves six entire segments for its own use. This only leaves the 10 64-Kbyte segments starting at address 0 available to applications (and the lowest addresses in 0 block are also reserved for system use as buffers and MS-DOS working store). As Bill Gates said in 1981, "640 K ought to be enough for anybody." When the PC first came out, 640Kb seemed like a tremendous amount of memory. In fact, the first PC came configured with only 16K of RAM as standard.

Handy Heuristic

PC Memory Models

Microsoft C recognizes these memory models:

small	All pointers are 16 bits, limiting code and data to a single segment each, and the overall program size to 128 K.
large	All pointers are 32 bits. The program can contain many 64-K segments.
medium	Function pointers are 32 bits, so there can be many code segments. Data pointers are 16 bits, so there can only be one 64-K data segment.
compact	The other way around from medium: function pointers are 16 bits, so the code must be less than 64K. Data pointers are 32 bits so the data can occupy many segments. Stack data is still limited to a single 64-K segment, though.

Microsoft C recognizes these non-standard keywords; when applied to an object pointer or a function pointer, they override the memory model for that particular pointer only.

`__near`	A 16-bit pointer
`__far`	A 32-bit pointer, but the object pointed to must be all in one segment (no object may be larger than 64 K), i.e., once you load the segment register you can address all of the object from it.
`__huge`	A 32-bit pointer, and the restriction about all being in one segment is lifted.

Example: `char __huge * banana;`

Note that these keywords modify the item immediately to their right, in contrast to the `const` and `volatile` type qualifiers which modify the pointer immediately to their left.

In addition to the defaults, you can always explicitly declare near, far, and huge pointers in any model. Huge pointers always do comparisons and pointer arithmetic based on canonical[1] values. In canonical form, a pointer offset is always in the range 0 to 15. If two pointers are in canonical form, then an unsigned long comparison will produce accurate results.

It is difficult and error-prone to compile the interaction between array and struct sizes, pointer sizes, memory models, and 80x86 hardware operating modes.

1. We know, we know. We're using "canonical" in the canonical way.

As the spreadsheets and word processors gradually proved themselves, they placed ever-increasing demands on memory. People have devoted a tremendous amount of energy to coping with the limited address space of the IBM PC. A variety of memory expanders and extenders have been produced, but there is no satisfactory portable solution. MS-DOS 1.0 was essentially a port of CP/M to 8086. All later versions retained compatibility with the earliest one. This is why DOS 6.0 is still single-tasking and still uses the "real-address" (8086-compatible) mode of an 80x86, thus maintaining the limits on user program address space. The 8086 memory model has other undesirable effects. Every program that runs on MS-DOS runs with unlimited privilege, permitting easy attacks by virus software. PC viruses would be almost unknown if MS-DOS used the memory and task protection hardware built into every Intel x86 processor from the 80286 onwards.

Virtual Memory

If it's there and you can see it—it's real

If it's not there and you can see it—it's virtual

If it's there and you can't see it—it's transparent

If it's not there and you can't see it—you erased it!

—IBM poster explaining virtual memory, circa 1978

It is very inconvenient for a program to be restricted by the amount of main memory installed on a machine, as happens on MS-DOS. So early on in computing, the concept of virtual memory was developed to remove this restriction. The basic idea is to use cheap but slow disk space to extend your fast but expensive main memory. The regions of memory that are actually in use by a program at any given instant are brought into physical memory. When regions of memory lie untouched for a while, they are likely to be saved off to disk, making room to bring in other memory areas that are being used. All modern computer system from the largest supercomputers to the smallest workstations, with the sole exception of PC's, use virtual memory.

Moving unused parts out to disk used to be done manually by the programmer, back in the early days of computing when snakes could walk. Programmers had to expend vast amounts of effort keeping track of what was in memory at a given time, and rolling segments in and out as needed. Older languages like COBOL still contain a large vocabulary of features for expressing this memory overlaying—totally obsolete and inexplicable to the current generation of programmers.

Multilevel store is a familiar concept. We see it elsewhere on a computer (e.g., in registers vs. main memory). In theory, every memory location could be a register. In practice, this would be prohibitively expensive, so we trade off access speed for a cheaper implementation. Virtual memory just extends this one stage further, using disk instead of main memory to hold the image of a running process. So we have a continuum.

Handy Heuristic

Memory Media Trade-Offs

Slow Access ← **Fast Access**

Mag Tape **Disk** **Main Memory** **Cache Memory** **CPU Registers**

Cheap per-bit
High Capacity → **Expensive per-bit**
Low Capacity

Exercise: fill in actual figures for typical access times, cost, and capacity for a system that you are familiar with.

$per bit:	______	______	______	______	______
access time:	______	______	______	______	______
max capacity:	______	______	______	______	______

Processes on SunOS execute in a 32-bit address space. The OS arranges matters so that each process thinks it has exclusive access to the entire address space. The illusion is sustained by "virtual memory," which shares access to the machine's physical memory and uses disk to hold data when memory fills up. Data is continually moved from memory to disk and back again as a process runs. Memory management hardware translates virtual addresses to physical addresses, and lets a process run anywhere in the system's real memory. Application programmers only ever see the virtual addresses, and don't have any way to tell when their process has migrated out to disk and back into memory again, except by observing elapsed time or looking at system commands like "ps". Figure 7-3 illustrates the virtual memory basics.

Virtual memory is organized into "pages." A page is the unit that the OS moves around and protects, typically a few Kbytes in size. You can look at the pagesize on your system by typing /usr/ucb/pagesize. When a memory image travels between disk and physical memory we say it is being paged in (if going to memory) or paged out (going to disk).

Potentially, all the memory associated with a process will need to be used by the system. If the process is unlikely to run soon (perhaps it is low-priority or is sleeping), all of the physical memory resources allocated to it can be taken away and backed up on disk. The process is then said to be "swapped out." There is a special "swap area" on disk that holds memory that has been paged or swapped. The swap area will usually be several times bigger than the physical memory on the machine. Only user processes ever page and swap. The SunOS kernel is always memory-resident.

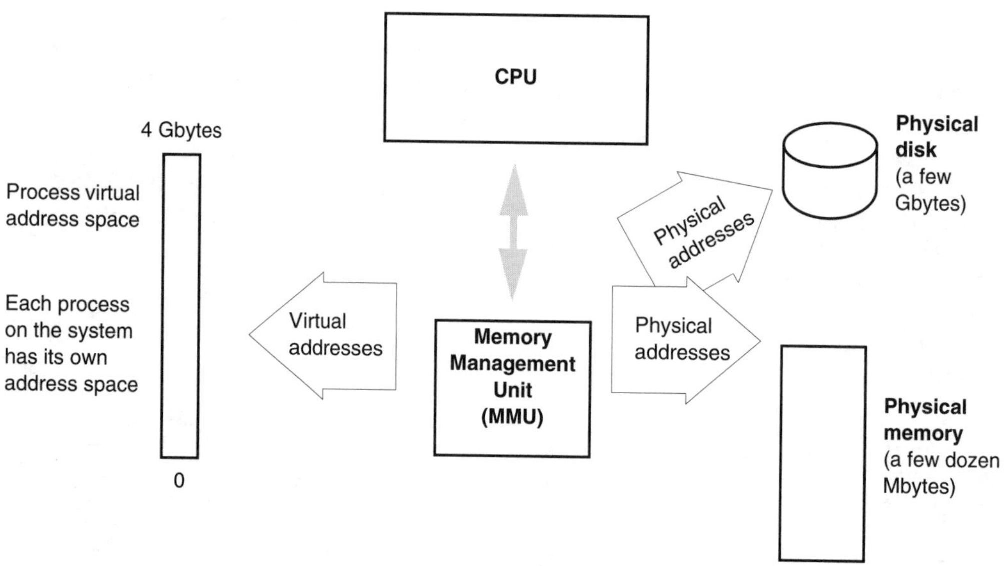

Figure 7-3 The Basics of Virtual Memory

A process can only operate on pages that are in memory. When a process makes a reference to a page that isn't in memory, the MMU generates a page fault. The kernel responds to the event and decides whether the reference was valid or invalid. If invalid, the kernel signals "segmentation violation" to the process. If valid, the kernel retrieves the page from the disk. Once the page gets back into memory, the process becomes unblocked and can start running again—without ever knowing it had been held up for a page-in event.

SunOS has a unified view of the disk filesystem and main memory. The OS uses an identical underlying data structure (the vnode, or "virtual node") to manipulate each. All virtual memory operations are organized around the single philosophy of mapping a file region to a memory region. This has improved performance and allowed considerable code reuse. You may also hear people talk about the "hat layer"—this is the "hardware address translation" software that drives the MMU. It is very hardware-dependent and has to be rewritten for each new computer architecture.

Virtual memory is an indispensable technique in operating system technology now, and it allows a quart of processes to run in a pint pot of memory. The light relief section at the end of this chapter has an additional description of virtual memory, written as a fable. It's a classic.

Programming Challenge

How Much Memory Can You Allocate?

Run the following program to see how much memory you can allocate in your process.

```
#include <stdio.h>
#include <stdlib.h>
main() {
    int Mb = 0;
    while ( malloc(1<<20)) ++Mb;
    printf("Allocated %d Mb total\n", Mb);
}
```

The total will depend on the swap space and process limits with which your system was configured. Can you get more if you allocate smaller chunks than a Mbyte? Why?

To run this program on the memory-limited MS-DOS, allocate 1-Kbyte chunks instead of 1-Mbyte chunks.

Cache Memory

Cache memory is a further extension of the multi-level store concept. It is a small, expensive, but extremely fast memory buffer that sits somewhere between the CPU and the physical memory. The cache may be on the CPU side of the memory management unit (MMU), as it is in the Sun SPARCstation 2. In this case it caches *virtual* addresses and must be flushed on each context switch. (See Figure 7-4.) Or the cache may be on the physical memory side of the MMU, as it is in the SPARCstation 10. This allows easy cache sharing with multiprocessor CPU's by caching *physical* addresses.

All modern processors use cache memory. Whenever data is read from memory, an entire "line" (typically 16 or 32 bytes) is brought into the cache. If the program exhibits good locality of reference (e.g., it's striding down a character string), future references to adjacent data can be retrieved from the fast cache rather than the slow main memory. Cache operates at the same speed as the cycle time of the system, so for a 50 MHz processor, the cache runs at 20 nanoseconds. Main memory might typically be four times slower than this! Cache is more expensive, and needs more space and power than regular memory, so we use it as an adjunct rather than as the exclusive form of memory on a system.

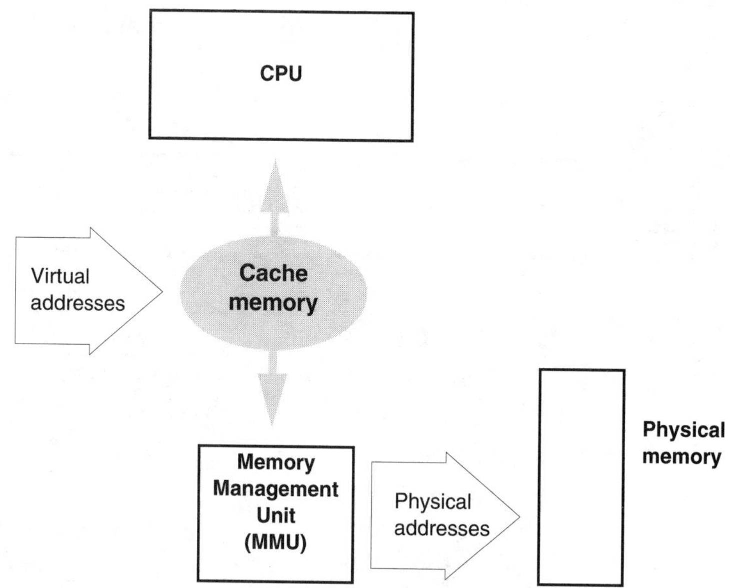

Figure 7-4 The Basics of Cache Memory

The cache contains a list of addresses and their contents. Its list of addresses is constantly changing, as the processor references new locations. Both reads and writes go through the cache. When the processor wants to retrieve data from a particular address, the request goes first to the cache. If the data is already present in the cache, it can be handed over immediately. Otherwise, the cache passes the request on, and a slower access to main memory takes place. A new line is retrieved, and it takes its place in the cache.

If your program has somewhat perverse behavior and just misses cache every time, you end up with worse performance than if there was no cache at all. This is because all the extra logic of figuring out what is where doesn't come free.

Sun currently uses two types of cache:

- Write-through cache—This always initiates a write to main memory at the same time it writes to the cache.

- Write-back cache—In the first instance, this writes only to cache. The data is transferred to main memory when the cache line is about to be written again and a save hasn't taken place yet. It will also be transferred on a context switch to a different process or the kernel.

In both cases, the instruction stream continues as soon as the cache access completes, without waiting for slower memory to catch up.

The cache on a SPARCstation 2 holds 64 Kbytes of write-through data, and a line is 32 bytes in size. Much larger caches are becoming commonplace: the SPARCserver 1000 has a 1-Mbyte write-back cache memory. There may be a separate cache for the I/O bus if the processor uses memory-mapped I/O, and there are often separate caches for instructions and data. There can also be multi level caches, and caches also can be applied whenever there is an interface between fast and slow devices (e.g., between disk and memory). PC's often use a main memory cache to help a slow disk. They call this "RAMdisk". In UNIX, disk inodes are cached in memory. This is why the filesystem can be corrupted by powering the machine off without first flushing the cache to disk with the "sync" command.

Cache and virtual memory are both invisible to the applications programmer, but it's important to know the benefits that they provide and the manner in which they can dramatically affect performance.

Table 7-1 Cache Memories Are Made of This

Term	Definition
Line	A line is the unit of access to a cache. Each line has two parts: a data section, and a tag specifying the address that it represents.
Block	The data content of a line is referred to as a block. A block holds the bytes moved between a line and main memory. A typical block size is 32 bytes. The contents of a cache line represent a particular block of memory, and it will respond if a processor tries to access that address range. The cache line "pretends" to be that address range in memory, only considerably faster. "Block" and "line" are used loosely and interchangeably by most people in the computer industry.
Cache	A cache consists of a big (typically 64 Kbytes to 1 Mbyte or more) collection of lines. Sometimes associative memory hardware is used to speed up access to the tags. Cache is located next to the CPU for speed, and the memory system and bus are highly tuned to optimize the movement of cache-block-sized chunks of data.

Handy Heuristic

One Experience with Cache

Run the following program to see if you can detect cache effects on your system.

```
#define DUMBCOPY for (i = 0; i < 65536; i++) \
 destination[i] = source[i]

#define SMARTCOPY memcpy(destination, source, 65536)

main()
{
    char source[65536], destination[65536];
    int i, j;
    for (j = 0; j < 100; j++)
 SMARTCOPY;

}

% cc -O cache.c
% time a.out
1.0 seconds user time

# change to DUMBCOPY and recompile
% time a.out
7.0 seconds user time
```

Compile and time the run of the above program two different ways, first as it is, and then with the macro call changed to DUMBCOPY. We measured this on a SPARCstation 2, and there was a consistent large performance degradation with the dumb copy.

The slowdown happens because the source and destination are an exact multiple of the cache size apart. Cache lines on the SS2 aren't filled sequentially—the particular algorithm used happens to fill the same line for main memory addresses that are exact multiples of the cache size apart. This arises from optimized storage of tags—only the high-order bits of each address are put in the tag in this design.

One Experience with Cache (Continued)

All machines that use a cache (including supercomputers, modern PC's, and everything in between) are subject to performance hits from pathological cases like this one. Your mileage will vary on different machines and different cache implementations.

In this particular case both the source and destination use the same cache line, causing every memory reference to miss the cache and stall the processor while it waited for regular memory to deliver. The library `memcpy()` routine is especially tuned for high performance. It unrolls the loop to read for one cache line and then write, which avoids the problem. Using the smart copy, we were able to get a huge performance improvement. This also shows the folly of drawing conclusions from simple-minded benchmark programs.

The Data Segment and Heap

We have covered the background on system-related memory issues, so it's time to revisit the layout of memory inside an individual process. Now that you know the system issues, the process issues will start making a lot more sense. Specifically, we'll begin by taking a closer look at the data segment within a process.

Just as the stack segment grows dynamically on demand, so the data segment contains an object that can do this, namely, the heap, shown in Figure 7-5. The heap area is for dynamically allocated storage, that is, storage obtained through `malloc` (memory allocate) and accessed through a pointer. Everything in the heap is anonymous—you cannot access it directly by name, only indirectly through a pointer. The `malloc` (and friends: calloc, realloc, etc.) library call is the only way to obtain storage from the heap. The function **c**`alloc` is like malloc, but **c**lears the memory to zero before giving you the pointer. Don't think that the "**c**" in **c**`alloc`() has anything to do with C programming—it means "allocate zeroized memory". The function `realloc()` changes the size of a block of memory pointed to, either growing or shrinking it, often by copying the contents somewhere else and giving you back a pointer to the new location. This is useful when growing the size of tables dynamically—more about this in Chapter 10.

Heap memory does not have to be returned in the same order in which it was acquired (it doesn't have to be returned at all), so unordered malloc/free's eventually cause heap fragmentation. The heap must keep track of different regions, and whether they are in use or available to malloc. One scheme is to have a linked list of available blocks (the "free store"), and each block handed to malloc is preceded by a size count that goes with it. Some people use the term *arena* to describe the set of blocks managed by a memory allocator (in SunOS, the area between the end of the data segment and the current position of the break).

Malloced memory is always aligned appropriately for the largest size of atomic access on a machine, and a malloc request may be rounded up in size to some convenient power of two. Freed memory goes back into the heap for reuse, but there is no (convenient) way to remove it from your process and give it back to the operating system.

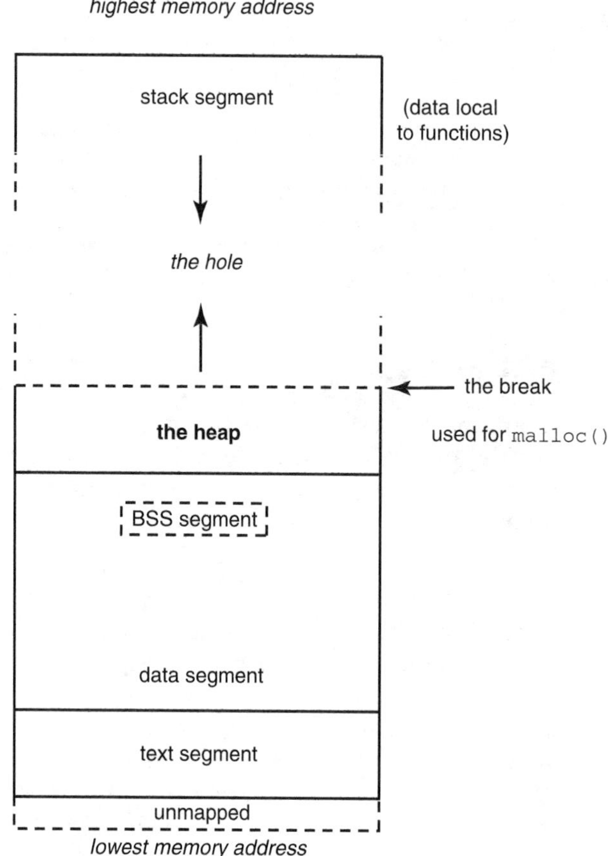

Figure 7-5 Where the Heap Lives

The end of the heap is marked by a pointer known as the "break".[2] When the heap manager needs more memory, it can push the break further away using the system calls `brk` and `sbrk`. You typically don't call brk yourself explicitly, but if you malloc enough memory, brk will eventually be called for you. The calls that manage memory are:

`malloc` and `free`—get memory from heap and give it back to heap

`brk` and `sbrk`—adjust the size of the data segment to an absolute value/by an increment

2. Your programs will "break" if they reference past the break...

One caution: your program may not call both `malloc()` and `brk()`. If you use malloc, malloc expects to have sole control over when brk and sbrk are called. Since sbrk provides the only way for a process to return data segment memory to the kernel, if you use malloc you are effectively prevented from ever shrinking the program data segment in size. To obtain memory that can later be returned to the kernel, use the mmap system call to map the /dev/zero file. To return this memory, use munmap.

Memory Leaks

Some programs don't need to manage their dynamic memory use; they simply allocate what they need, and never worry about freeing it. This class includes compilers and other programs that run for a fixed or bounded period of time and then terminate. When such a program finishes, it automatically relinquishes all its memory, and there is little need to spend time giving up each byte as soon as it will no longer be used.

Other programs are more long-lived. Certain utilities such as calendar manager, mailtool, and the operating system itself have to run for days or weeks at a time, and manage the allocation and freeing of dynamic memory. Since C does not usually have garbage collection (automatic identification and deallocation of memory blocks no longer in use) these C programs have to be very careful in their use of `malloc()` and `free()`. There are two common types of heap problems:

- freeing or overwriting something that is still in use (this is a "memory corruption")
- not freeing something that is no longer in use (this is a "memory leak")

These are among the hardest problems to debug. If the programmer does not free each malloced block when it is no longer needed, the process will acquire more and more memory without releasing the portions no longer in use.

Handy Heuristic

Avoiding Memory Leaks
Whenever you write `malloc`, write a corresponding `free` statement. If you don't know where to put the "free" that corresponds to your "malloc", then you've probably created a memory leak!

Avoiding Memory Leaks (Continued)

One simple way to avoid this is to use `alloca()` for your dynamic needs when possible. The `alloca()` routine allocates memory on the stack; when you leave the function in which you called it, the memory is automatically freed.

Clearly, this can't be used for structures that need a longer lifetime than the function invocation in which they are created; but for stuff that can live within this constraint, dynamic memory allocation on the stack is a low-overhead choice. Some people deprecate the use of alloca because it is not a portable construct. `alloca()` is hard to implement efficiently on processors that do not support stacks in hardware.

We use the term "memory leak" because a scarce resource is draining away in a process. The main user-visible symptom of a memory leak is that the guilty process slows down. This happens because larger processes are more likely to have to be swapped out to give other processes a chance to run. Larger processes also take a longer time to swap in and out. Even though (by definition) the leaked memory itself isn't referenced, it's likely to be on a page with something that is, thus enlarging the working set and slowing performance. An additional point to note is that a leak will usually be larger than the size of the forgotten data structure, because `malloc()` usually rounds up a storage request to the next larger power-of-two. In the limiting case, a process with a memory leak can slow the whole machine down, not just the user running the offending program. A process has a theoretical size limit that varies from OS to OS. On current releases of SunOS, a process address space can be up to 4 Gbytes; in practice, swap space would be exhausted long before a process leaked enough memory to grow that big. If you're reading this book five years after it was written, say around the turn of the millenium, you'll probably get a good laugh over this by then long-obsolete restriction.

How to Check for a Memory Leak

Looking for a memory leak is a two-step process. First you use the swap command to see how much swap space is available:

```
/usr/sbin/swap -s
total: 17228k bytes allocated + 5396k reserved = 22624k used, 29548k
available
```

Type the command three or four times over the space of a minute or two, to see if available swap space keeps getting smaller. You can also use others of the `/usr/bin/*stat` tools, `netstat`, `vmstat`, and so on. If you see an increasing amount of memory being used and never released, one possible explanation is that a process has a memory leak.

Handy Heuristic

Listening to the Network's Heartbeat: Click to Tune

Of all the network investigative tools, the absolute tops is `snoop`.
The SVr4 replacement for `etherfind`, `snoop` captures packets from the network and displays them on your workstation. You can tell snoop just to concentrate on one or two machines, say your own workstation and your server. This can be useful for troubleshooting connectivity problems—snoop can tell you if the bytes are even leaving your machine.

The absolute best feature of snoop, though, is the `-a` option. This causes snoop to output a click on the workstation loudspeaker for each packet. You can *listen* to your network ether traffic. Different packet lengths have different modulation. If you use `snoop -a` a lot, you get good at recognizing the characteristic sounds, and can troubleshoot and literally tune a net "by ear"!

The second step is to identify the suspected process, and see if it is guilty of a memory leak. You may already know which process is causing the problem. If not, the command `ps -lu` *`username`* shows the size of all your processes, as in the example below:

```
F S UID PID PPID C PRI NI ADDR      SZ  WCHAN    TTY    TIME  COMD
8 S 5303 226 224 80 1 20 ff38f000  199 ff38f1d0 pts/3  0:01  csh
8 O 5303 921 226 29 1 20 ff38c000  143          pts/3  0:00  ps
```

The column headed `SZ` is the size of the process in pages. (The `pagesize` command will tell you how big that is in Kbytes if you really must know.) Again, repeat the command several times; any program that dynamically allocates memory can be observed growing in size. If a process appears to be constantly growing and never leveling off, then suspect a memory leak. It's a sad fact of life that managing dynamic memory is a very difficult programming task. Some public domain X-Window applications are notorious for leaking like the Apple Computer board of directors.

Systems often have different malloc libraries available, including ones tuned for optimal speed or optimal space usage, and to help with debugging. Enter the command

```
man -s 3c malloc
```

to look at the manpage, and to see all the routines in the malloc family. Make sure you link with the appropriate library. The SPARCWorks debugger on Solaris 2.x has extensive features to help detect memory leaks; these have supplanted the special malloc libraries on Solaris 1.x.

Software Dogma

The President and the Printtool—A Memory Leak Bug

The simplest form of memory leak is:

```
for (i=0; i<10; i++)
     p = malloc(1024);
```

This is the *Exxon Valdez* of software; it leaks away everything you give it.

With each successive iteration, the previous address held in p is overwritten, and the Kbyte block of memory that it points to "leaks away". Since nothing now points to it, there is no way to access or free that memory. Most memory leaks aren't quite as blatant as overwriting the only pointer to the block before it can be freed, so they are harder to identify and debug.

An interesting case occurred with the printtool software here at Sun. An internal test release of the operating system was installed on the desktop system of Scott McNealy, the company president.[1] The president soon noticed that over the course of a couple of days, his workstation became slower and slower. Rebooting fixed it instantly. He reported the problem, and nothing concentrates the mind like a bug report filed by the company president.

We found that the problem was triggered by "printtool", a window interface around the print command. "Printtool" is the kind of software much used by company presidents but not by OS developers, which is why the problem had lain undiscovered. Killing printtool caused the memory leak to stop, but `ps -lu scott` showed that printtool was only triggering the leak, not growing in size itself. It was necessary to look at the system calls that printtool used.

The design of printtool had it allocate a named pipe (a special type of file that allows two unrelated processes to communicate) and use it to talk to the line printer process. A new pipe was created every few seconds, then destroyed if printtool didn't have anything interesting to tell the printer. The real memory leak bug was in the pipe creation system call. When a pipe was created, kernel memory was allocated to hold the vnode data structure to control it, but the code that kept a reference count for the structure was off by one.

1. Actually, this *is* quite a good idea. Having the president run early release software and participate in the internal testing process keeps everyone on their toes. It ensures that upper management has a good understanding of the evolving product and how fast it is improving. And it provides product engineering with both the motivation and resources to shake out the last few bugs.

The President and the Printtool—A Memory Leak Bug (Continued)

As a result, when the true number of pipe users dropped to zero, the count stayed at 1, so the kernel always thought the pipe was in use. Thus, the vnode struct was never freed as it should have been when the pipe was closed. Every time a pipe was closed, a few hundred bytes of memory leaked away in the kernel. This added up to megabytes lost per day—enough to bring the entry-level workstation that we give presidents to its knees after two or three days.

We corrected the off-by-one bug in the vnode reference count algorithm, and the regular kernel memory free routine kicked in just as it was supposed to. We also changed printtool to use a smarter algorithm than just continually yammering at the printer every few seconds. The memory leak was plugged, the programmers breathed a sigh of relief, the engineering manager started to smile again, and the president went back to using printtool.

The operating system kernel also manages its memory use dynamically. Many tables of data in the kernel are dynamically allocated, so that no fixed limit is set in advance. If a kernel programming error causes a memory leak, the machine slows down; in the limiting case the machine hangs or even panics. When kernel routines ask for memory they usually wait until it becomes available. If memory is leaking away, eventually there is none available, and everyone ends up waiting—the machine is hung. Memory leaks in the kernel usually show up rapidly, as most paths through the kernel are pretty well travelled. We also have specialized software tools to test for and exercise kernel memory management.

Bus Error, Take the Train

When I first started programming on UNIX in the late 1970's, like many people I quickly ran into two common runtime errors:

```
bus error (core dumped)
```

and

```
segmentation fault (core dumped)
```

At the time these errors were very frustrating: there was no simple explanation of the kind of source errors that caused them, the messages gave no clue where to look in the code, and the difference between them wasn't at all clear. And it's still the same today.

Most of the problem lies in the fact that the errors represent an anomaly the operating system has detected, and the anomaly is reported in terms most convenient to the operating system. The precise causes of a bus error and a segmentation fault will thus vary among different versions of operating system. Here, we describe what they mean on SunOS running on the SPARC architecture, and what causes them.

Both errors occur when hardware tells the OS about a problematic memory reference. The OS communicates this to the faulting process by sending it a signal. A *signal* is an event notification or a software-generated interrupt, much used in UNIX systems programming and hardly ever used in applications programming. By default, on receiving the "bus error" or the "segmentation fault" signal, a process will dump core and terminate; but you can impose some different action by setting up a signal handler for these signals.

Signals were modeled on hardware interrupts. Interrupt programming is hard because things happen asynchronously (at unpredictable times); therefore, signal programming and debugging is hard. You can glean more information by reading the manpage for signal, and looking at the include file `/usr/include/sys/signal.h`.

Programming Challenge

Catching Signals on the PC

Signal handling functions are a part of ANSI C now, and they apply equally to PCs as well as UNIX. For example, a PC programmer can use the signal() function to catch Ctrl-Break and prevent a user breaking out of the program.

Write a signal handler to catch the INT 1B (Ctrl-Break) signal on a PC. Have it print a user-friendly message, but not exit.

If you use UNIX, write a signal handler, so that on receiving a control-C (control-C is passed to a UNIX process as a `SIGINT` signal) the program restarts, rather than quits. The typedefs that will help you define a signal handler are shown in Chapter 3 on declarations.

The header file `<signal.h>` needs to be included in any source file that uses signals.

The "core dump" part of the message is just a throwback to the days when all memory was made of ferrite rings, or "cores". Semiconductor memory has been the rule for 15 years or more, but "core" persists as a synonym for "main memory".

Bus Error

In practice, a bus error is almost always caused by a misaligned read or write. It's called a bus error, because the address bus is the component that chokes if a misaligned load or store is requested. Alignment means that data items can only be stored at an address that is a multiple of their size. On modern architectures, especially RISC architectures, data alignment is required because the extra logic associated with arbitrary alignment makes the whole memory system much larger and slower. By forcing each individual memory access to remain in one cache line or on a single page, we greatly simplify (and therefore speed up) hardware like cache controllers and memory management units.

The way we express the "no data item may span a page or cache boundary" rule is somewhat indirect, in that we state it in terms of address alignment rather than a prohibition on crossing page boundaries, but it comes down to the same thing. For example, accesses to an 8-byte double are only permitted at addresses that are an exact multiple of 8 bytes. So a double can be stored at address 24, address 8008, or address 32768, but not at address 1006 (since it is not exactly divisible by 8). Page and cache sizes are carefully designed so that keeping the alignment rule will ensure that no atomic data item spills over a page or cache block boundary.

The requirement for data to be stored aligned always reminds us of the kids' game of walking down a sidewalk without placing a foot on a crack in the paving stones. *"Step on a crack, break your mother's back"* has mutated to *"dereference nonaligned then cuss, cause an error on the bus."* Maybe it's Freudian or something; Mother was frightened by a Fortran I/O channel at an impressionable age. A small program that will cause a bus error is:

```
union { char a[10];
        int  i;
      } u;
int  *p= (int*) &(u.a[1]);
*p = 17;    /* the misaligned addr in p causes a bus error! */
```

This causes a bus error because the array/int union ensures that character array "a" is also at a reasonably aligned address for an integer, so "a+1" is definitely not. We then try to store 4 bytes into an address that is aligned only for single-byte access. A good compiler will warn about misalignment, but it cannot spot all occurrences.

The compilers automatically allocate and pad data (in memory) to achieve alignment. Of course, there is no such alignment requirement on disk or tape, so programmers can remain blissfully unaware of alignment—until they cast a char pointer to an int pointer, leading to mysterious bus errors. A few years ago bus errors were also generated if a memory parity error was detected. These days memory chips are so reliable, and so well protected by error detection and correction circuitry, that parity errors are almost unheard of at the application programming level. A bus error can also be generated by referencing memory that does not physically exist; you probably won't be able to screw up this badly without help from a naughty device driver.

Segmentation Fault

The segmentation fault or violation should already be clear, given the segment model explained earlier. On Sun hardware, segmentation faults are generated by an exception in the memory management unit (the hardware responsible for supporting virtual memory). The usual cause is dereferencing (looking at the contents of the address contained in) a pointer with an uninitialized or illegal value. The pointer causes a memory reference to a segment that is not part of your address space, and the operating system steps in. A small program that will cause a segmentation fault is:

```
int *p=0;
*p = 17;        /* causes a segmentation fault */
```

One subtlety is that it is usually a different programmatic error that led to the pointer having an invalid value. Unlike a bus error, a segmentation fault will therefore be the indirect symptom rather than the cause of the fault.

A worse subtlety is that if the value in the uninitialized pointer happens to be misaligned for the size of data being accessed, it will cause a bus error fault, not a segmentation violation. This is true for most architectures because the CPU sees the address before sending it to the MMU.

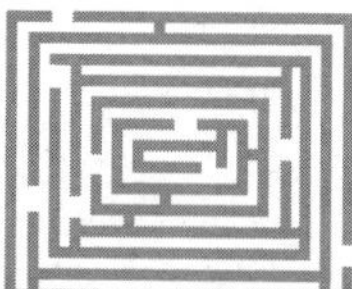

Programming Challenge

Test Crash Your Software
Complete the test program fragments above.
Try running them to see how these bugs are reported by the OS.
Extra Credit: Write signal handlers to catch the bus error and segmentation fault signals. Have them print a more user-friendly message, and exit.
Rerun your program.

The dereferencing of the illegal pointer value may be done explicitly in your code as shown above, or it may occur in a library routine if you pass it a bad value. Unhappily, changing your program (e.g., compiling for debugging or adding extra debugging statements) can easily change the contents of memory such that the problem moves or disappears. Segmentation faults are tough to solve, and only the strong will survive. You know it's a really tough bug when you see your colleagues grimly carrying logic analyzers and oscilloscopes into the test lab!

Software Dogma

A Segmentation Violation Bug in SunOS

We recently had to solve a segmentation fault that was occurring when the ncheck utility was run on a corrupted filesystem. This was a very distressing bug, because you are most likely to use ncheck to investigate filesystems that you suspect of corruption.

The symptom was that ncheck was failing in printf, by dereferencing a null pointer and causing a segmentation violation. The faulty statement was:

```
(void) printf("%s", p->name);
```

Most junior programmers from Yoyodyne Software Corp. would fix this in a long-winded way:

```
if (p->name != NULL)
        (void) printf("%s", p->name );
else
        (void) printf("(null)");
```

In cases like this, however, the conditional operator can be used instead to simplify the code and maintain locality of reference:

```
(void) printf("%s", p->name ? p->name : "(null)");
```

A lot of people prefer not to use the — ? — : — conditional operator, because they find it confusing. The operator makes a whole lot more sense when compared with an if statement:

```
if ( expression ) statement-when-non-zero else statement-when-zero
     expression ?  expression-when-non-zero : expression-when-zero
```

When looked at this way, the conditional operator is quite intuitive, and allows us to feel happy with the one-liner instead of needlessly inflating the size of the code. But never nest one conditional operator inside another, as it quickly becomes too hard to see what goes with what.

Common immediate causes of segmentation fault:

- dereferencing a pointer that doesn't contain a valid value
- dereferencing a null pointer (often because the null pointer was returned from a system routine, and used without checking)
- accessing something without the correct permission—for example, attempting to store a value into a read-only text segment would cause this error
- running out of stack or heap space (virtual memory is huge but not infinite)

It's a little bit of an oversimplification, but for most architectures in most cases, a bus error means that the CPU disliked something about that memory reference, while a segv means that the MMU disliked something about it.

The common programming errors that (eventually) lead to something that gives a segmentation fault, in order of occurrence, are:

1. **Bad pointer value errors:** using a pointer before giving it a value, or passing a bad pointer to a library routine. (Don't be fooled by this one! If the debugger shows that the segv occurred in a system routine, it doesn't mean that the system caused it. The problem is still likely to be in your code.) The third common way to generate a bad pointer is to access something after it has been freed. You can amend your free statements to clear a pointer after freeing what it points to:

```
free(p); p = NULL;
```

   This ensures that if you do use a pointer after you have freed it, at least the program core dumps at once.

2. **Overwriting errors:** writing past either end of an array, writing past either end of a malloc'd block, or overwriting some of the heap management structures (this is all too easy to do by writing before the beginning of a malloc'd block).

```
p=malloc(256); p[-1]=0; p[256]=0;
```

3. **Free'ing errors:** freeing the same block twice, freeing something that you didn't malloc, freeing some memory that is still in use, or freeing an invalid pointer. A very common free error is to cdr[3] down a linked list in a `for (p=start; p; p=p->next)` loop, then in the loop body do a `free(p)`. This leads a freed pointer to be dereferenced on the next loop iteration, with unpredictable results.

Handy Heuristic

How to Free Elements in a Linked List

The correct way to free an element while traversing down a linked list is to use a temporary variable to store the address of the next element. Then you can safely free the current element at any time, and not have to worry about referencing it again to get the address of the next. The code is:

```
struct node *p, *start, *tmp;
for (p=start; p; p=tmp) {
        tmp=p->next;
        free(p);
}
```

3. Car and cdr are two LISP terms for the head and remainder of a list, respectively. Cdr'ing down a list is processing the list by picking successive elements off the front. Car and cdr come from the IBM 704, a 36-bit vacuum-tube processor with 15-bit addresses. Core memory locations were called "registers". CAR meant "contents of address part of register", and CDR was "contents of decrement part of register". These were brief routines, and the LISP 1.5 manual (MIT Press, 1962) lists them in their entirety. Here's CAR

```
CAR     SXA  CARX,4
        PDX  0,4
        CLA  0,4
        PAX  0,4
        PXD  0,4
CARX    AXT  **,4
        TRA  1,4
```

LISP 1.0 originally had CTR and CXR, too, contents of tag part of register and contents of index part of register. These weren't very useful, and were dropped from LISP 1.5.

Software Dogma

Is Your Program Out of Space?

If your program needs more memory than the operating system can give it, it will be terminated with a "segmentation fault". You can distinguish this type of segmentation fault from one of the more bug-based ones by the method described here.

To tell if it ran off the stack, run it under dbx:

```
% dbx a.out


(dbx) catch SIGSEGV
(dbx) run
 ...
signal SEGV (segmentation violation) in <some_routine> at 0xeff57708
(dbx) where
```

If you now see a call chain, then it hasn't run out of stack space.

If instead you see something like:

```
fetch at 0xeffe7a60 failed -- I/O error
(dbx)
```

then it probably has run out of stack space. That hex number is the stack address which could not be mapped or retrieved.

You can also try adjusting the segment limits in C-shell:

```
limit stacksize 10
```

You can adjust the maximum size of the stack and the data segments in the C-shell. The line above sets it to 10 Kbytes. Try giving your program less stack space, and see if it fails at an earlier point. Try giving it more stack space, and see if it now runs successfully. A process will still be limited overall by the size of swap space, which can be found by typing the `swap -s` command.

Anything can happen with a bad pointer value. The accepted wisdom is that if you're "lucky," it will point outside your address space, so the first use will cause the program to dump core and stop. If you're "unlucky," it will point inside your address space and corrupt (overwrite) whatever area of memory it points at. This leads to obscure bugs that are very hard to track down. A number of excellent software tools have come on the market in recent years to aid in solving this kind of problem.

Some Light Relief— The Thing King and the Paging Game

The section that follows was written by Jeff Berryman in 1972 when he was working on project MAC and running one of the early virtual memory systems. Jeff somewhat ruefully comments that of all the papers he has ever written, this one is the most popular and widely read. It's as applicable today as it was twenty years ago.

The Paging Game

This note is a formal non-working paper of the Project MAC Computer Systems Research Division. It should be reproduced and distributed wherever levity is lacking, and may be referenced at your own risk in other publications.

Rules

1. Each player gets several million things.
2. Things are kept in crates that hold 4096 things each. Things in the same crate are called crate-mates.
3. Crates are stored either in the workshop or the warehouse. The workshop is almost always too small to hold all the crates.
4. There is only one workshop but there may be several warehouses. Everybody shares them.
5. Each thing has its own thing number.
6. What you do with a thing is to zark it. Everybody takes turns zarking.
7. You can only zark your things, not anybody else's.
8. Things can only be zarked when they are in the workshop.
9. Only the Thing King knows whether a thing is in the workshop or in a warehouse.
10. The longer a thing goes without being zarked, the grubbier it is said to become.
11. The way you get things is to ask the Thing King. He only gives out things in multiples of eight. This is to keep the royal overhead down.
12. The way you zark a thing is to give its thing number. If you give the number of a thing that happens to be in a workshop it gets zarked right away. If it is in a warehouse, the Thing King packs the crate containing your thing back into the

workshop. If there is no room in the workshop, he first finds the grubbiest crate in the workshop, whether it be yours or somebody else's, and packs it off with all its crate-mates to a warehouse. In its place he puts the crate containing your thing. Your thing then gets zarked and you never know that it wasn't in the workshop all along.

13. Each player's stock of things have the same numbers as everybody else's. The Thing King always knows who owns what thing and whose turn it is, so you can't ever accidentally zark somebody else's thing even if it has the same thing number as one of yours.

Notes

1. Traditionally, the Thing King sits at a large, segmented table and is attended to by pages (the so-called "table pages") whose job it is to help the king remember where all the things are and who they belong to.
2. One consequence of Rule 13 is that everybody's thing numbers will be similar from game to game, regardless of the number of players.
3. The Thing King has a few things of his own, some of which move back and forth between workshop and warehouse just like anybody else's, but some of which are just too heavy to move out of the workshop.
4. With the given set of rules, oft-zarked things tend to get kept mostly in the workshop while little-zarked things stay mostly in a warehouse. This is efficient stock control.

Long Live the Thing King!

Now doesn't that look a lot more interesting than the non-allegorical translated version below?

Rules

1. Each player gets several million "bytes."
2. Bytes are kept in "pages" that hold 4096 bytes each. Bytes on the same page have "locality of reference".
3. Pages are stored either in memory or on a disk. The memory is almost always too small to hold all the pages.
4. There is only one memory but there may be several disks. Everybody shares them.
5. Each byte has its own "virtual address."
6. What you do with a byte is to "reference" it. Everybody takes turns referencing.
7. You can only reference your bytes, not anybody else's.
8. Bytes can only be referenced when they are in memory.
9. Only the "VM manager" knows whether a byte is in memory or on a disk.

10. The longer a byte goes without being referenced, the "older" it is said to become.
11. The way you get bytes is to ask the VM manager. It only gives out bytes in multiples of powers of two. This is to keep overhead down.
12. The way you reference a byte is to give its virtual address. If you give the address of a byte that happens to be in the memory it gets referenced right away. If it is on disk, the VM manager brings the page containing your byte back into the memory. If there is no room in the memory, it first finds the oldest page in the memory, whether it be yours or somebody else's, and packs it off with the rest of the page to a disk. In its place it puts the page containing your byte. Your byte then gets referenced and you never know that it wasn't in the memory all along.
13. Each player's stock of bytes have the same virtual addresses as everybody else's. The VM manager always knows who owns what byte and whose turn it is, so you can't ever accidentally reference somebody else's byte even if it has the same virtual address as one of yours.

Notes

1. Traditionally, the VM manager uses a large, segmented table and "page tables" to remember where all the bytes are and who they belong to.
2. One consequence of Rule 13 is that everybody's virtual addresses will be similar from run to run, regardless of the number of processes.
3. The VM manager has a few bytes of his own, some of which move back and forth between memory and disk just like anybody else's, but some of which are just too heavily used to move out of the memory.
4. With the given set of rules, oft-referenced bytes tend to get kept mostly in the memory while little-used bytes stay mostly in a disk. This is efficient memory utilization.

Long Live the VM Manager!

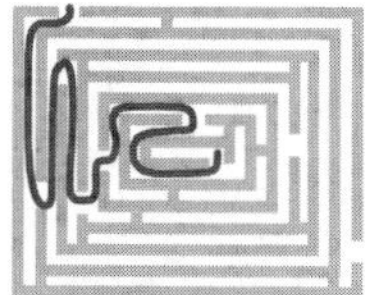

Programming Solution

A Signal Handler to Catch the segv Signal

```
#include <signal.h>
#include <stdio.h>

void handler(int s)
{
    if (s == SIGBUS) printf(" now got a bus error signal\n");
    if (s == SIGSEGV) printf(" now got a segmentation violation signal\n");
    if (s == SIGILL) printf(" now got an illegal instruction signal\n");
    exit(1);
}

main () {
    int *p=NULL;
    signal(SIGBUS, handler);
    signal(SIGSEGV, handler);
    signal(SIGILL, handler);
    *p=0;
}
```

Running this program results in this output:

```
% a.out

now got a segmentation violation signal
```

Note: this is an example for teaching purposes. Section 7.7.1.1 of the ANSI standard points out that in the circumstances we have here, the behavior is undefined when the signal handler calls any function in the standard library such as printf.

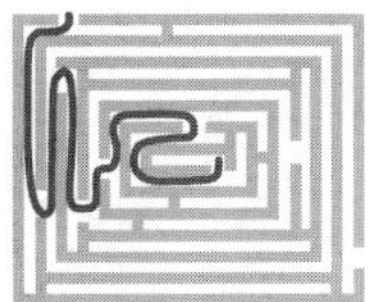

Programming Solution

Using setjmp/longjmp to Recover from a Signal

This program uses `setjmp/longjmp` and signal handling, so that on receiving a control-C (passed to a UNIX process as a `SIGINT` signal) the program restarts, rather than quits.

```
#include <setjmp.h>
#include <signal.h>
#include <stdio.h>
jmp_buf buf;
void handler(int s)
{
    if (s == SIGINT) printf(" now got a SIGINT signal\n");
    longjmp(buf, 1);
    /*NOTREACHED*/
}
main () {
    signal(SIGINT, handler);
    if (setjmp(buf))  {
        printf("back in main\n");
        return 0;
    }else
        printf("first time through\n");
loop:
    /* spin here, waiting for ctrl-c */
    goto loop;
}
```

Note: signal handlers are not supposed to call library functions (except under restricted circumstances stated in the standard). If the signal is raised during the "first time" printf, then the printf in the signal handler, coming in the middle of all this, may get confused. We cheat here, because interactive I/O is the best way to see what's going on. Don't cheat in real world code, OK?

Using setjmp/longjmp to Recover from a Signal (Continued)

Running this program results in this output:

```
% a.out

first time through
^C now got a SIGINT signal
back in main
```

Using setjmp/longjmp to Recover from a Signal (Continued)

This program uses `setjmp/longjmp` and signal handling, so that on receiving a control-C (passed to a UNIX process as a `SIGINT` signal) the program restarts, rather than quits.

Why Programmers Can't Tell Halloween from Christmas Day 8

Are you fed up with the slow speed of your workstation?
Would you like to run your programs twice as fast?

Here's how to do it in UNIX. Just follow these three easy steps:

1. *Design and code a high-performance UNIX vm kernel. Be careful! Your algorithm needs to run twice as fast as the present one to see the full 100% speed-up.*
2. *Put your code in a file called* `/kernel/unix.c`
3. *Issue the command*
   `cc -O4 -o /kernel/unix /kernel/unix.c`
   and reboot your machine.

It's as simple as that. And remember, Beethoven wrote his first symphony in C.

—A.P.L. Byteswap's *Big Book of Tuning Tips and Rugby Songs*

---

the Potrzebie system of weights and measures...making a glyph from bit patterns...types changed while you wait...prototype painfulness... read a character without newline...implementing a finite state machine in C... program the simple cases first...how and why to cast... some light relief—the international obfuscated C competition

---

The Potrzebie System of Weights and Measures

Of course, when Picasso made the comment about computers being uninteresting, we know that he was really seeking to advance a discourse in which it was the rôle of artists to challenge the establishment, ask questions, or at least see that the correct serving of fries accompanied each order. How appropriate, therefore, that this chapter opens with the old question among computer folk that asks why programmers can't tell Halloween from Christmas Day. Before we provide the punchline, we should say a few words about the work of world-class computer scientist Donald Knuth. Professor Knuth, who has taught at Stanford University for many years, wrote the massive and definitive reference work, *The Art of Computer Programming,*[1] and designed the TeX typesetting system.

A little-known fact is that Professor Knuth's first publication was not in a prestigious peer-reviewed scientific journal, but in a much more popular gazette. "The Potrzebie System of Weights and Measures" by Donald Knuth appeared in *MAD Magazine,* issue number 33, in June 1957. The article, by the very same Donald Knuth who later became known as an eminent computer scientist, parodied the then-novel metric system of weights and measures. Most of Knuth's subsequent papers have tended to be more conventional. We think that's a shame, and look for a return to roots. The basis of all measurements in the Potrzebie system is the thickness of *MAD Magazine*'s issue number 26.

Knuth's article was a consistent application of metric-decaded prefixes using units that were more familiar to *MAD* readers, such as *potrzebies, whatmeworrys,* and *axolotls.* For many of *MAD*'s readers it was a gentle introduction to the concepts of the metric system. People in the U.S. just weren't familiar with *kilo, centi,* and other prefixes, so Knuth's Potrzebie paved the way for a greater understanding. Had the Potrzebie system actually been adopted, perhaps the later American experiment with the metric system would have been more successful.

Like the Potrzebie system, the joke about programmers' confusion over Halloween and Christmas Day depends on inside knowledge of numbering systems. The reason that programmers can't tell Halloween from Christmas Day is because 31 in octal (base eight) equals 25 in decimal (base ten). More succinctly, OCT 31 equals DEC 25!

When I wrote to Professor Knuth asking his permission to tell the story, and including a draft copy of the chapter, he not only agreed, he marked numerous proofreading improvements on the text, and pointed out that programmers can't distinguish NOV 27 from the other two dates, either.

This chapter presents a selection of C idioms that similarly depend on inside knowledge of programming. Some of the examples here are useful tips to try, while others are cautionary tales of trouble spots to avoid. We start off with a delightful way to make icons self-documenting.

---

1. Professor Knuth later identified his long-standing colleague Art Evans as the *Art* in *The Art of Computer Programming* book title. Back in 1967, when the series of volumes started to appear, Knuth gave a seminar at Carnegie Tech. Knuth remarked that he was glad to see his old friend Art Evans in the audience since he had named his series of books after him. Everyone groaned in appreciation once they grasped the awful pun, and Art was more amazed than anyone.
Later, when Knuth won the ACM's Turing Award, he ensured that the pun entered the official record by mentioning Art again in his Turing Award Lecture. You can read it in *Communications of the ACM,* vol. 17, no. 12, p. 668. Art claims that "it hasn't affected my life much at all."

Making a Glyph from Bit Patterns

An icon, or a glyph, is a small graphic for a bit-mapped screen. A single bit represents each pixel in the image. If the bit is set, then the pixel is "on"; if the bit is clear, then the pixel is "off". So a series of integer values encodes the image. Tools like Iconedit are used to draw the picture, and they output an ASCII file of integers that can be included in a windowing program. One problem has been that the icon appears in a program as just a bunch of hex numbers. A typical 16-by-16 black and white glyph might look like this in C:

```
static unsigned short stopwatch[] = {
    0x07C6,
    0x1FF7,
    0x383B,
    0x600C,
    0x600C,
    0xC006,
    0xC006,
    0xDF06,
    0xC106,
    0xC106,
    0x610C,
    0x610C,
    0x3838,
    0x1FF0,
    0x07C0,
    0x0000
};
```

As you can see, the C literals don't provide any clue about how the image actually looks. Here is a breathtakingly elegant set of #defines that allow the programmer to build the literals so that they look like the glyph on the screen.

```
#define X )*2+1
#define _ )*2
#define s ((((((((((((((((0 /* For building glyphs 16 bits wide */
```

They enable you to create the hex patterns for icons, glyphs, etc., by drawing a picture of the image you want! What could be better for making a program self-documenting? Using these defines, the example is transformed into:

```
static unsigned short stopwatch[] =
{
    s _ _ _ _ _ X X X X X _ _ _ X X _ ,
    s _ _ _ X X X X X X X X X _ X X X ,
    s _ _ X X X _ _ _ _ _ X X X _ X X ,
    s _ X X _ _ _ _ _ _ _ _ _ X X _ _ ,
    s _ X X _ _ _ _ _ _ _ _ _ X X _ _ ,
    s X X _ _ _ _ _ _ _ _ _ _ _ X X _ ,
    s X X _ _ _ _ _ _ _ _ _ _ _ X X _ ,
    s X X _ X X X X X _ _ _ _ _ X X _ ,
    s X X _ _ _ _ _ X _ _ _ _ _ X X _ ,
    s X X _ _ _ _ _ X _ _ _ _ _ X X _ ,
    s _ X X _ _ _ _ X _ _ _ _ X X _ _ ,
    s _ X X _ _ _ _ X _ _ _ _ X X _ _ ,
    s _ _ X X X _ _ _ _ _ X X X _ _ _ ,
    s _ _ _ X X X X X X X X X _ _ _ _ ,
    s _ _ _ _ _ X X X X X _ _ _ _ _ _ ,
    s _ _ _ _ _ _ _ _ _ _ _ _ _ _ _ _
};
```

certainly quite a bit more meaningful than the equivalent literal values. Standard C has octal, decimal, and hexadecimal constants, but not binary constants, which would otherwise be a simpler way of picturing the pattern.

If you hold the book at the right angle and squint at the page, you might even have a chance of guessing that this is the little stopwatch "cursor busy" glyph used on popular window systems. We got this tip from the Usenet comp.lang.c newsgroup some years ago.

Don't forget to undefine the macros after your pictures; you don't want them mysteriously interfering with later code.

Types Changed While You Wait

We saw in Chapter 1 the type conversions that occur when operators are supplied operands of different types. These are known as the "usual arithmetic conversions", and they govern conversions between two different types to a common type, which is usually also the result type.

Type conversions in C are much more widespread than is generally realized. They can also occur in any expression that involves a type smaller than `int` or `double`. Take the following code, for example:

```
printf(" %d ", sizeof 'A' );
```

The code prints out the size of the type that holds a character literal. Surely this will be the size of a character, and hence "1"? Try running the code. You will see you actually get "4" (or whatever size `int` is on your system). Character literals have type `int` and they get there by following the rules for promotion from type `char`. This is too briefly covered in K&R 1, on page 39 where it says:

> Every char in an expression is converted into an `int`....Notice that all `float`'s in an expression are converted to `double`....Since a function argument is an expression, type conversions also take place when arguments are passed to functions: in particular, `char` and `short` become `int`, `float` becomes `double`.
>
> —*The C Programming Language*, first edition

The feature is known as *type promotion*. When it happens to integer types it's called "integral promotion". The concept of automatic type promotion carried over to ANSI C, although it was watered down in places. The ANSI C standard has this to say about it:

> In executing the fragment

```
char c1, c2;
/* ... */
c1 = c1 + c2;
```

> the "integral promotions" require that the abstract machine promote the value of each variable to `int` size and then add the two `ints` and truncate the sum. Provided the addition of two `chars` can be done without creating an overflow exception, the actual execution need only produce the same result, possibly omitting the promotions.

Similarly, in the fragment

```
float f1, f2;
double d;
/* ... */
f1 = f2 * d;
```

the multiplication may be executed using single-precision arithmetic if the implementation can ascertain that the result would be the same as if it were executed using double-precision arithmetic (for example, if `d` were replaced by the constant `2.0`, which has type `double`).

—*ANSI C Standard*, Section 5.1.2.3

Table 8-1 provides a list of all the usual type promotions. These occur in every expression, not just in expressions involving operators and mixed-type operands.

Table 8-1 Type Promotions in C

Original Type	Usually Promoted To
`char`	`int`
`bit-field`	`int`
`enum`	`int`
`unsigned char`	`int`
`short`	`int`
`unsigned short`	`int`
`float`	`double`
`array` *of anything*	`pointer` *to anything*

The integral promotions are: `char`, `short int` and bit-field types (and signed or unsigned versions of these), and enumeration types, will be promoted to `int` if they can be represented as such. Otherwise they are promoted to `unsigned int`. ANSI C says that the promotion doesn't have to be done if the compiler can guarantee that the same result occurs without it—this usually means a literal operand.

Software Dogma

Alert! Really Important Point—Arguments Are Promoted Too!

An additional place where implicit type conversion occurs is in argument passing. Under K&R C, since a function argument is an expression, type promotion takes place there, too. In ANSI C, arguments are not promoted if a prototype is used; otherwise, they are. Widened arguments are trimmed down to their declared size in the called function.

This is why the single `printf()` format string `"%d"` works for all the different types, `short`, `char`, or `int`. Whichever of these you passed, an `int` was actually put on the stack (or in a register, or whatever) and can be dealt with uniformly in `printf`[1], or any callee at the other end. You can see this in effect if you use printf to output a type longer than `int` such as `long long` on Sun's. Unless you use the long long format specifier `%lld`, you will not get the correct value. This is because in the absence of further information, printf assumes it is dealing with an `int`.

1. Even if a prototype is in scope for `printf()`, note that its prototype ends with an ellipsis:

```
int printf(const char *format, ...);
```

This means it is a function that takes variable arguments. No information about the parameters (other than the first one) is given, and the usual argument promotions always take place.

Type conversion in C is far more widespread than in other languages, which usually restrict themselves to making operands of different types match. C does this too, but also boosts matching types that are smaller than the canonical forms of `int` or `double`. There are three important points to note about implicit type conversions:

- It's a kludge in the language, dating from a desire to simplify the earliest compilers. Converting all operands to a uniform size greatly simplified code generation. Parameters pushed on the stack were all the same length, so the runtime system only needed to know the number of parameters, and not their sizes. Doing all floating-point calculations at double precision meant that the PDP-11 could just be set in "double" mode and left to crank away, without keeping track of the precision.
- You can do a lot of C programming without ever becoming aware of the default type promotions. And many C programmers do.
- You can't call yourself an expert C programmer unless you know this stuff. It gains particular importance in the context of prototypes, described in the next section.

Prototype Painfulness

The purpose of ANSI C function prototypes is to make C a more reliable language. Prototypes are intended to reduce a common (and hard-to-find) class of errors, namely a mismatch between formal and actual parameter types.

This is accomplished by a new form of function declaration that includes the parameter declarations. The function definition is also changed in a similar way, to match the declaration. The compiler can thus check use against declaration. As a reminder, the old and new forms of declaration and definition are shown in Table 8-2.

Table 8-2 K&R C Function Declarations Compared with ANSI C Prototypes

<table>
<tr><th>K&R C</th><th>ANSI C</th></tr>
<tr><td>Declaration:<pre>int foo();</pre></td><td>Prototype:<pre>int foo(int a, int b);</pre>or<pre>int foo(int, int);</pre></td></tr>
<tr><td>Definition:<pre>   int foo(a,b)
        int a;
        int b;
{
        ...
}</pre></td><td>Definition:<pre>int foo(int a, int b)
{
    ...
}</pre></td></tr>
</table>

Notice that a K&R function declaration differs from an ANSI C function declaration (prototype), and a K&R function definition differs from an ANSI C function definition. You express "no parameters" in ANSI C as `int foo(void);` so even this case looks different from classic C.

However, ANSI C didn't and couldn't insist on the use of prototypes exclusively, because that would have destroyed upward compatibility for billions of lines of existing pre-ANSI code. The standard does stipulate that the use of function declarators with empty parentheses (i.e., without specifying argument types) is officially declared obsolescent, and support for it may be withdrawn from future versions of the standard. For the foreseeable future both styles will coexist, because of the volume of pre-ANSI code. So, if prototypes are "a good thing," should we use them everywhere, and go back and add prototypes to existing code when we conduct maintenance on it? Emphatically not!

Function prototypes not only change the syntax of the language; they also introduce a subtle (and arguably undesirable) difference into the semantics. As we know from the previous section, under K&R, if you passed anything shorter than an int to a function it actually got an int, and floats were expanded to doubles. The values are automatically trimmed back to the corresponding narrower types in the body of the called function, if they are declared that way there.

At this point, you might be wondering, why bother expanding them at all, only to shrink them back? It was originally done to simplify the compiler—everything became a standard size. With just a few types it especially simplified argument passing, especially in very old K&R C where you couldn't pass structs as arguments. There were exactly three types: int, double, and pointer. All arguments became a standard size, and the callee would narrow them if necessary.

In contrast, if you use a function prototype, the default argument promotions do not occur. If you prototype something as a `char`, a `char` actually gets passed. If you use the new-style function definition (where argument types are given in the parentheses following the function name), then the compiler generates code on the assumption that the parameters are exactly as declared, without the default type widening.

Where Prototypes Break Down

There are four cases to consider here:

1. **K&R function declaration, and K&R function definition**
   call works ok, promoted types are passed
2. **ANSI C declaration (prototype), and ANSI C definition**
   call works ok, actual types are passed
3. **ANSI C declaration (prototype), and K&R function definition**
   ☞ Failure if you use a narrow type! Call passes actual types, function expects promoted types.
4. **K&R function declaration, and ANSI C definition**
   ☞ Failure if you use a narrow type! Call passes promoted types, function expects actual types.

So if you add a prototype for a K&R C definition including a `short`, the prototype will cause a `short` to be passed, but the definition will expect an `int`, so it will retrieve junk from whatever happens to be adjacent to the parameter. You can force cases 3 and 4 to work by writing the prototype to use the widened type. This will detract from portability and confuse maintenance programmers. The examples below show the two cases that fail.

file 1

```
/* old style definition, but has prototype */
olddef (d,i)
 float d;
 char i;
{
 printf("olddef: float= %f, char =%x \n", d, i);
}
```

```
/* new style definition, but no prototype */
newdef (float d, char i)
{
 printf("newdef: float= %f, char =%x \n", d, i);
}
```

file 2:

```
/* old style definition, but has prototype */
int olddef (float d, char i);


main() {
 float d=10.0;
 char j=3;

 olddef(d, j);


/* new style definition, but no prototype */
 newdef (d, j);
}
```

Expected output:

```
olddef: float= 10.0, char =3
newdef: float= 10.0, char =3
```

Actual output:

```
olddef: float= 524288.000000, char =4
newdef: float= 2.562500, char =0
```

Note that if you put the functions in the same file where they are called (file 2, here), the behavior changes. The compiler will detect the mismatch of `olddef()` because it now sees the prototype and K&R definition together. If you place the definition of `newdef()` before it is called, the compiler will silently do the right thing because the definition acts as a prototype, providing consistency. If you place the definition after the call, the compiler should complain about the mismatch. Since C++ requires prototypes, you may be tempted to add them willy-nilly if using a C++ compiler to brute-force some antique K&R C code.

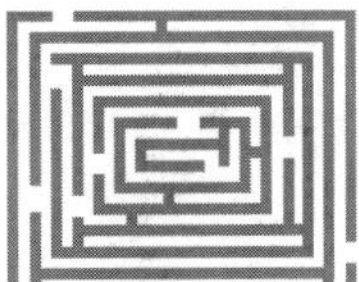

Programming Challenge

How to Fake Out Prototypes

Try a few examples to clarify the issues here. Create the following function in a file of its own:

```
void banana_peel(char a, short b, float c) {
    printf("char = %c, short =%d, float = %f \n", a,b,c);
}
```

In a separate file, create a main program that calls `banana_peel()`.

1. Try calling it with and without a prototype, and with a prototype that doesn't match the definition.
2. In each case, predict what will happen before trying it. Check your prediction by writing a `union` that allows you to store a value of one type, and retrieve another of a different size.
3. Does changing the order of the parameters (in the declaration and the definition) affect how the values are perceived in the called function? Account for this. How many of the error cases does your compiler catch?

Earlier we mentioned that prototypes allow the compiler to check use against declaration. Even if you don't mix'n'match old style with new style, the convention is not foolproof, as there is no guarantee that a prototype actually matches the corresponding definition. In practice we guard against this by putting the prototype into a header file and including the header in the function declaration file. The compiler sees them both at once and will detect a mismatch. Woe betide the programmer who doesn't do this!

Handy Heuristic

Don't Mix Old and New Styles in Function Declaration and Definition

Never mix the old and new styles of function declaration and definition. If the function has a K&R-style declaration in the header file, then use K&R syntax in the definition.

```
int foo();      int foo(a,b) int a; int b; { /* ... */ }
```

If the function has an ANSI C prototype, use ANSI C-style syntax in the definition.

```
int foo(int a, int b);      int foo(int a, int b) { /* ... */ }
```

It would have been possible to create a foolproof mechanism for checking function calls across multiple files. Special magic would be used (as it currently is) on functions like printf that take a variable number of arguments. This could even have been applied to the existing syntax. All that would be needed is a constraint in the standard specifying that each call to a function must be consistent with name, number, and type of parameters and return type in the function definition. The "prior art" was there, as this is done for the Ada language. It could be done in C too, with an additional pre-linker pass. Big hint: use lint.

In practice, the ANSI C committee members were quite cautious about extending C—arguably too cautious. The Rationale shows how they agonized over whether or not they could remove the existing six-character case-insensitive limitation on the significance of external names. In the end, they decided they couldn't remove this restriction, somewhat feebly in the view of some language experts. Maybe the ANSI C committee should have bitten the bullet on this as well, and stipulated a complete solution even if it needs a pre-linker pass, instead of adopting a cockamamie partial solution from C++ with its own conventions, syntax, semantics, and limitations.

Getting a Char Without a Carriage Return

One of the first questions that MS-DOS programmers ask on encountering a UNIX system is, "How do I read characters from the terminal without requiring the user to hit `RETURN`?" Terminal input in UNIX is "cooked" by default, meaning that the raw input is first processed so that line-editing characters (backspace, delete, and so on) can be used, and these keys take effect without being passed through to the running program. Usually this is a desirable convenience, but it does mean that a read won't get the data until the user presses RETURN to signify that the line is finished. Input is effectively line-by-line, whereas some applications need to see each character as each individual key is pressed.

This feature is essential for many kinds of software and is trivial on a PC. The C libraries there support this, often with a function called `kbhit()`, which indicates if a character is waiting to be read. The C compilers from Microsoft and Borland provide `getch()` (or `getche()` to echo the character) to get input character-by-character without waiting for the whole line.

People often wonder why ANSI C didn't define a standard function to get a character if a key has been pressed. Without a standard function every system has a different method, and program portability is lost. The argument against providing `kbhit()` as part of the standard is that it is mostly useful for games software, and there are many other terminal I/O features that are not standardized. In addition, you don't want to promise a standard library function that some OS's will find difficult to provide. The argument for providing it is that it is mostly useful for games software, and that games writers don't need the myriad of other terminal I/O features that could be standardized. Whichever view you hold, it's true that X3J11 missed an opportunity to reinforce C as the language of choice for a generation of student programmers writing games on UNIX.

Handy Heuristic

The Boss Key

Games software is more important than generally thought. Microsoft realizes this, and thoughtfully provides all their new games software with a "boss key". You hit the boss key when you notice in the corner of your eye that your manager is sneaking up on you. It causes the game to instantly disappear, so when the boss strides over to your terminal, it looks like you were working. We're still looking for the boss key that will collapse MS-Windows to reveal a proper window system underneath...

On UNIX, there's a hard way and an easy way to get character-by-character input. The easy way is to let the stty program do the work. Although it is an indirect means of getting what you want, it's trivial to program.

```
#include <stdio.h>
main()
{
int c;

/* The terminal driver is in its ordinary line-at-a-time mode */
system("stty raw");

/* Now the terminal driver is in character-at-a-time mode */
c = getchar();

system("stty cooked");
/* The terminal driver is back in line-at-a-time mode */
}
```

That last line—`system("stty cooked");`—is necessary because the terminal characteristics persist after the program finishes. If a program sets the terminal into a funny mode, it will stay in a funny mode. This is quite unlike, say, setting an environment variable, which disappears when the process does.

Raw I/O achieves a blocking read—if no character is available, the process waits there until one comes in. If you need a nonblocking read, you can use the `ioctl()` (I/O control) system call. It provides a fine level of control over terminal characteristics, and can tell you if a key has been pressed under SVr4. This code uses an ioctl to only do a read if there is a character waiting to be read. This type of I/O is known as *polling*, as you continually ask the device for its opinion on whether it has a character to give you yet.

```
#include <sys/filio.h>
int kbhit()
{
 int i;
 ioctl(0, FIONREAD, &i);
 return i;   /* return a count of chars available to read */
}
```

```
main()
{
 int i = 0;
 int c = ' ';

 system("stty raw -echo");
 printf("enter 'q' to quit \n");
 for (;c!='q';i++) {
    if (kbhit()) {
         c=getchar();
        printf("\n got %c, on iteration %d",c, i);
    }
 }
 system("stty cooked echo");
}
```

Handy Heuristic

Check errno After Library Calls

Whenever you're using system calls (like `ioctl()`), it's a good idea to check the global variable `errno` that is part of ANSI standard C.

If a library or system call encounters problems, it will set `errno` to indicate the cause of the problem. However, the value of `errno` is only valid if there was a problem—the call will have some way of indicating this (usually by its return code).

A typical use might be:

```
errno=0;
if (ioctl(0, FIONREAD, &i)<0) {
    if (errno==EBADF) printf("errno: bad file number");
    if (errno==EINVAL) printf("errno: invalid argument");}
```

You can get as fancy as you like, and encapsulate the checking in a single function that is called after each system call while you are debugging your program. This really helps a lot in isolating the errors. The library call `perror()` will print out an error message when you know you have one.

If you're interested in single-character I/O like this, you're often also interested in doing other display control, and the curses library provides various portable routines for both. Curses (think "cursor") is a library of screen management calls, with implementations on all popular platforms. Rewriting the main function above to use curses instead of stty gives:

```
#include <curses.h>
/* uses curses library, and the kbhit() function defined above */
main()
{
 int c=' ', i=0;

 initscr(); /* initialize curses functions */
 cbreak();
 noecho(); /* do not echo pressed character */

 mvprintw(0, 0, "Press 'q' to quit\n");
 refresh();

 while (c!='q')
 if (kbhit()) {
    c = getch(); /* won't block, as we know a character is waiting */
    mvprintw(1, 0, "got char '%c' on iteration %d \n",c, ++i);
    refresh();
 }

 nocbreak();
 echo();
 endwin(); /* finish curses */
}
```

Compile this with `cc foo.c -lcurses`. Notice how much neater the output is when run under curses. There's a Nutshell book titled *UNIX Curses Explained* (which is not at all the book of programmer swear words most people think it is when they pick it up) that describes curses well. The curses library only offers character-based screen control functions. It's a lower common denominator than software written using specific bit-mapped graphics windowing libraries, but the curses software is far more portable.

Finally, there is a non-polling read in which the operating system will send your process a signal each time it has some input ready.

If a program uses interrupt-driven I/O, when it is not handling input it can be doing other processing in the main function. This is a very efficient use of resources if input is sporadic and there is much processing to be done. Interrupt-driven programs are much more complex and difficult to get working, but the paradigm enables a process to make productive use of time otherwise spent waiting for input. The use of threads diminishes the need to use interrupt-driven I/O techniques.

Programming Challenge

Write an Interrupt-Driven Input Routine on Your System

Interrupt-driven input is a breeze on MS-DOS. The system provides such spartan services that it is easy to brush them aside and pluck characters direct from the I/O port. Under SVr4, you will need to do the following:

1. Create a signal handler routine that will be invoked to read a character when the OS sends a signal that one is ready. The signal to catch is `SIGPOLL`.
2. The signal handler should read a character, and also reset itself as the handler for this signal each time it is invoked. Have it echo the character it just read, and quit if it was a 'q'. Note: this is just for teaching purposes. In practice the results are usually undefined if you call any standard library function from within a signal handler.
3. Make an `ioctl()` call to inform the OS that you require a signal to be sent every time input comes in on the standard input. Look at the manpages for streamio. You will need a command of `I_SETSIG` and an argument of `S_RDNORM`.
4. Once the signal handler has been set up, the program can do something else until input comes in. Have it increment a counter. Print the value of the counter in the handler routine.

Every time a character is sent from the keyboard, the `SIGPOLL` signal will be sent to the process. The signal handler will read the character, and reset itself to be the handler.

Implementing a Finite State Machine in C

A finite state machine is a mathematical concept that can be very useful when embodied in a program. It's a protocol for progressing through a limited ("finite") number of subroutines ("states"), each of which does some processing and then chooses the next state, usually based on the next piece of input.

A finite state machine (FSM) can be used as the control structure of a program. FSMs are well-suited to programs that loop over several different alternative actions based on input. A coin-operated vending machine is a good candidate for an FSM. It will have states like "accept coin", "select item", "deliver item", and "make change". The inputs will be coins, and the outputs will be the items for sale.

The basic idea is to have a table that holds all the possible states, and lists the actions to do when you enter each state. The last action is to calculate (often by a further table lookup based on the state you are in and the next input token) what state to enter next. You start in a state known as the "initial state." Along the way, your transition table might tell you to enter an error state, signifying an unexpected or erroneous input. You continue to make state transitions until you arrive at the end state.

There are several ways to express an FSM in C, but most of them are based on an array of pointers to functions. An array of pointers to functions can be declared like this:

```
void ( *state[MAX_STATES] )();
```

If you know the function names, you can initialize the array like so:

```
extern int a(), b(), c(), d();
int (*state[])() = { a, b, c, d };
```

A function can be called through a pointer in the array like this:

```
(*state[i])();
```

The functions must all take the same arguments and have the same return value (unless you make the array element a union...). Pointers to functions are funny. Notice, too, how the pointer can be dropped, so our call can equally be made as

```
state[i]();
```

or even

```
(******state[i])();
```

This is an unfortunate quirk popularized with ANSI C: calls to a function and calls to a function through a pointer (or any level of pointer indirection) can use the same syntax. There's a corresponding quirk applying to arrays. It further undermines the flawed "declaration looks like use" philosophy.

Programming Challenge

Write an FSM Program

Implement the C declaration analyzer from Chapter 3 as a finite state machine.

1. Review the "decoder ring" diagram, Figure 3-3 on page 76. This is a simple state machine diagram! Program it this way, perhaps by modifying the cdecl program you wrote back in Chapter 3. (You *did* write it, didn't you?)
2. First, write the code to control progress from state to state. Make each action routine simply print out the fact that it has been invoked. Debug this fully.
3. Add the code to process and decode the input declaration.

The decoder ring is a simple state machine; most of the state transitions are in serial order regardless of the input. This means that you don't have to create a *table* of transitions matching state/input to get the next state. You can have a simple variable (of type pointer-to-function). In each state, one of the things you will do is assign the next state. In the main loop, the program will call the function pointed at, and so on until the end function or an error state is reached.

How does the FSM-based program compare with the non-FSM version in terms of ease of coding and debugging? In terms of ease of adding a different action, or modifying the order in which actions occur?

If you want to get fancier, you can have the state function return a pointer to a generic successor function, which you cast to the appropriate type. Then you don't need a global variable. If you want to get less fancy, you can use a switch statement as a poor man's state machine, by assigning to the control variable and putting the switch inside a loop. One final point on FSMs. If your state functions seem to need a variety of arguments, consider using an argument count and an array of pointers to strings, just as the main routine does. The familiar `int argc, char *argv[]` mechanism is very general and can be borrowed with equal success for functions that you define.

Software Is Harder than Hardware!

Did you ever notice that software and hardware are named the wrong way round—software is easier to change, but harder in all other respects? Because software is so difficult to develop and get right, as programmers we need to find ways to make it as easy as possible. One way to do that (and it applies to all languages, not just C) is to code for debuggability. When you write the program, provide the debugging hooks.

Handy Heuristic

Debugging Hooks

Did you know that most debuggers allow you to make function calls from the debugger command line? This can be very useful if you have complicated data structures. Write and compile a function to traverse the data structure and print it out. The function won't be called anywhere in the code, but it will be part of the executable. It is a "debugger hook."

When you debug the code and you're stopped at a breakpoint you can easily check the integrity of your data structures by manually issuing a call to your print routine. Obvious once it's pointed out to you; not obvious if you've never seen it before.

We already hinted at coding for debuggability in the previous section, where we suggested coding an FSM in two distinct phases: first do the state transitions, and only when they are working provide the actions. Don't confuse incremental development with "debugging code into existence"—a technique common among junior programmers, and those writing under too-strict time deadlines. Debugging code into existence means writing a fast slapdash first attempt, and then getting it working by successive refinements over a period of weeks by changing parts that don't work. Meanwhile, anyone who relies on that system component can pull their hair out. "Sendmail" and "make" are two well known programs that are pretty widely regarded as originally being debugged into existence. That's why their command languages are so poorly thought out and difficult to learn. It's not just you—everyone finds them troublesome.

Coding for debuggability means breaking the system down into parts, and getting the program structure working first. Only when you have got the basic program working should you code the complicated refinements, the performance tweaks, and the algorithm optimizations.

Handy Heuristic

Hash with Panache

Hashing is a way to speed up access to an element in a table of data. Instead of searching the table serially, you get a jumpstart to the likeliest element to contain your value.

This is achieved by loading the table carefully, and not in serial order. What you do instead is apply some kind of transformation (known as a hashing function) on a data value from an element to be stored. The hashing function will yield a value in the range 0...tablesize-1, and that becomes the index where you try to store that record.

If the slot is already taken, search forward from that point in the table for the next empty slot.

Alternatively, you can set up a linked list hanging off that element, and simply add it to the end (either end, by the way). Or you can even hang a second hash table off the element.

When you look up a data item, you don't need to start searching entries from element zero. Instead, again hash the value you want to locate, and start looking from that point in the table.

Hashing is a tried and tested table lookup optimization, and it's used everywhere in systems software: in databases, operating systems, and compilers.

If I were stranded on a desert island and could only take one data structure with me, it would be the hash table.

A colleague had to write a program that at one point stored filenames and information about each file. The data was stored in a table of structs, and he decided to use hash lookup. Here's where the coding for debuggability came in. He didn't try to get every part of the program working in one swell foop. He got it working for the simplest case first, by making the hash function always return the constant zero. The function looked like this:

```
/* hash_file: Placeholder for more sophisticated future routine */
int hash_filename (char *s)
{
 return 0;
}
```

The code that called it looked like this:

```
/*
 * find_file: Locate a previously created file descriptor or
 *      make a new one if necessary.
 */
file find_filename (char *s)
{
 int hash_value = hash_filename(s);
 file f;

 for (f = file_hash_table[hash_value]; f != NIL; f = f->flink) {
   if (strcmp(f->fname, s) == SAME) {
     return f;
   }
 }

 /* file not found, so make a new one: */
 f = allocate_file(s);
 f->flink = file_hash_table[hash_value];
 file_hash_table[hash_value] = f;
 return f;
}
```

The effect was as though a hash table was not used; all the elements would be stored in a linked list off element zero. This made it simple to debug, because you didn't have to calculate where anything really should be. The ace programmer was able to quickly get the rest of the code working because he did not have to worry about the interaction with hashing. When he was satisfied that the main routines worked perfectly, he took some performance measurements, and decided to activate the hash function. This was a two-line change in a single function. Here's the current version involving, as he put it, "brain, pain, and gain".

```
int hash_filename (char *s)
{
 int length = strlen(s);
 return (length + 4 * (s[0] + 4 * s[length/2])) % FILE_HASH;
}
```

Sometimes taking the time to break a programming problem into smaller parts is the fastest way of solving it.

Programming Challenge

Write a Hash Program
Type in the fragment of code above, and supply enough of the missing types, data, and code to get it running as a program. Then (horrors!) debug it into existence.

How and Why to Cast

The term "cast" has been applied since the dawn of C to mean both "type conversion" and "type disambiguation." If you say something like

```
(float) 3
```

it's a type conversion and the actual bits change. If you say

```
(float) 3.0
```

it's a type disambiguation, and the compiler can plant the correct bits in the first place. Some people say that casts are so-named because they help something broken to limp along.

It is easy to cast something to an elementary type: write the name of the new type (for example, `int`) in brackets before the expression you wish to cast. It is not quite so obvious how to cast to a more complicated type. Say you have a pointer to a void that you know actually contains a function pointer. How do you do the typecast and call the function all in one statement?

Even complicated casts can be written following this three-step process.

1. Look at the declaration of the object to which you wish to assign the casted result.

2. Remove the identifier (and any storage class specifiers like `extern`), and enclose what remains in parentheses.

3. Write the resulting text immediately to the left of the object you wish to cast.

As a practical example, programmers frequently discover that they need to cast to use the qsort() library routine. The routine takes four parameters, one of which is a pointer to a comparison routine. Qsort is declared as

```
void qsort(void *base, size_t nel, size_t width,
        int (*compar) (const void *, const void *));
```

When you call qsort() you will provide a pointer to your favorite comparison routine as argument compar. Your comparison routine will take an actual type rather than void * arguments, so will likely look somewhat like this:

```
int intcompare(const int *i, const int *j)
{
      return(*i - *j);
}
```

This does not exactly match what qsort expects for argument compar() so a cast is required.[2] Let's assume we have an array a of ten integers to sort. Following the three step cast process outlined above, we can see that the call will look like

```
qsort(
      a,
      10,
      sizeof(int),
      (int (*)(const void *, const void *)) intcompare
);
```

As an impractical example, you can create a pointer to, for example printf(), with

```
extern int printf(const char*,...);
void *f = (void*)printf;
```

2. If you have a perverse and unpopular computer that makes the size of a pointer vary according to the type it points to, then you will have to do the cast in your comparison routine, rather than the call. Try to move to a better designed architecture as soon as possible.

You can then call printf through a properly-cast pointer, in this manner:

```
(*(int(*)(const char*,...))f)("Bite my shorts. Also my chars and ints\n");
```

Some Light Relief—
The International Obfuscated C Code Competition

> *The C language combines all the power of assembly language with all the ease-of-use of assembly language.*
>
> —Ancient Peasant Proverb

It's possible to abuse any programming language. Most good programmers can write programs that are so intense, it hurts your eyes just to look at them. Code that you can proudly show to programmers in the next office, and challenge them to figure out what it does. Code that, six months after writing it, *you* can't figure out what it does. You can write these kinds of programs in any language; it just seems to be easier with C.

The International Obfuscated C Code Competition (IOCCC) is an annual contest run since 1984 over USENET by Landon Curt Noll and Larry Bassel. It started when Landon looked at the source for the Bourne shell and decided, "Nah! It's just too outré." He began to wonder how far you could go if you actively tried to make C code look confusing, rather than just achieving this as an accidental side effect.

The competition has become an annual tradition. Entries are accepted in Winter, judging takes place over the Spring, and the winners are announced at the Summer Usenix conference. There are usually about ten categories of winner: "strangest abuse of the rules," "most creative source layout," "best one-liner," and so on. The overall "best of show" winner is whoever produces the most unreadable, and bizarre (but working) C program.

The IOCCC is a lot of fun, and can extend your knowledge in surprising ways, whether you enter or merely analyze the prize-winning code afterward. For example, in 1987, David Korn of Bell Labs submitted this winning entry:

```
main() { printf(&unix["\021%six\012\0"],(unix)["have"]+"fun"-0x60);}
```

What does *that* print? (Hint: it's not "have fun"!) David wrote the eponymous Korn shell, which is widely regarded as much cleaner than the version 7 /bin/sh, so presumably the IOCCC also acts as a safety valve for the happy hacker.

A 1988 winner was an obfuscated version of cdecl, submitted by programmer Gopi Reddy. Recall that we needed about 150 lines to program this unobfuscated. The obfuscated code is less than a dozen lines

```
#include<stdio.h>
#include<ctype.h>
#define w printf
#define p while
#define t(s) (W=T(s))
char*X,*B,*L,I[99];M,W,V;D(){W==9?(w("`%.*s' is ",V,X),t(0)):W==40?
(t(0),D(),t(41)):W==42?(t(0),D(),w("ptr to ")):0;p(W==40?(t(0),
w("func returning "),t(41)):W==91?(t(0)==32?(w("array[0..%d] of ",
atoi(X)-1),t(0)):w("array of "),t(93)):0);}main(){p(w("input: "),
B=gets(I))if(t(0)==9)L=X,M=V,t(0),D(),w("%.*s.\n\n",M,L);}T(s){if(!s||s==W)
{p(*B==9||*B==32)B++;X=B;V=0;if(W=isalpha(*B)?9:isdigit(*B)?32:*B++)
if(W<33)p(isalnum(*B))B++,V++;}return W;}
```

This kind of obfuscation, using excessive `?` and `,` operators, is a little vieux chapeau now, but at the time it was novel and the program's conciseness is certainly astonishing. Figuring out how it works is left as an exercise for the reader. (Ha! I've always wanted to say that.) To get you started, there are two subroutines, `T()`, which lexes the next token and says whether it is an identifier, number, etc., and `D()`, which does the parsing. Try unscrambling it by running it through the preprocessor and formatting it. Then turn all the `?` expressions into `if` statements. Iterate until readable.

The final obfuscated C example is a BASIC interpreter, submitted by University of London graduate student Diomidis Spinellis and written in about 1,500 characters! It was accompanied by an instruction manual that explained how to use the interpreter, and provided a sample BASIC program.

Software Dogma

DDS-BASIC Interpreter (Version 1.00)

Immediate commands:

`RUN` `LIST` `NEW` `BYE` `OLD` *filename* `SAVE` *filename*

Program commands:

variable names A to Z	variables initialized to 0 on RUN
FOR var = exp TO exp	NEXT variable
GOSUB exp	RETURN
GOTO exp	IF exp THEN exp
INPUT variable	PRINT string
PRINT exp	var = exp
REM any text	END

Expressions (ranked by precedence):

bracketed expressions

number (leading 0 for octal, 0x for hex, else decimal), variable

Unary -

* /

\+ -

= <>

\> <

<= >=

* and + are also used for boolean AND and boolean OR

boolean expressions evaluate to 0 for false and 1 for true

Editing:

Line editor using line re-entry.

A line number with nothing following it deletes the line.

DDS-BASIC Interpreter (Version 1.00) (Continued)

Input format:

Free format positioning of tokens on the line.

No space is allowed before the line number.

Exactly one space is needed between the OLD or SAVE command and the filename.

ALL INPUT MUST BE UPPERCASE.

Limits:

Line numbers:	1–10000
Line length:	999 characters
FOR nesting:	26
GOSUB:	999 levels
Program:	Dynamically allocated
Expressions:	-32768–32767 for 16-bit machines, -2147483648–2147483647 for 32-bit machines

Error checking / error reports:

No error checking is performed.

The message "core dumped" signifies a syntax or semantic error.

Hosting environment:

ANSI C, traditional K&R C
ASCII or EBCDIC character set
48 Kbytes memory

The sample BASIC program provided was the old lunar lander game:

```
10 REM Lunar Lander
20 REM By Diomidis Spinellis
30 PRINT "You are on the Lunar Lander about to leave the spacecraft."
60 GOSUB 4000
70 GOSUB 1000
80 GOSUB 2000
90 GOSUB 3000
100 H = H - V
110 V = ((V + G) * 10 - U * 2) / 10
```

```
120 F = F - U
130 IF H > 0 THEN 80
135 H = 0
140 GOSUB 2000
150 IF V > 5 THEN 200
160 PRINT "Congratulations! This was a very good landing."
170 GOSUB 5000
180 GOTO 10
200 PRINT "You have crashed."
210 GOTO 170
1000 REM Initialise
1010 V = 70
1020 F = 500
1030 H = 1000
1040 G = 2
1050 RETURN
2000 REM Print values
2010 PRINT " Meter readings"
2015 PRINT " --------------"
2020 PRINT "Fuel (gal):"
2030 PRINT F
2040 GOSUB 2100 + 100 * (H <> 0)
2050 PRINT V
2060 PRINT "Height (m):"
2070 PRINT H
2080 RETURN
```

```
2100 PRINT "Landing velocity (m/sec):"
2110 RETURN
2200 PRINT "Velocity (m/sec):"
2210 RETURN
3000 REM User input
3005 IF F = 0 THEN 3070
3010 PRINT "How much fuel will you use?"
3020 INPUT U
3025 IF U < 0 THEN 3090
3030 IF U <= F THEN 3060
3040 PRINT "Sorry, you have not got that much fuel!"
3050 GOTO 3010
3060 RETURN
3070 U = 0
3080 RETURN
3090 PRINT "No cheating please! Fuel must be >= 0."
3100 GOTO 3010
4000 REM Detachment
4005 PRINT "Ready for detachment"
4007 PRINT "-- COUNTDOWN --"
4010 FOR I = 1 TO 11
4020 PRINT 11 - I
4025 GOSUB 4500
4030 NEXT I
4035 PRINT "You have left the spacecraft."
4037 PRINT "Try to land with velocity less than 5 m/sec."
4040 RETURN
4500 REM Delay
4510 FOR J = 1 TO 500
4520 NEXT J
4530 RETURN
5000 PRINT "Do you want to play again? (0 = no, 1 = yes)"
5010 INPUT Y
5020 IF Y = 0 THEN 5040
5030 RETURN
5040 PRINT "Have a nice day."
```

If you type this into a file called `LANDER.BAS`, you can compile and run it with these commands in the BASIC interpreter:

```
OLD LANDER.BAS
RUN
```

The obfuscated BASIC interpreter itself looks like this:

```
#define O(b,f,u,s,c,a) \
 b(){int o=f();switch(*p++){X u:_ o s b();X c:_ o a b();default:p--;_ o;}}
#define t(e,d,_,C)X e:f=fopen(B+d,_);C;fclose(f)
#define U(y,z) while(p=Q(s,y))*p++=z,*p=’ ‘
#define N for(i=0;i<11*R;i++)m[i]&&
#define I “%d %s\n”,i,m[i]
#define X ;break;case
#define _ return
#define R 999
typedef char*A;int*C,E[R],L[R],M[R],P[R],l,i,j;char B[R],F[2];A m[12*R],malloc
(),p,q,x,y,z,s,d,f,fopen();A Q(s,o)A s,o;{for(x=s;*x;x++){for(y=x,z=o;*z&&*y==
*z;y++)z++;if(z>o&&!*z)_ x;}_ 0;}main(){m[11*R]=”E”;while(puts(“Ok”),gets(B)
)switch(*B){X’R’:C=E;l=1;for(i=0;i<R;P[i++]=0);while(l){while(!(s=m[l]))l++;if
(!Q(s,”\””)){U(“<>”,’#’);U(“<=”,’$’);U(“>=”,’!’);}d=B;while(*F=*s){*s==’”’&&j
++;if(j&1||!Q(“ \t”,F))*d++=*s;s++;}*d--=j=0;if(B[1]!=’=’)switch(*B){X’E’:l=-1
X’R’:B[2]!=’M’&&(l=*--C)X’I’:B[1]==’N’?gets(p=B),P[*d]=S():(*(q=Q(B,”TH”))=0,p
=B+2,S()&&(p=q+4,l=S()-1))X’P’:B[5]==’”’?*d=0,puts(B+6):(p=B+5,printf(“%d\n”,S
()))X’G’:p=B+4,B[2]==’S’&&(*C++=l,p++),l=S()-1 X’F’:*(q=Q(B,”TO”))=0;p=B+5;P[i
=B[3]]=S();p=q+2;M[i]=S();L[i]=l X’N’:++P[*d]<=M[*d]&&(l=L[*d]);}else p=B+2,P[
*B]=S();l++;}X’L’:N printf(I)X’N’:N free(m[i]),m[i]=0   X’B’:_ 0 t(‘S’,5,”w”,N
fprintf(f,I))t(‘O’,4,”r”,while(fgets(B,R,f))(*Q(B,”\n”)=0,G()))X 0:default:G()
;}_ 0;}G(){l=atoi(B);m[l]&&free(m[l]);(p=Q(B,” “))?strcpy(m[l]=malloc(strlen(p
)),p+1):(m[l]=0,0);}O(S,J,’=’,==,’#’,!=)O(J,K,’<‘,<,’>’,>)O(K,V,’$’,<=,’!’,>=)
O(V,W,’+’,+,’-’,-)O(W,Y,’*’,*,’/’,/)Y(){int o;_*p==’-’?p++,-Y():*p>=’0’&&*p<=
‘9’?strtol(p,&p,0):*p==’(‘?p++,o=S(),p++,o:P[*p++];}
```

Watch for the difference between the letter "l" and the digit "1" when you type this in! If it's on the left-hand side of an assignment, it must be the letter "l".

This is an incredible program, and it's well worth reverse-engineering it to remove the obfuscation and see how it works. If this fires your imagination, you'll be pleased to hear that you too can enter the IOCCC. Just read the comp.lang.c newsgroup on Usenet and follow the instructions posted there in late Autumn. Be warned that the winners are among the best programmers in the world, and they're doing their worst.

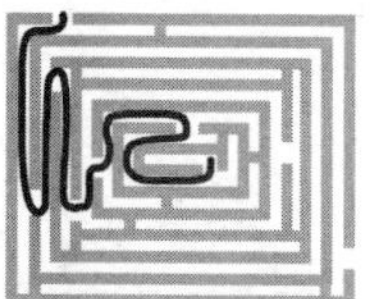

Programming Solution

Type Promotion Mix-Up in Prototypes

```
main() {
    union {
        double d;
        float f;
    } u;

    u.d = 10.0;
    printf(" put in a double, pull out a float f= %f \n", u.f);

    u.f=10.0;
    printf(" put in a float, pull out a double d= %f \n", u.d);
}

%a.out
 put in a double, pull out a float f= 2.562500
 put in a float, pull out a double d= 524288.000000
```

Programming Solution

Asynchronous I/O

The code below causes an SVr4-based OS to send an interrupt for each character entered on the standard input.

```
#include <errno.h>
#include <signal.h>
```

Asynchronous I/O (Continued)

```
#include <stdio.h>
#include <stropts.h>
#include <sys/types.h>
#include <sys/conf.h>

int iteration=0;
char crlf []={0xd,0xa, 0};

void handler(int s)
{
    int c=getchar(); /* read a character */
    printf("got char %c, at count %d %s",c,iteration,crlf);

    if (c=='q') {
            system("stty sane");
            exit(0);
    }
}

main()
{
    sigset(SIGPOLL, handler); /* set up the handler */
    system("stty raw -echo");
    ioctl(0, I_SETSIG, S_RDNORM); /* ask for interrupt driven input */

    for(;;iteration++);
     /* can do other stuff here */
}
```

Use sigset() instead of signal() and you won't have to re-register the signal handler each time. Sample output is:

```
% a.out
got char a, at count 1887525
got char b, at count 5979648
got char c, at count 7299030
got char d, at count 9802103
got char e, at count 11060214
got char q, at count 14551814
```

Programming Solution

cdecl as an FSM

```
#include <stdio.h>
#include <string.h>
#include <ctype.h>

#define MAXTOKENS 100
#define MAXTOKENLEN 64

enum type_tag { IDENTIFIER, QUALIFIER, TYPE };

struct token {
    char type;
    char string[MAXTOKENLEN];
};

int top = -1;

/* holds all the tokens before first identifier */
struct token stack[MAXTOKENS];

/* holds the token just read */
struct token this;

#define pop stack[top--]
#define push(s) stack[++top]=s

enum type_tag
classify_string(void)
/* figure out the identifier type */
{
    char *s = this.string;
```

cdecl as an FSM (Continued)

```
    if (!strcmp(s, "const")) {
        strcpy(s, "read-only");
        return QUALIFIER;
    }
    if (!strcmp(s, "volatile")) return QUALIFIER;
    if (!strcmp(s, "void")) return TYPE;
    if (!strcmp(s, "char")) return TYPE;
    if (!strcmp(s, "signed")) return TYPE;
    if (!strcmp(s, "unsigned")) return TYPE;
    if (!strcmp(s, "short")) return TYPE;
    if (!strcmp(s, "int")) return TYPE;
    if (!strcmp(s, "long")) return TYPE;
    if (!strcmp(s, "float")) return TYPE;
    if (!strcmp(s, "double")) return TYPE;
    if (!strcmp(s, "struct")) return TYPE;
    if (!strcmp(s, "union")) return TYPE;
    if (!strcmp(s, "enum")) return TYPE;
    return IDENTIFIER;
}

void gettoken(void)
{               /* read next token into "this" */
    char *p = this.string;

    /* read past any spaces */
    while ((*p = getchar()) == ' ');

    if (isalnum(*p)) {
        /* it starts with A-Z,1-9 read in identifier */
        while (isalnum(*++p = getchar()));
        ungetc(*p, stdin);
        *p = '\0';
        this.type = classify_string();
        return;
    }
    this.string[1] = '\0';
    this.type = *p;
    return;
```

cdecl as an FSM (Continued)

```
}

void initialize(),
 get_array(), get_params(), get_lparen(), get_ptr_part(), get_type();

void (*nextstate)(void) = initialize;


int main()
/* Cdecl written as a finite state machine */
{
    /* transition through the states, until the pointer is null */
    while (nextstate != NULL)
        (*nextstate)();

    return 0;
}

void initialize()
{
    gettoken();
    while (this.type != IDENTIFIER) {
        push(this);
        gettoken();
    }
    printf("%s is ", this.string);
    gettoken();
    nextstate = get_array;
}

void get_array()
{
    nextstate = get_params;
    while (this.type == '[') {
        printf("array ");
        gettoken();/* a number or ']' */
        if (isdigit(this.string[0])) {
            printf("0..%d ", atoi(this.string) - 1);
```

cdecl as an FSM (Continued)

```
            gettoken();/* read the ']' */
        }
        gettoken();/* read next past the ']' */
        printf("of ");
        nextstate = get_lparen;
    }
}

void get_params()
{
    nextstate = get_lparen;
    if (this.type == '(') {
        while (this.type != ')') {
            gettoken();
        }
        gettoken();
        printf("function returning ");
    }
}

void get_lparen()
{
    nextstate = get_ptr_part;
    if (top >= 0) {
        if (stack[top].type == '(') {
            pop;
            gettoken();/* read past ')' */
            nextstate = get_array;
        }
    }
}

void get_ptr_part()
{
    nextstate = get_type;
    if (stack[top].type == '*') {
        printf("pointer to ");
        pop;
```

cdecl as an FSM (Continued)

```
        nextstate = get_lparen;
    } else if (stack[top].type == QUALIFIER) {
        printf("%s ", pop.string);
        nextstate = get_lparen;
    }
}

void get_type()
{
    nextstate = NULL;
    /* process tokens that we stacked while reading to identifier */
    while (top >= 0) {
        printf("%s ", pop.string);
    }
    printf("\n");
}
```

More about Arrays 9

Never eat at a place called "Mom's." Never play cards with a man called "Doc."

And never, ever, forget that C treats an l-value of type array-of-T in an expression as a pointer to the first element of the array.

—C programmers' saying (Traditional)

when an array **is** a pointer...why the confusion?...an "array name in an expression" is a pointer...why C treats array subscripts as pointer offsets...an "array name as a function parameter" is a pointer... why C treats array parameters as pointers...how an array parameter is referenced...indexing a slice...arrays and pointers interchangeability summary...C has multi-dimensional arrays...but every other language calls them "arrays of arrays"...how arrays are laid out in memory... how to initialize arrays...some light relief—hardware/software trade-offs

When an Array *Is* a Pointer

An earlier chapter emphasized the most common circumstance when an array may not be written as a pointer. This chapter starts by describing when it can. There are many more occasions in practice when arrays are interchangeable with pointers than when they aren't. Let us consider "declaration" and "use" (with their conventional intuitive meanings) as individual cases.

Declarations themselves can be further split into three cases:

- declaration of an external array
- definition of an array (remember, a definition is just a special case of a declaration; it allocates space and may provide an initial value)
- declaration of a function parameter

All array names that are function parameters are always converted to pointers by the compiler. In all other cases (and the main interesting case is the "defined as an array in one file/declared as a pointer in another" described in the previous chapter) the declaration of an array gives you an array, the declaration of a pointer gives you a pointer, and never the twain shall meet. But the *use* (reference in a statement or expression) of an array can always be rewritten to use a pointer. A diagram summary is shown in Figure 9-1.

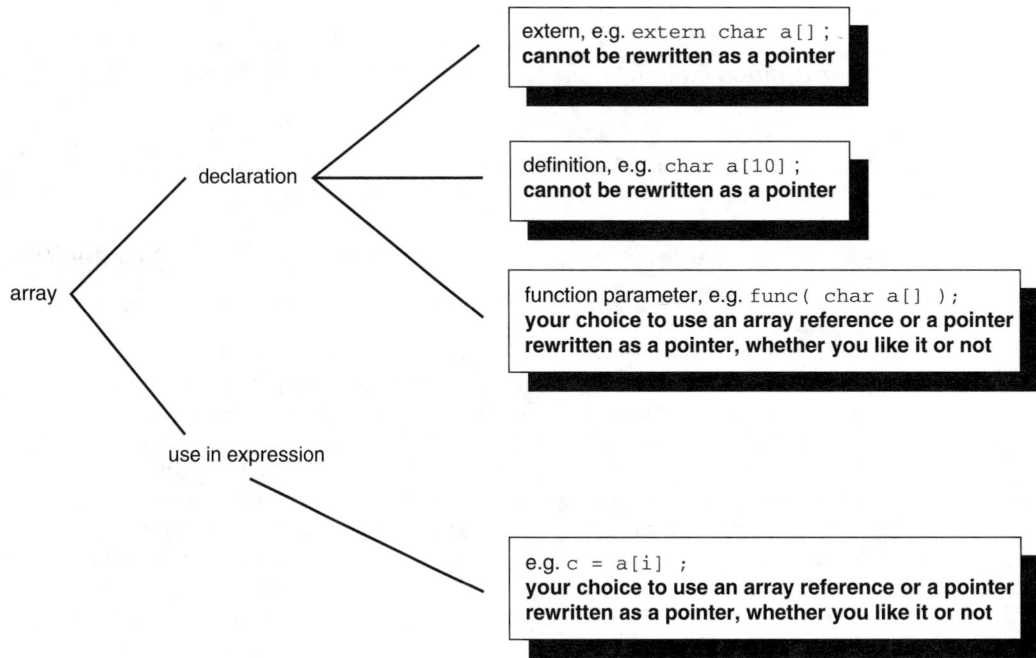

Figure 9-1 When Arrays are Pointers

However, arrays and pointers are processed differently by the compiler, represented differently at runtime, and may generate different code. To a compiler, an array is an address, and a pointer is the address of an address. Choose the right tool for the job.

Why the Confusion?

Why do people wrongly think that arrays and pointers are completely interchangeable? Because they read the standard reference literature!

The C Programming Language, 2nd Ed, Kernighan & Ritchie, foot of page 99:

> As formal parameters in a function definition

turn leaf to page 100:

```
   char s[];
and
   char *s;
are equivalent; . . .
```

Argggghhh! Argv! Argc! What a truly unfortunate place to break the page in K&R2! It is easy to miss that the statement of equivalence is made only for the ***one specific case of formal parameters in a function definition***—especially since it is emphasized that subscripted array expressions can always be written as pointer-plus-offset expressions.

"The C Programming Language," Ritchie, Johnson, Lesk & Kernighan, *The Bell System Technical Journal*, vol. 57, no. 6, July-Aug 1978, pages 1991-2019:

> includes a general rule that, whenever the name of an array appears in an expression, it is converted to a pointer to the first member of the array.

The key term "expression" is not defined in the paper.

When people learn to program, they usually start by putting all their code in one function, then progress to several functions, and finally learn how to structure a program over several files. Thus, they get a lot of practice seeing arrays and pointers in function arguments where they *are* fully interchangeable, like this:

```
char my_array[10];
 char * my_ptr;
 . . .
 i = strlen( my_array );
 j = strlen( my_ptr );
```

Programmers also see a lot of statements like

```
printf("%s %s", my_ptr, my_array);
```

which clearly demonstrate the interchangeability of pointers and arrays. It's too easy to overlook that this only happens in the specific context of actual parameters in a function call. Worse, you can write

```
printf("array at location %x holds string %s",a ,a);
```

in which the same statement uses an array name as an address (pointer) and as an array of characters. This only works because `printf` is a function, so the array is passed as a pointer. We are also accustomed to seeing the parameter of `main` declared as `char **argv` or `char *argv[]` quite interchangeably. Again, this is only permitted because `argv` is a function parameter, but it does lull the programmer into wrongly concluding that "C is consistent and regular in its approach to address arithmetic." When you add to this the detailed and lengthy treatment of how subscripted array expressions can always be written in terms of pointers, it is easy to see how the confusion has arisen.

The box below is really important, and will be explained then referred to many times in this chapter and the next one. Pay attention, mark the page, and be prepared to refer to it again several times!

Software Dogma

When Arrays *Are* Pointers

The C standard has the following to say about the matter.

Rule 1. An array name **in an expression** (in contrast with a declaration) is treated by the compiler as a pointer to the first element of the array[1] (paraphrase, ANSI C Standard, paragraph 6.2.2.1).

Rule 2. A subscript is always equivalent to an offset from a pointer (paraphrase, ANSI C Standard, paragraph 6.3.2.1).

Rule 3. An array name **in the declaration of a function parameter** is treated by the compiler as a pointer to the first element of the array (paraphrase, ANSI C Standard, paragraph 6.7.1).

1. OK nitpickers, there are a few minuscule exceptions that concern arrays treated as a whole. A reference to an array is not replaced by a pointer to the first element when:
   - the array appears as the operand of `sizeof()`—obviously you want the size of the whole array here, not just a pointer to it.
   - the array's address is taken with the `&` operator.
   - the array is a string or wide-string literal initializer.

The executive summary of this is roughly that arrays and pointers are like limericks and haikus: they are related art forms, but each has its own different practical expression. The following sections describe what these rules actually mean in practice.

Rule 1: An "Array Name in an Expression" Is a Pointer

Rules 1 and 2 (above) in combination mean that subscripted array references can always be written equally well as a pointer-to-base-of-array plus offset. For example, if we declare

```
int a[10], *p, i=2;
```

then `a[i]` can equally be accessed in any of these ways:

```
p=a;
p[i];
```

```
p=a;
*(p+i);
```

```
p=a+i;
*p;
```

In fact, it's even stronger than this. An array reference `a[i]` is always rewritten to `*(a + i)` by the compiler at compiletime. The C standard requires this conceptual behavior. Perhaps an easy way to follow this is to remember that square brackets `[ ]` represent a subscript operator, just as a plus sign represents the addition operator. The subscript operator takes an integer and pointer-to-type-T, and yields an object of type T. An array name in an expression becomes a pointer, and there you are: pointers and arrays are interchangeable in expressions because they all boil down to pointers in the end, and both can be subscripted. Just as with addition, the subscript operator is commutative (it doesn't care which way round the arguments come, 5 + 3 equals 3 + 5). This is why, given a declaration like int `a[10];`, both the following are correct:

```
a[6] = ....;
6[a] = ....;
```

The second version is never seen in production code, and has no known use apart from confusing those new to C.

The compiler automatically scales a subscript to the size of the object pointed at. If integers are 4 bytes long, then `a[i+1]` is actually 4 bytes (not 1) further on from `a[i]`. The compiler takes care of scaling before adding in the base address. This is the reason why pointers are always typed—constrained to point to objects of only one type—so that the compiler knows how many bytes to retrieve on a pointer dereference, and it knows by how much to scale a subscript.

Rule 2: C Treats Array Subscripts as Pointer Offsets

Treating array subscripts as a pointer-plus-offset is a technique inherited from BCPL (the language that was C's ancestor). This is the convention that renders it impractical to add runtime support for subscript range-checking in C. A subscript operator hints, but does not ensure, that an array is being accessed. Alternatively, subscripting might be by-passed altogether in favor of pointer access to an array. Under these conditions, range-checking could only be done for a restricted subset of array accesses. In practice it has usually not been considered worthwhile.

Word has gotten out that it is "more efficient" to program array algorithms using pointers instead of arrays.

The popular belief is usually wrong. With modern production-quality optimizing compilers, there is not necessarily a difference in the code generated for one-dimensional arrays and that for references through a pointer. After all, array subscripts are defined in terms of pointers, so it is often possible for the optimizer to make the transformation to the most efficient representation, and output machine instructions for that. Let's take a look at those array/pointer alternatives again, and separate out the initialization from an access in a loop:

```
int a[10], *p, i;
```

Variable `a[i]` can equally be accessed in any of the ways shown in Figure 9-2.

Even with a simple-minded translation into different generated code, stepping through a one-dimensional array is often no faster with a pointer than with a subscript. Scaling needs to be done when striding through consecutive memory locations with a pointer or an array. Scaling is done by multiplying the offset by the size of an element; the result is the true byte offset from the start of the array. The scaling factor is often a power of 2 (e.g., 4 bytes to an integer, 8 bytes in a double, etc.). Instead of doing a slow multiplication, the scaling can be done by shifting left. A "shift-left-by-three" is equivalent to multiplying a binary number by eight. If you have array elements the size of which isn't a power of two (e.g., an array of structs), all bets are off.

However, striding down an int array is an idiom that's easily recognized. If a good optimizing compiler does code analysis, and tries to keep base variables in fast registers and to recognize loop paradigms, the end result may be identical generated code for pointers and array accesses in a loop.

Pointers are not necessarily any faster than subscripts when processing one-dimensional arrays. The fundamental reason that C treats array subscripts as pointer offsets is because that is the model used by the underlying hardware.

Array Access

```
for (i=0;i<10;i++)
        a[i] = 0;
```

Intermediate code

```
load l-value(a) into R1    (can be hoisted out of loop)
load l-value(i) into R2    (can be hoisted out of loop)

load [R2] into R3
if necessary, scale R3
add R1 + R3 into R4
store 0 into [R4]
```

Pointer Alternative 1

```
p=a;

for (i=0;i<10;i++)
        p[i] = 0;
```

```
load l-value(p) into R0    (can be hoisted out of loop)
load [R0] into R1          (can be hoisted out of loop)
load l-value(i) into R2    (can be hoisted out of loop)

load [R2] into R3
if necessary, scale R3
add R1 + R3 into R4
store 0 into [R4]
```

Pointer Alternative 2

```
p=a;

for (i=0;i<10;i++)
        *(p+i) = 0;
```

identical to Pointer Alternative 1.
(Mini challenge: Why?)

Pointer Alternative 3

```
p=a;

for (i=0;i<10;i++)
        *p++ = 0;
```

```
load size of what-p-points-at into R5
                           (can be hoisted out of loop)
load l-value(p) into R0    (can be hoisted out of loop)

load [R0] into R1
store 0 into [R1]
add R5 + R1 into R1
store R1 into [R0]
```

The examples above show a simple intermediate code translation for these alternatives. Optimization can make the generated code different from that shown here. The notation R0, R1, etc., represents CPU registers. In each example we use

R0 to hold the l-value of `p`	R1 to hold the l-value of `a`, or the r-value of `p`
R2 to hold the l-value of `i`	R3 to hold the r-value of `i`

The notation [R0] means load from or store into indirectly, using the address indicated by the register (a common notation for many assemblers). "Can be hoisted" means that the data is not changed by the loop, so the loop can be made faster by moving these statements out of it.

Figure 9-2 Array/Pointer Code Trade-offs

Rule 3: An "Array Name as a Function Parameter" Is a Pointer

Rule 3 also needs explaining. First, let's review some terminology laid down in Kernighan and Ritchie.

Term	Definition	Example
Parameter	is a variable defined in a function definition or a function prototype declaration. Some people call this a "formal parameter."	`int power( int base, int n);` `base` and `n` are parameters.
Argument	is a value used in a particular call to a function. Some people call this an "actual parameter."	`i = power(10, j);` `10` and `j` are arguments. The argument can be different for the different calls of a function.

The standard stipulates that a declaration of a parameter as "array of *type*" shall be adjusted to "pointer to *type*". In the specific case of a definition of a formal function parameter, the compiler is *obliged* to rewrite an array into a pointer to its first element. Instead of passing a copy of the array, the compiler just passes its address. Parameters that are functions are similarly treated as pointers, but let's just stick with arrays for now. The implicit conversion means that

```
my_function( int * turnip ) { . . . }
my_function( int turnip[] ) { . . . }
my_function( int turnip[200] ) { . . . }
```

are all completely equivalent. Therefore, `my_function()` can quite legally be called with an array, or really with a pointer, as its actual argument.

Why C Treats Array Parameters as Pointers

The reason arrays are passed to functions as pointers is efficiency, so often the justification for transgressions against good software engineering practice. The Fortran I/O model is tortuous because it was thought "efficient" to re-use the existing (though clumsy and already obsolete) IBM 704 assembler I/O libraries. Comprehensive semantic checking was excluded from the Portable C Compiler on the questionable grounds that it is more "efficient" to implement `lint` as a separate program. That decision has been implicitly revoked by the enhanced error checking done by most ANSI C compilers.

The array/pointer equivalence for parameters was done for efficiency. All non-array data arguments in C are passed "by value" (a copy of the argument is made and passed to the called function; the function cannot change the value of the actual variable used as an argument, just the value of the copy it has). However, it is potentially very expensive in memory and time to copy an array; and most of the time, you don't actually want a copy of the array, you just want to indicate to the function which particular array you are interested in at the moment. One way to do this might be to allow parameters to have a storage specifier that says whether it is passed by value or by reference, as occurs in Pascal. It simplifies the compiler if the convention is adopted that all arrays are passed as a pointer to the start, and everything else is passed by making a copy of it. Similarly the return value of a function can never be an array or function, only a *pointer* to an array or function.

Some people like to think of this as meaning that all C arguments are call-by-value by default, except arrays and functions; these are passed as call-by-reference parameters. Data can be explicitly passed as call-by-reference by using the "address of" operator. This causes the address of the argument to be sent, rather than a copy of the argument. In fact, a major use of the address-of operator `&` is simulating call-by-reference. This "by reference" viewpoint isn't strictly accurate, because the implementation mechanism is explicit—in the called procedure you still only have a pointer to something, and not the thing itself. This makes a difference if you take its size or copy it.

How an Array Parameter Is Referenced

Figure 9-3 shows the steps involved in accessing a subscripted array parameter.

```
func( char p[]);          . . .          c = p[i];

func( char *p);           . . .          c = p[i];
```

compiler symbol table shows `p` is addressable as offset 14 from the stack-pointer SP

runtime step 1: get the argument from the procedure activation record at offset 14 from the stack top, contains say '5081'

runtime step 2: get value `i`, and add it to 5081

runtime step 3: get the contents from address (5081+`i`)

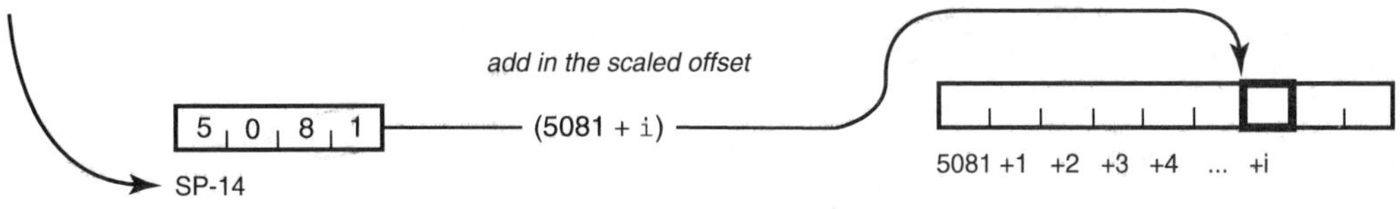

Figure 9-3 How a Subscripted Array Parameter Is Referenced

Note well that this is identical to Diagram C on page 101, showing how a subscripted pointer is looked up. The C language permits the programmer to declare and refer to this parameter as either an array (what the programmer intends to pass to the function) or as a pointer (what the function actually gets). The compiler knows that whenever a formal parameter is declared as an array, inside the function it will in fact always be dealing with a pointer to the first element of an array of unknown size. Thus, it can generate the correct code, and does not need to distinguish between cases.

No matter which of these forms the programmer writes, the function doesn't automatically know how many elements there are in the pointed-to thing. There has to be some convention, such as a NUL end marker or an additional parameter giving the array extent. This is not true in, for example, Ada, where every array carries around with it a bunch of information about its element size, dimensions, and indices.

Given these definitions:

```
    func( int * turnip ) { . . . }
or
    func( int turnip[] ) { . . . }
or
    func( int turnip[200] ) { . . . }

int my_int; /* data definitions */
int * my_int_ptr;
int my_int_array[10];
```

you can legally call any of the function prototypes above with any of the following arguments. They are often used for very different purposes:

Table 9-1 Common Uses of Array/Pointer Actual Parameters

Actual Argument in Call	Type	Common Purpose
`func(&my_int );`	Address of an integer	"Call-by-reference" of an int
`func( my_int_ptr );`	A pointer to an integer	To pass a pointer
`func( my_int_array );`	An array of integers	To pass an array
`func(&my_int_array[i] );`	Address of an element of int array	To pass a slice of an array

Conversely, if you are inside `func()`, you don't have any easy way of telling which of these alternative arguments, and hence with which purpose, the function was invoked. All arrays that are function arguments are rewritten by the compiler at compiletime into pointers. Therefore, any reference inside a function to an array parameter generates code for a pointer reference. Figure 9-3 on page 247 shows what this means in practice.

Interestingly, therefore, there is no way to pass an array itself into a function, as it is always automatically converted into a pointer to the array. Of course, using the pointer inside the function, you can pretty much do most things you could have done with the original array. You won't get the right answer if you take the size of it, though.

You thus have a choice when declaring such a function. You can define the parameter as either an array or a pointer. Whichever you choose, the compiler notices the special case that this object is a function argument, and it generates code to dereference the pointer.

Programming Challenge

Play Around with Array/Pointer Arguments

Write and execute a program to convince yourself that the preceding information is true.

1. Define a function that takes a character array `ca` as an argument. Inside the function, print out the values of `&ca` and `&(ca[0])` and `&(ca[1])`.
2. Define another function that takes a character pointer `pa` as an argument. Inside the function, print out the values of `&pa` and `&(pa[0])` and `&(pa[1])` and `++pa`.
3. Set up a global character array `ga` and initialize it with the letters of the alphabet. Call the two functions using this global as the parameter. Compare the values that you print out.
4. In the main routine, print out the values of `&ga` and `&(ga[0])` and `&(ga[1])`.
5. Before running your program, write down which values you expect to match, and why. Account for any discrepancies between your expected answers and observed results.

It takes some discipline to keep all this straight! Our preference is always to define the parameter as a pointer, since that is what the compiler rewrites it to. It's questionable programming style to name something in a way that wrongly represents what it is. But on the other hand, some people feel that:

`int table[]`   instead of   `int *table`

explains your intentions a bit better. The notation `table[]` makes plain that there are several more int elements following the one that table points to, suggesting that the function will process them all.

Note that there is one thing that you can do with a pointer that you cannot do with an array name: change its value. Array names are not modifiable l-values; their value cannot be altered. See Figure 9-4 (the functions have been placed side by side for comparison; they are all part of the same file).

pointer argument	**array argument**	**pointer non-argument**

`fun1(int *ptr)`
`{`
`    ptr[1]=3;`
`    *ptr = 3;`
`    ptr = array2;`
`}`
	`fun2(int arr[])`
	`{`
	`    arr[1]=3;`
	`    *arr = 3;`
	`    arr = array2;`
	`}`
		`int array[100], array2[100];`
		`main()`
		`{`
		`    array[1]=3;`
		`    *array = 3;`
		`    array = array2;/*FAILS*/`
		`}`

Figure 9-4 Valid Operations on Arrays that are Arguments

The statement `array = array2;` will cause a compiletime error along the lines of "cannot change the value of an array name". But it is valid to write `arr = array2;` because `arr`, though declared as an array, is actually a pointer.

Indexing a Slice

An entire array is passed to a function by giving it a pointer to the zeroth element, but you can give it a pointer to any element, and pass in just the last part of the array. Some people (primarily Fortran programmers) have extended this technique the other way. By passing in an address that is one before the start of the array (`a[-1]`), you can effectively give the array an index range of 1 to N, instead of 0 to N - 1.

If, like many Fortran programmers, you are used to programming algorithms where all the arrays have bounds 1 to N, this is very attractive to you. Unhappily, this trick goes completely outside the Standard (Section 6.3.6, "Additive Operators," is where it is prohibited), and indeed is specifically labelled as causing undefined behavior, so don't tell anyone you heard it from me.

It is very simple to achieve the effect that Fortran programmers want: just declare all your arrays one element larger than needed so that the index ranges from 0 to N. Then only use elements 1 to N. No muss, no fuss. It's that easy.

Arrays and Pointers Interchangeability Summary

Caution: don't read this unless you've read and understood the preceding chapter, or it may cause permanent brain-fade.

1. An array access `a[i]` is always "rewritten" or interpreted by the compiler as a pointer access `*(a+i);`
2. Pointers are always just pointers; they are never rewritten to arrays. You can apply a subscript to a pointer; you typically do this when the pointer is a function argument, and you know that you will be passing an array in.
3. An array declaration in the specific context (only) of a function parameter can equally be written as a pointer. An array that is a function argument (i.e., in a call to the function) is always changed, by the compiler, to a pointer to the start of the array.
4. Therefore, you have the choice for defining a function parameter which is an array, either as an array or as a pointer. Whichever way you define it, you actually get a pointer inside the function.
5. In all other cases, definitions should match declarations. If you defined it as an array, your extern declaration should be an array. And likewise for a pointer.

C Has Multidimensional Arrays...

Some people claim that C doesn't have multidimensional arrays. They're wrong. Section 6.5.4.2 of the ANSI standard and its footnote number 69 says:

> When several "array of" specifications *(i.e., the square brackets that denote an index)* are adjacent, a multidimensional array is declared.

...But Every Other Language Calls Them "Arrays of Arrays"

What these people mean is that C doesn't have multidimensional arrays **as they appear in other languages**, like Pascal or Ada. In Ada you can declare a multidimensional array as shown in Figure 9-5.

```
apples : array(0..10, 1..50) of real;
```

or an array of arrays, like this:

```
type vector is array(1..50) of real;
    oranges : array(0..10) of vector;
```

Ada

Figure 9-5 Ada Example

But you can't mix apples and sauerkraut. In Ada, multidimensional arrays and arrays of arrays are two completely different beasts.

The opposite approach was taken by Pascal, which regards arrays of arrays and multidimensional arrays as completely interchangeable and equivalent at all times. In Pascal you can declare and access a multidimensional array as shown in Figure 9-6.

```
var M : array[a..b] of array[c..d] of char;
    M[i][j] := c;
```

Pascal

It is customary to make the convenient abbreviations:

```
var M : array[a..b,c..d] of char;
    M[i,j] := c;
```

Figure 9-6 Pascal Example

The Pascal User Manual and Report[1] explicitly says that arrays of arrays are equivalent to and interchangeable with multidimensional arrays. The Ada language is more tightly buttoned, and strictly maintains the distinction between the arrays of arrays and multidimensional arrays. In memory they look the same, but it makes a big difference as to what types are compatible and can be assigned to individual rows of an array of arrays. It's rather like choosing between a float and an int for a variable: you choose the type that most closely reflects the underlying data. In Ada, you would typically use a multidimensional array when you have independently varying indices, such as the Cartesian coordinates specifying a point. You would typically use an array of arrays when the data is more hierarchical, for example, an array [12] months of [5] weeks of [7] days for

1. *The Pascal User Manual and Report,* Springer-Verlag, 1975, p. 39.

keeping a daily record of something, but also being able to manipulate an entire week or month at a time.

Handy Heuristic

What "Multidimensional" Means in Different Languages
The Ada standard explicitly says arrays of arrays and multidimensional arrays are different.
The Pascal standard explicitly says arrays of arrays and multidimensional arrays are the same.
C only has what other languages call arrays of arrays, but it also calls these "multidimensional."

C's approach is somewhat unique: The only way to define and reference multidimensional arrays is with arrays of arrays. Although C refers to arrays of arrays as multidimensional arrays, there is no way to "fold" several indices such as `[i][j][k]` into one Pascal-style subscript expression such as `[i,j,k]`. If you know what you're doing, and you don't mind a nonconforming program, you can calculate what the equivalent offset to `[i][j][k]` is, and just reference with one subscript `[z]`. This is not recommended practice. Worse still, `[i,j,z]` is a legal (comma-separated) expression. It doesn't reference several subscripts, though. C thus supports what other languages generally call "arrays of arrays," but C blurs the distinction and confuses the hell out of many people by also calling these "multidimensional arrays." (See Figure 9-7.)

In C, you can declare a 10-by-20 multidimensional array of characters like this:

```
char carrot[10][20];
```

or (in a way that is a little more "array of array"-ish) like this:

```
typedef char vegetable[20];
vegetable carrot[10];
```

In either case, an individual character is accessed by `carrot[i][j]`

The compiler will resolve that to `*( *(carrot + i) +j)` at compiletime.

Figure 9-7 Arrays of Arrays

Although its terminology refers to "multidimensional arrays," C really only supports "arrays of arrays." It greatly simplifies this rather taxing area if your mental model is that whenever you see "array" in C, think "vector" (i.e., one-dimensional array of something, possibly another array).

Handy Heuristic

Arrays in C Are One-Dimensional

Whenever you see "array" in C, think "vector," that is, a **one-dimensional** array of *something*, possibly another array.

How Multidimensional Arrays Break into Components

Note carefully how multidimensional arrays can be broken into their individual component arrays. If we have the declaration

```
int apricot[2][3][5];
```

this tells us that the same storage can be looked at in any of the ways shown in Figure 9-8.

Normally, one assigns between two identical types, integer to integer, double to double, and so on. In Figure 9-8, we see that each individual array within the array-of-array-of-arrays is compatible with a pointer. This is because an array-name in an expression decays into a "pointer-to-element" (Rule 1 on page 242). In other words, you can't assign an array to something of the same type because an array cannot be assigned to as a whole. You can load a *pointer* with the value of the array-name because of the "array-name in an expression decays into a pointer" rule.

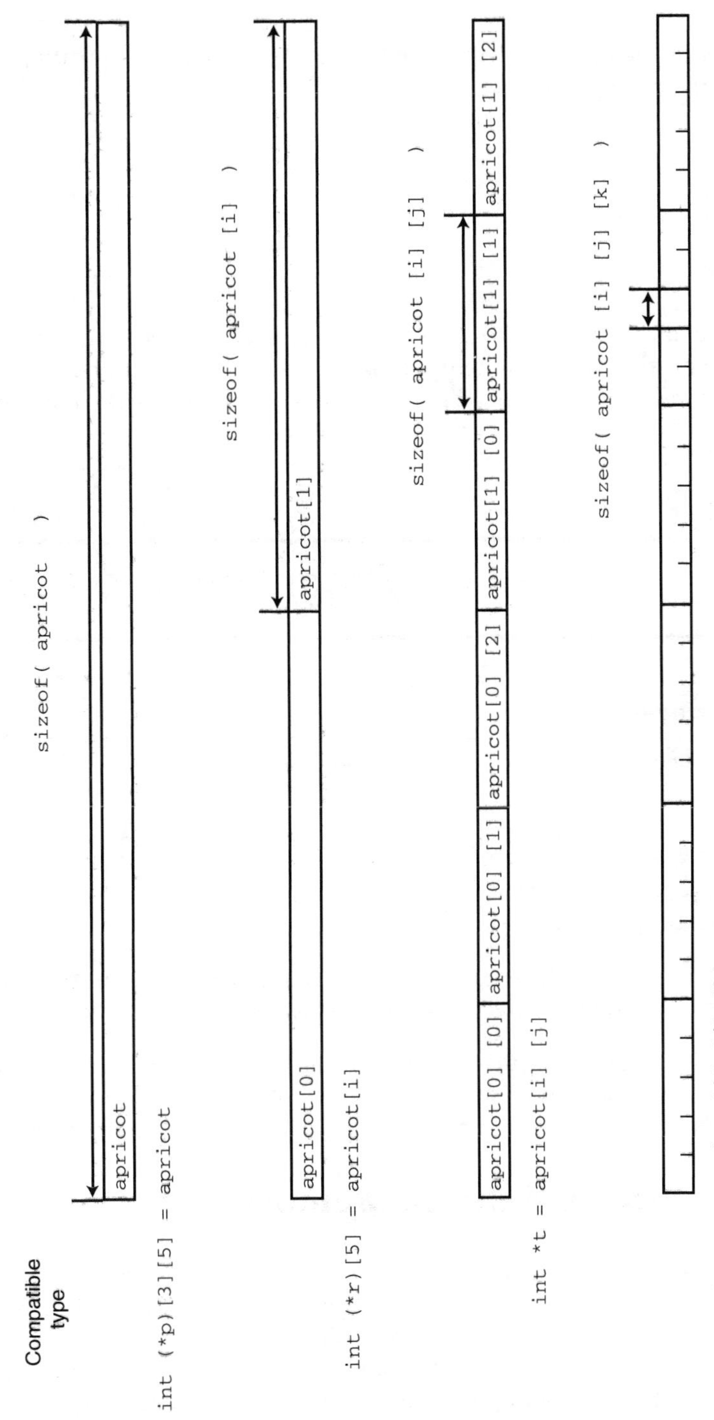

Figure 9-8 Multidimensional Array Storage

The dimensions of the array that the pointer points to make a big difference. Using the declarations in the example above,

```
r++;
t++;
```

will increment `r` and `t` to point to their next respective element, (in both cases, this element is itself an array). The increment will be scaled by quite different amounts, because `r` points to array elements that are three times larger than the array elements to which `t` points.

Programming Challenge

Hooray for Arrays!

Using the declarations:

```
int apricot[2][3][5];

int (*r)[5] = apricot[0];
int *t = apricot[0][0];
```

write a program to print out the initial values of `r` and `t` in hex (use the `%x` printf conversion character to print a hex value), increment these two pointers, and print out their new values.

Before running the program, predict how many bytes the increment will actually cause to be added to each pointer. Use Figure 9-8 on page 255 to help you.

How Arrays Are Laid Out in Memory

With multidimensional arrays in C the rightmost subscript varies fastest, a convention known as "row major addressing". Since the "row/column major addressing" term really only makes sense for arrays with exactly two dimensions, a preferred term is "rightmost subscript varies fastest". Most algorithmic languages use "rightmost subscript varies fastest", the major exception being Fortran, which prefers leftmost, or column major addressing. The subscript that varies fastest makes a difference to the way in which arrays are laid out in memory. Indeed, if you pass a C matrix to a Fortran routine, the matrix will appear transposed—a huge kludge, advantage of which is occasionally taken.

		lowest address		⟷		highest address		
C	int a[2][3]	a[0][0]	a[0][1]	a[0][2]	a[1][0]	a[1][1]	a[1][2]	rightmost sub. varies fastest
Fortran	dim a(2,3)	a(1,1)	a(2,1)	a(1,2)	a(2,2)	a(1,3)	a(2,3)	leftmost sub. varies fastest

Figure 9-9 Row Major versus Column Major Order

The most common use of multidimensional arrays in C is to store several strings of characters. Some people point out that rightmost-subscript-varies-fastest is advantageous for this (adjacent characters in each string are stored next to each other); this is not true for multidimensional arrays of characters in leftmost-subscript-varies-fastest order.

How to Initialize Arrays

In the simplest case, one-dimensional arrays can be given an initial value by enclosing the list of values in the usual curly braces. As a convenience, if you leave out the size of the array, it creates it with the exact size to hold that number of initial values.

```
float banana [5] = { 0.0, 1.0, 2.72, 3.14, 25.625 };

float honeydew[] = { 0.0, 1.0, 2.72, 3.14, 25.625 };
```

You can only assign to an entire array during its declaration. There's no good reason for this restriction.

Multidimensional arrays can be initialized with nested braces:

```
short cantaloupe[2][5] = {
 {10, 12, 3, 4, -5},
 {31, 22, 6, 0, -5},
 } ;
```

```
int rhubarb[][3] ={ {0,0,0}, {1,1,1}, };
```

Note that you can include or omit that comma after the last initializer. You can also omit the most significant dimension (*only* the most significant dimension), and the compiler will figure it out from the number of initializers given.

If the array dimension is bigger than the number of initial values provided, the remaining elements are set to zero. If they are pointers they are set to NULL. If they are floating point elements, they are set to 0.0. In the popular IEEE 754 standard floating point implementation, as used on the IBM PC and Sun systems, the bit pattern for 0.0 is the same as integer zero in any case.

Programming Challenge

Check Those Bit Patterns

Write a one-liner to check whether or not the bit pattern for floating point 0.0 is the same as integer zero on your system.

Here's how you initialize a two-dimensional array of strings:

```
char vegetables[][9] = { "beet",
                         "barley",
                         "basil",
                         "broccoli",
                         "beans" };
```

One useful facility is to set up an array of pointers. String literals can be used as array initializers, and the compiler will correctly store the addresses in the array. Thus,

```
char *vegetables[] = { "carrot",
                       "celery",
                       "corn",
                       "cilantro",
                       "crispy fried potatoes" }; /* works fine */
```

Notice how the initialization part is identical to the array of arrays of characters initialization. Only string literals have this privilege of initializing pointer arrays. Arrays of pointers can't be directly initialized with non-string types:

```
int *weights[] = {            /* will NOT compile successfully */
                  {1,2,3,4,5},
                  {6,7},
                  {8,9,10}
                };            /* will NOT compile successfully */
```

The secret to doing this kind of initialization is to create the rows as individual arrays, and use those array names to initialize the original array.

```
int row_1[] = {1,2,3,4,5,-1};  /* -1 is end-of-row marker */
int row_2[] = {6,7,-1};
int row_3[] = {8,9,10,-1};

int *weights[] = {
                  row_1,
                  row_2,
                  row_3
 };
```

More about this in the next chapter, on pointers. But first, a little light relief.

Some Light Relief—Hardware/Software Trade-Offs

To be a successful programmer, you have to have a good understanding of the software/hardware trade-offs. Here's an example that I heard from a friend of a friend. Many years ago there was a large mail order company which used an old IBM legacy mainframe to maintain their names and addresses database. This machine had no batch control mechanism at all.

The IBM system was obsolete, and was due to be replaced by a Burroughs system. That shows you how long ago it was—Burroughs (or "Rubs-rough" as we anagramatically adapted it) hasn't existed since the mid 1980's when it merged with Sperry to produce Unisys. Meanwhile, back at the data processing ranch, the IBM was running at full capacity, including a night shift. The sole task of the night operator was to wait until the day jobs finished, then start up four more jobs at intervals throughout the night.

The data processing manager realized that he could free up the night operator to work on the day shift if he could find a way to start batch jobs at certain times. IBM quoted a figure in the tens of thousands of dollars for the software upgrade to provide this. Nobody wanted to spend that much on a machine that was soon to be decommissioned. It so happened that the machine was divided into several partitions, each with an attached terminal. It was possible to arrange the night jobs so that each one was initiated from a different terminal. Each terminal could be set up so that the job would start as soon as the return key was pressed. The manager then designed and built four copies of a device he called the "phantom finger," illustrated in Figure 9-10.

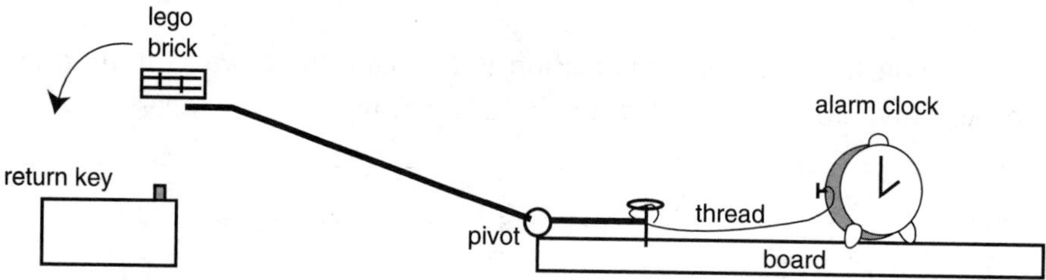

Figure 9-10 The Phantom Finger

Each night a phantom finger was set up behind each terminal. At 2 a.m., the first alarm would go off. The winder on the alarm wound up the thread, pulling out a pin, which caused the arm to drop onto the return key. The Lego brick snapped off, avoiding key bounce or repetition, and the job started.

Although everyone laughed at this contraption, it worked for six months until the new system was in place! Within hours of the new system being commissioned, systems engineers from both Burroughs and IBM were begging for a surviving example of these Rube Goldberg devices. And that is the essence of a successful software-hardware trade-off.

Programming Solution

Playing Around with Array/Pointer Arguments

```
char ga[] = "abcdefghijklm";

void my_array_func( char ca[10] )
{
    printf(" addr of array param = %#x \n",&ca);
    printf(" addr (ca[0]) = %#x \n",&(ca[0]));
    printf(" addr (ca[1]) = %#x \n",&(ca[1]));
    printf(" ++ca = %#x \n\n", ++ca);
}

void my_pointer_func( char *pa )
{
    printf(" addr of ptr param = %#x \n",&pa);
    printf(" addr (pa[0]) = %#x \n",&(pa[0]));
    printf(" addr (pa[1]) = %#x \n",&(pa[1]));
    printf(" ++pa = %#x \n", ++pa);
}

main()
{
    printf(" addr of global array = %#x \n",&ga);
    printf(" addr (ga[0]) = %#x \n",&(ga[0]));
    printf(" addr (ga[1]) = %#x \n\n",&(ga[1]));
    my_array_func( ga );
    my_pointer_func( ga );
}
```

Playing Around with Array/Pointer Arguments (Continued)

And the output is:

```
% a.out
 addr of global array = 0x20900
 addr (ga[0]) = 0x20900
 addr (ga[1]) = 0x20901

 addr of array param = 0xeffffa14
 addr (ca[0]) = 0x20900
 addr (ca[1]) = 0x20901
 ++ca = 0x20901

 addr of ptr param = 0xeffffa14
 addr (pa[0]) = 0x20900
 addr (pa[1]) = 0x20901
 ++pa = 0x20901
```

It looks a little weird at first sight, to see the address of an array parameter not equal to the address of the first element of the array parameter, but it's true enough.

You can win a lot of money-making bets with novice C programmers about what the sizeof operator will produce in this circumstance.

More About Pointers 10

Never forget that when you point the finger at someone, three of your own fingers are pointing back at you...

—Suspicious spy's proverb

---

the layout of multidimensional arrays...an array of pointers is an "Iliffe vector"...using pointers for ragged arrays... passing a one-dimensional array to a function... using pointers to pass a multidimensional array to a function... using pointers to return an array from a function... using pointers to create and use dynamic arrays... some light relief—the limitations of program proofs

---

The Layout of Multidimensional Arrays

Multidimensional arrays are uncommon in systems programming and, not surprisingly, C does not define the elaborate runtime routines that other languages require to support this feature. For some constructs, like dynamic arrays, programmers must allocate and manipulate memory explicitly with pointers rather than have the compiler do the work. For another construct (multidimensional arrays as parameters), there is no way of expressing the general case in C at all. This chapter covers these issues. By now, everyone is familiar with the layout of a multidimensional array in memory. If we have the declaration

```
char pea[4][6];
```

some people think of the two-dimensional array having its individual rows laid out in a table, as in Figure 10-1.

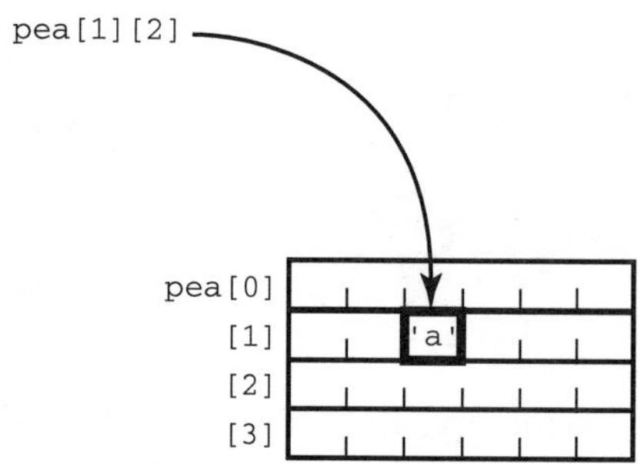

Figure 10-1 Presumed Memory Layout of a Two-dimensional Array

Never allow a programmer like this to park your car. The storage and a reference to an individual element are actually laid out in linear memory as shown in Figure 10-2.

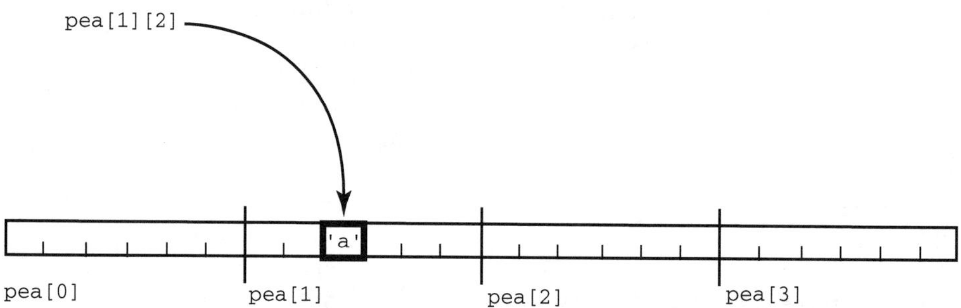

Figure 10-2 Actual Memory Layout of a Two-dimensional Array

The rules for array subscripting (see Chapter 9, page 242) tell us that to evaluate the l-value `pea[i][j]`, we take whatever is at `pea[i]` and then get the character at offset `[j]` from there. Thus, `pea[i][j]` is resolved by the compiler as

```
* ( *(pea + i) + j )
```

But (and here's the key point!) the meaning of "`pea[i]`" varies depending on how `pea` was defined. We'll come back to this expression in a minute, but first let's take a look at a very common and important C data structure: the one-dimensional array of pointers to strings.

An Array of Pointers Is an "Iliffe Vector"

A similar effect to a two-dimensional array of char can be obtained by declaring a one-dimensional array of *pointers*, each of which points to a character string.[1] The C declaration for this is

```
char * pea[4];
```

Software Dogma

Reminder on Declaration Syntax

Note that `char *turnip[23]` declares "turnip" to be a 23-element array, each element of which is a pointer to a character (or a character-string—there's no way to distinguish from the declaration). Think of it as parenthesized—`(char *) turnip[23]`. It is not what it appears to be if you read it from left to right: a pointer to a 23-element array of characters. This is because index brackets have a higher precedence than the pointer asterisk. This is fully covered in Chapter 3 on declarations.

An array of pointers that implements support for a multidimensional array is variously termed an "Iliffe vector," a "display," or a "dope vector." A display is also used in Britain to mean a vector of pointers to active stack frames of lexically enclosing procedures (as an alternative to a static link followed by a linked list). An array of pointers like this is a powerful programming technique that has wide applicability outside C. In diagram form, we have the structure shown in Figure 10-3.

1. We're simplifying things very slightly here—the pointer is actually declared as a pointer to a single character. By declaring a pointer-to-character we leave open the possibility that other characters can be stored adjacent to the first, implicitly forming a string. A declaration like

```
char (* rhubarb[4])[7];
```

is truly the way we declare an array of pointers to strings. This is never seen in practice, as it constrains the size of the pointed-to arrays unnecessarily (to be exactly seven characters long).

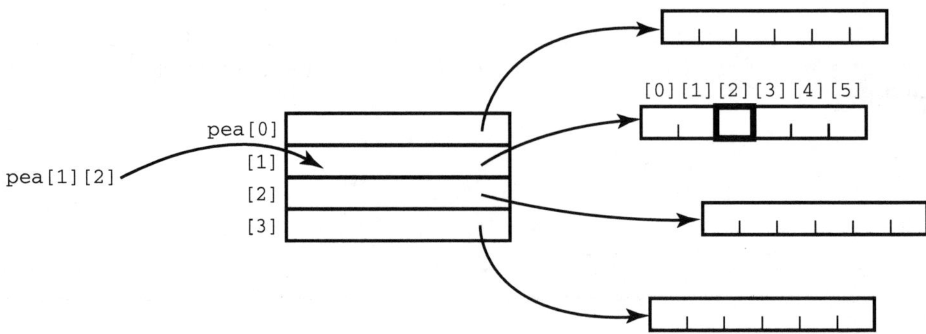

Figure 10-3 An Array of Pointers-to-String

The array must be initialized with pointers to memory allocated for the strings, either at compile time with a literal initializer, or at runtime with code like this:

```
for (j=0;j<=4;j++) {
    pea[j] = malloc( 6 );
```

Another approach is to malloc the entire x by y data array at once,

```
malloc(row_size * column_size * sizeof(char) ) ;
```

then use a loop to assign pointers to locations within that region. The entire array is guaranteed to be stored in contiguous memory in the order that C allocates static arrays. It reduces the bookkeeping overhead of calls to malloc, but prevents you from freeing an individual string when you're done with it.

Software Dogma

When You See squash[i][j]—You Don't Know How It Was Declared!

One problem with being able to double-subscript a two-dimensional array and a one-dimensional array of pointers is that looking at the reference `squash[i][j]` does not tell you whether squash was declared as:

```
int squash[23][12];        /* array [23] of array[12] of int */
```

or

```
int * squash[23];          /* an Iliffe vector of 23 pointers-to-int */
```

or

```
int ** squash;             /* pointer to a pointer to int */
```

or even

```
int (* squash)[12];        /* pointer to array-of-12-ints */
```

This is similar to the inability (inside a function) to tell whether an array or a pointer was passed as the actual argument, of course, for the same reason: array names as l-values "decay" into pointers.

The identical reference `squash[i][j]` works for accessing any of these definitions, though the kind of access is different in the different cases.

Just as with an array of arrays, an individual character in an Iliffe vector will be referenced with two indices, (e.g., `pea[i][j]`). The rules for pointer subscripting (see Chapter 9, page 242) tell us that `pea[i][j]` becomes:

```
* ( *(pea + i) + j )
```

Does this look familiar? It should. It's exactly the same expression to which a multidimensional array reference decomposes, and it is explained this way in many C books. There's one big problem, however. Although the two subscripts look identical in the source, and both decompose to the identical pointer expression, a different kind of reference is done in each case. Tables 10-1 and 10-2 show the distinction.

Table 10-1 `char a[4][6]`*—An Array-of-Arrays*

`char a[4][6]`—An Array-of-Arrays

compiler symbol table has `a` as address 9980

runtime step 1: get value `i`, scale it by the size of a row (6 bytes here), and add it to 9980

runtime step 2: get value `j`, scale it by the size of an element (1 byte here), add it to previous step's result

runtime step 3: get the contents from address (9980 + `i`*scale-factor1 + `j`*scale-factor2)

`a[i][j]`

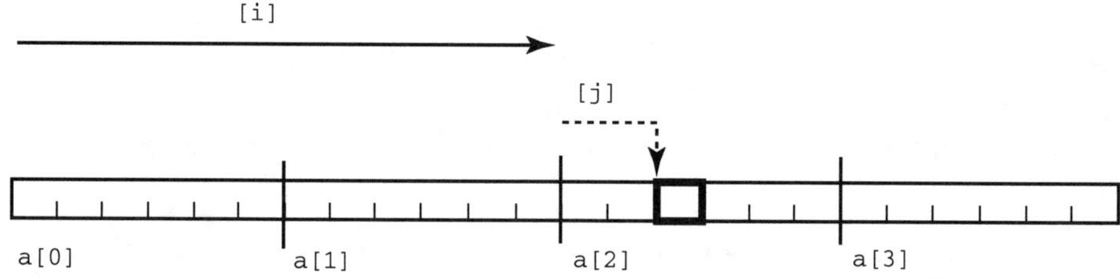

The definition `char a[4][6]` says `a` is an array [4], each element of which is an array [6], each element of which is a `char`. So the look-up goes to the *i*'th of the four arrays (steps over *i* six-byte arrays to get there), then gets the *j*'th character in that array.

Table 10-2 `char *p[4]`*—An Array of Pointers-to-String*

`char *p[4]`—An Array of Pointers-to-String

compiler symbol table has `p` as address 4624

runtime step 1: get value `i`, scale it by the size of a pointer (4 bytes here), and add it to 4624

runtime step 2: get the contents from address (4624+ scaled value `i`), say '5081'

runtime step 3: get value `j`, scale it by the size of an element (1 byte here), add it to 5081

runtime step 4: get the contents from address (5081+`j`)

`p[i][j]`

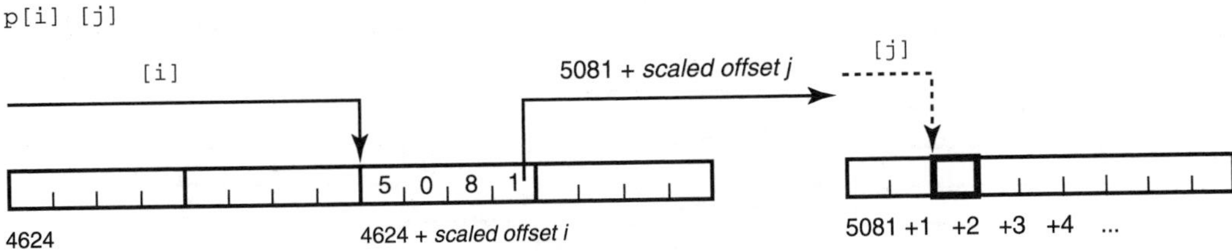

The definition `char * p[4]` says `p` is an array [4], each element of which is a pointer-to-char. So the look-up can't even be completed unless the pointers have been filled in to point to characters (or arrays of characters). Assuming everything has been given a value, the look-up goes to the *i*'th element of the array (each element is a pointer), retrieves the pointer value there, adds j to it, and retrieves whatever is at *that* address.

This works because of rule 2 in Chapter 8: *a subscript is always equivalent to an offset from a pointer.* Thus, `turnip[i]` selects an individual element, which happens to be a pointer; then applying subscript `[j]` to this yields `*(pointer + j)`, which reaches a single character. This is merely an extension of a[2] and p[2] both evaluating to a character, as we saw in the previous chapter.

Using Pointers for Ragged Arrays

Iliffe vectors are an old compiler-writing technique, first used in Algol-60. They were originally used to speed up array references, and on limited-memory machines to simplify keeping only part of an array in main memory. Neither of these uses is as applicable on modern systems, but Iliffe vectors are valuable in two other ways: for storing tables where the rows are different lengths, and for passing arrays of strings in a function call. If you need to store 50 strings which can vary in length up to 255 characters, you could declare the following two-dimensional array:

```
char carrot[50][256];
```

This reserves the 256 characters for each of the fifty strings, even if in practice some of them are only one or two bytes long. If you do this a lot, it can be wasteful of memory. One alternative is to use an array of pointers-to-strings, and note that the second level arrays don't all have to be the same size, as shown in Figure 10-4.

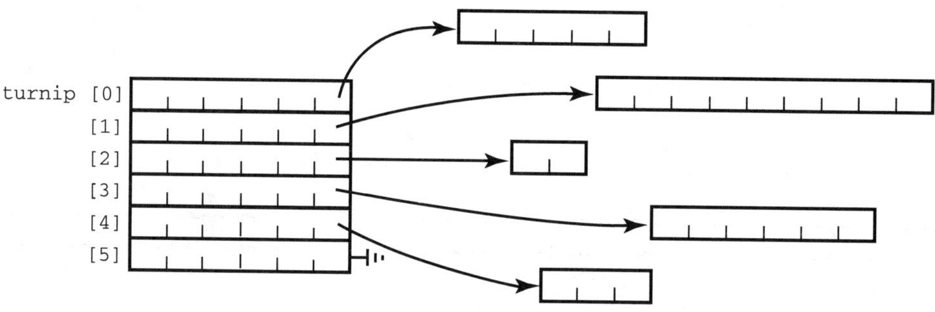

Figure 10-4 A Ragged String Array

If you declare an array of pointers to strings, and allocate memory for these strings as needed, you will be much more frugal with machine resources. Some people call these "ragged arrays" because of the uneven right-hand ends. You can create one by filling the Iliffe vector with pointers to strings which already exist, or by allocating memory for a fresh copy of the string. Both of these approaches are shown in Figure 10-5.

```
char * turnip[UMPTEEN];
char my_string[] = "your message here";
```

```
        /* share the string */
turnip[i] = &my_string[0];
```

```
        /* copy the string */
turnip[j] =
    malloc( strlen(my_string) + 1 );
strcpy(turnip[j], my_string);
```

Figure 10-5 Creating a Ragged String Array

Wherever possible with strings, don't make a fresh copy of the entire string. If you need to reference it from two different data structures, it's much faster and uses less store to duplicate the pointer, not the string. Another performance aspect to consider is that Iliffe vectors may cause your strings to be allocated on different pages in memory. This could detract from locality of reference and cause more paging, depending on how, and how frequently, you reference the data.

Handy Heuristic

How Array and Pointer Parameters Are Changed by the Compiler

The "array name is rewritten as a pointer argument" rule isn't recursive. An array of arrays is rewritten as a "pointer to arrays" *not* as a "pointer to pointer".

Argument is:		Matches Formal Param:	
array of array	`char c[8][10];`	`char (*c)[10];`	pointer to array
array of pointer	`char *c[15];`	`char **c;`	pointer to pointer
pointer to array	`char (*c)[64];`	`char (*c)[64];`	*doesn't change*
pointer to pointer	`char **c;`	`char **c;`	*doesn't change*

The reason you see `char ** argv` is that `argv` is an array of *pointers* (i.e., `char *argv[]`). This decays into a pointer to the element, namely a pointer to a pointer. If the `argv` parameter were actually declared as an array of *arrays* (say, `char argv[10][15]`) it would decay to `char (* argv)[15]` (i.e., a pointer to an array of characters) *not* `char ** argv`.

For Advanced Students Only

Take a moment to refer back to Figure 9-8, "Multidimensional Array Storage," on page 255. See how the variables labelled "compatible type" down the left side of that diagram exactly match how you would declare the corresponding array as a function argument (shown in the table above).

This is not too surprising. Figure 9-8 shows how an array name in an expression decays into a pointer; the table above shows how an array name as a function argument decays into a pointer. Both cases are governed by a similar rule about an array name being rewritten as a pointer in that specific context.

Figure 10-6 shows all combinations of valid code. We see:

- all three functions take same type of argument, an array [2][3][5] or a pointer to an array[3][5] of int.
- all three variables, `apricot, p, *q` match the parameter declaration of all three functions.

```
my_function_1( int fruit [2][3][5] ) { ; }
my_function_2( int fruit [][3][5] ) { ; }
my_function_3( int (*fruit)[3][5] ) { ; }
```

```
int apricot[2][3][5];

my_function_1( apricot );
my_function_2( apricot );
my_function_3( apricot );
```

```
int (*p) [3][5] = apricot;

my_function_1( p );
my_function_2( p );
my_function_3( p );
```

```
int (*q)[2][3][5] = &apricot;

my_function_1( *q );
my_function_2( *q );
my_function_3( *q );
```

Figure 10-6 All Combinations of Valid Code

Programming Challenge

Check It Out

Type in the C code in Figure 10-6 and try it for yourself.

Passing a One-Dimensional Array to a Function

One-dimensional arrays of any type can be used as function arguments in C. The parameter is rewritten as a pointer to its first element, so you may need a convention for indicating the total size of the array. There are two basic methods:

- Send an additional parameter that gives the number of elements (this is what `argc` does)
- Give the last element in the array a special value to indicate the end of data (this is what the nul character at the end of a string does). The special value must be one that can't otherwise occur in the data.

Two-dimensional arrays are a little bit trickier, as the array is rewritten as a pointer to the first row. You now need two conventions, one to indicate the end of an individual row, and one to indicate the end of all the rows. The end of an individual row can be signified by either of the two methods that work for one-dimensional arrays. So can the end of all the rows. We are passed a pointer to the first element of the array. Each time we increment the pointer, we get the address of the next row in the array, but how do we know when we have reached the limit of the array? We can add an additional row filled with some out-of-bound value that won't otherwise occur—if there is one. When you increment the pointer, check to see if it has reached this row. Alternatively, define yet another parameter that gives the total number of rows.

Using Pointers to Pass a Multidimensional Array to a Function

The problem of marking the extent of the array would be solvable with the ugly methods described above. But we also have the problem of declaring the two-dimensional array argument inside the function, and that's where the real trouble lies. C has no way to express the concept "the bounds of this array can vary from call to call." The C compiler insists on knowing the bounds in order to generate the correct code for indexing. It is technically feasible to handle this at runtime, and plenty of other languages do, but this is not the C philosophy.

About the best we can do is to give up on two-dimensional arrays and change `array[x][y]` into a one-dimensional `array[x+1]` of pointers to `array[y]`. This reduces the problem to one we have already solved, and we can store a null pointer in the highest element `array[x+1]` to indicate the end of the pointers.

Software Dogma

There Is No Way in C to Pass a General Multidimensional Array to a Function

This is because we need to know the size of each dimension, to do the correct scaling for address arithmetic. There is no way in C of communicating this data (which will change with each call) between the actual and formal parameters. You therefore have to give the size of all but the leftmost dimension in the formal parameter. That in turn restricts the actual parameter to arrays where all but the leftmost dimension must match in size.

```
invert_in_place( int a[][3][5] );
```

can be called by either of:

```
int b[10][3][5]; invert_in_place( b );
int c[999][3][5]; invert_in_place( c );
```

But arbitrary 3-dimensional arrays like:

```
int fails1[10][5][5];  invert_in_place( fails1 );/* does NOT compile */
int fails2[999][3][6]; invert_in_place( fails2 );/* does NOT compile */
```

fail to compile.

Arrays of two or more dimensions cannot be used as parameters in the general case in C. You cannot pass a general multidimensional array to a function. You can pass specific arrays of known prespecified size, but it cannot be done in the general case.

The most obvious way is to declare a function prototype like this:

Attempt 1

```
my_function( int my_array [10][20] );
```

Although this is the simplest way, it is also the least useful, as it forces the function to process only arrays of exactly size 10 by 20 integers. What we really want is a means of specifying a more general multidimensional array parameter, such that the function can operate on arrays of any size. Note that the size of the most significant dimension does not have to be specified. All the function has to know is the sizes of all the other dimensions, and the base address of the array. This provides enough information to "step over" a complete row and reach the next one.

Attempt 2

We can legally drop the first dimension, and declare our multidimensional array as:

```
my_function( int my_array [][20] );
```

This is still not good enough, as all the rows are still constrained to be exactly 20 integers long. The function could equally be declared as:

```
my_function( int (* my_array)[20] );
```

The brackets around `(* my_array)` in the parameter list are absolutely necessary to ensure that it is translated as a single pointer to a 20-element array of int's, and not an array of 20 pointers-to-int. Again, though, we are tied to an array of size twenty in the rightmost dimension.

Software Dogma

Conformant Arrays

As originally designed, Pascal had the same functionality gap as C—there was no way to pass arrays of different sizes to the same function. In fact Pascal was worse, because it could not even support the case of one-dimensional arrays, which C can. Array bounds were part of the signature of a function, and a type mismatch would occur if argument sizes did not match in all respects. Pascal code like the following failed:

```
var apple : array[1..10] of integer;
procedure invert( a: array[1..15] of integer);
invert(apple); { fails to compile! }
```

Conformant Arrays (Continued)

To repair this defect, the Pascal standardization language-meisters dreamed up a concept called *conformant arrays*—a better name would have been *confuse 'em arrays*. It's a protocol for communicating array sizes between actual and formal parameters. It's not immediately apparent to normal programmers how it works, and it's not in any other mainstream languages. You have to write code like the following:

```
procedure a(fname: array[lo..hi:integer] of char);
```

The data names `lo` and `hi` (or whatever you called them) get filled in with the corresponding array bounds from the actual parameter in each call. Experience has shown that many programmers find this confusing. In solving for the general case, the language designers also made the simplest case of literal fixed array bounds illegal:

```
1 procedure a(fname: array[1..70] of char);
E --------------------------^--- Expected identifier
```

This aspect of the language definition clearly runs counter to the expectations of many programmers, and generates numerous support calls to this day. We regularly get an escalation about this "Pascal compiler bug" every couple of months on the Sun compiler team. There are other problems with Pascal-conformant arrays; for example, a conformant array of characters does not have string type (because its type isn't denoted by an array type), so even though it is an array of characters, it cannot be used where a string is expected! Conformant formal array parameters cause more grief for Pascal programmers than just about anything else, except maybe interactive I/O. Worse still, some people are now talking about adding conformant arrays to C.

Attempt 3

The third possibility is to give up on two-dimensional arrays and change the organization to an Iliffe vector; that is, create a one-dimensional array of pointers to something else. Think of the parameters of the main routine. We are used to seeing `char * argv[];` and even sometimes `char ** argv;`, reminding ourselves of this makes the notation easy to unscramble. Simply pass a pointer to the zeroth element as the parameter, like this (for a two-dimensional array):

```
my_function( char **my_array );
```

But you can only do this if you first change the two-dimensional array into an array of pointers to vectors!

The beauty of the Iliffe vector data structure is that it allows arbitrary arrays of pointers to strings to be passed to functions, but *only* arrays of pointers, and *only* pointers to strings. This is because both strings and pointers have the convention of an explicit out-of-bound value (`NUL` and `NULL`, respectively) that can be used as an end marker. With other types, there is no general foolproof out-of-bound value and hence no built-in way of knowing when you reach the end of a dimension. Even with an array of pointers to strings, we usually use a count `argc` of the number of strings.

Attempt 4

The final possibility is again to give up on multidimensional arrays, and provide your own indexing. This roundabout method was surely what Groucho Marx had in mind when he remarked, "If you stew cranberries like applesauce, they taste more like plums than rhubarb does."

```
char_array[ row_size * i + j ] = ...
```

This is easy to get wrong, and should make you wonder why you are using a compiler at all if you have to do this kind of thing by hand.

In summary, therefore, if your multidimensional arrays are all fixed at the exactly same size, they can be passed to a function without trouble. The more useful general case of arrays of arbitrary size as function parameters breaks down like this:

- One dimension—works OK, but you need to include count or end-marker with "out-of-bound" value. The inability of the called function to detect the extent of an array parameter is the cause of the insecurity in `gets()` that led to the Internet worm.

- Two dimensions—can't be done directly, but you can rewrite the matrix to a one-dimensional Iliffe vector, and use the same subscripting notation. This is tolerable for character strings; for other types, you need to include a count or end-marker with "out-of-bound" value. Again, it relies on protocol agreement between caller and called routines.

- Three or more dimensions—doesn't work for any type. You must break it down into a series of lesser-dimension arrays.

The lack of support for multidimensional arrays as parameters is an inherent limitation of the C language that makes it much harder to write particular kinds of programs (such as numerical analysis algorithms).

Using Pointers to Return an Array from a Function

The previous section analyzed passing an array to a function as a parameter. This section examines data transfer in the opposite direction: returning an array from a function.

Strictly speaking, an array cannot be directly returned by a function. You can, however, have a function returning a pointer to anything you like, including an array. Remember, declaration follows use. An example declaration is:

```
int (*paf())[20];
```

Here, paf is a function, returning a pointer to an array of 20 integers. The definition might be:

```
int (*paf())[20] {
    int (*pear)[20];          /* declare a pointer to 20-int array */
    pear = calloc( 20,sizeof(int));
    if (!pear) longjmp(error, 1);
    return pear;
}
```

You would call the function like this:

```
int (*result)[20];            /* declare a pointer to 20-int array */
        ...
result = paf();               /* call the function */

(*result)[3] = 12;            /* access the resulting array */
```

Or wimp out, and use a struct:

```
struct a_tag {
                int array[20];
            } x,y;

struct a_tag my_function() { ... return y }
```

which would also allow:

```
x=y;
x=my_function();
```

at the expense of having to use an extra selector x in accessing the elements:

```
x.array[i] = 38;
```

Make sure you don't return a pointer to an auto variable (see Chapter 2 for more details).

Handy Heuristic

Why Does a Null Pointer Crash `printf`?

One question that gets asked over and over again is, "Why does a null pointer argument to printf crash my program?" People seem to want to write code like this:

```
char *p = NULL;
    /* . . . */
printf("%s", p );
```

and not have it crash. Customers sometimes complain, "It doesn't crash when I do that on my HP/IBM/PC." They want printf to print the empty string when given a null pointer.

The problem is that the C standard lays down that the argument for a `%s` specifier shall be a pointer to an array of characters. Since `NULL` is not such a pointer (it's a pointer, but not to an array of characters), the call falls into "undefined behavior."

Why Does a Null Pointer Crash `printf`?

Since the programmer has coded something wrongly, the question is, "At what point do you wish to bring this to his or her attention?" If you insist that printf should handle a null pointer as though it were valid, which other routines in libc should also do this? What should strcmp() do if one of its arguments is null? Do you want to let printf helpfully do what it thinks the programmer meant (likely allowing the program to run into bigger trouble later on), or do you want to check the program at the earliest available point?

The Sun libc chooses the second of these alternatives. Other libc vendors have chosen the first which, while arguably friendlier, is also less safe. There is also the question of consistency. Which other routines in libc are you going to extend by allowing null pointers?

Using Pointers to Create and Use Dynamic Arrays

Programmers use dynamic arrays when we don't know the size of the data in advance. Most languages that have arrays also provide the ability to set their size at runtime. They allow the programmer to calculate the number of things to be processed, then create an array just big enough to hold them all. Historic languages like Algol-60, PL/I, and Algol-68 permitted this. Newer languages like Ada, Fortran 90, and GNU C (the language implemented by the GNU C compiler) also let you declare arrays the size of which is set at runtime.

However, arrays are static in ANSI C—the size of an array is fixed at compiletime. C is so poorly supported in this area that you can't even use a constant like this:

```
const int limit=100;
char plum[limit];
          ^^^
            error: integral constant expression expected
```

We won't ask embarrassing questions about why a `const int` isn't regarded as being an integral constant expression. The statement is legal in C++, for example.

It would have been easy to introduce dynamic arrays with ANSI C, since the necessary "prior art" was there. All that would be needed is to change the line in Section 5.5.4 from

```
direct-declarator [ constant-expression opt ]
```

to

```
direct-declarator [ expression opt ]
```

It would actually have simplified the definition by removing an artificial restriction. The language would still have been compatible with K&R C, and it would have provided some useful functionality. Because of the strong desire to adhere to the original simple design goals of C, this was not done. Fortunately, it is possible to get the effect of dynamic arrays (at the expense of doing some pointer manipulation ourselves).

Handy Heuristic

Learning from a Program's Messages

It can be instructive to use the `strings` utility to look inside a binary to see the error messages a program can generate. You don't even have to look in the binary if the software has been internationalized and keeps its messages in a separate file. If you did this for `yacc` you would notice that its error messages changed in a significant way between two recent releases. Specifically, the error message

```
% strings yacc
        :
        too many states
```

became

```
% strings yacc
        :
        cannot expand table of states
```

The reason is that yacc was upgraded so that its internal tables are now dynamically allocated, and expanded as needed.

Software Dogma

Meaningful Error Messages

Interesting strings also occur in compilers. The following strings were all allegedly found in an Apollo C compiler:

```
00  cpp says it's hopeless but trying anyway
14  parse error: I just don't get it
77  you learned to program in Fortran, didn't you?
```

and our own favorite:

```
033 linker attempting to "duct tape" this "gerbil" of a program
```

maybe that's why the linker is also called the binder...

These (possibly apocryphal) messages can be appreciated here as an in joke by an audience of computer programmers. However, only use humor appropriately. One programmer (not at Sun) coded a message into a networking driver that said "Bad bcb: we're in big trouble now." It was the default case in a switch statement that, according to the protocol manual, would never occur.

Naturally, it did occur; but not until the system was in production use in the field. The customer site that got the message had a dozen or so mainframes attended round-the-clock by operators. All console messages were printed and operators were expected to sign the log confirming that the messages were read.

When this one came out, they called their supervisor, at 6 a.m., who promptly called the vendor's programmer at 3 a.m. Pacific Time. The supervisor explained that, because their processing environment was crucial to staying in business, the operators had to take all such messages very seriously, so what did this one mean?

Note that the message wasn't profane, and it told the programmer what went wrong. The problem was that it needlessly alarmed the customer. An immediate new release was made with a single change. The message became:

```
"buffer control block 35 checksum failed."
"packet rejected - inform support - not urgent."
```

Two lines is quite acceptable for a rare message like this.

Keep messages informative, non-inflammatory, and try to avoid unprofessional language such as profanity, colloquialisms, humor, or even exaggerations. Especially when it will save you being called out at 3 a.m.

Here's how a dynamic array can be effected in C. Fasten your seat belt; this may be a bumpy ride. The basic idea is to use the `malloc()` (memory allocation) library call to obtain a pointer to a large chunk of memory. Then reference it like an array, using the fact that a subscripted array decays to a pointer plus offset.

```
#include <stdlib.h>
#include <stdio.h>
 . . .
int     size;
char    *dynamic;
char    input[10];
printf("Please enter size of array: ");
size = atoi(fgets(input,7,stdin));
dynamic = (char *) malloc(size);
 . . .
dynamic[0] = 'a';
dynamic[size-1] = 'z';
```

Dynamic arrays are also useful for avoiding predefined limits. The classic example of this is in a compiler. We don't want to restrict the number of symbols by having tables of fixed sizes; but we don't want to start with a huge fixed-size table, as we may run out of room for other stuff. So far, so good.

Handy Heuristic

Reporting Bugs Improves Products

A few years ago we added some code to one of our Pascal compilers so that it would grow an internal table of include filenames on demand. This table started out with a dozen empty slots, and when a source file nested include statements more than 12 deep, the table was supposed to grow automatically to cope with it.

All significant software has bugs of one kind or another, and in this case, a programmer got the code wrong. The net result was that when the compiler tried to grow the table, it core dumped. This is very bad; a compiler should never abort, no matter what input you give it.

It caused particular problems for one large customer in Europe, who had a large suite of power generation control Pascal software that it was trying to port to Sun workstations. Most of their programs had nested includes more than 12 deep, so they frequently found the compiler core dumping. At this point the customer made two mistakes: it did not report the problem, and it did not adequately investigate the problem.

Fixing reported problems is one of our highest priorities, but we can only fix problems that we know about. It is unusual in Pascal to nest include files deeply (the include mechanism is not even part of standard Pascal). None of our test suites or other customers reported the problem. As a result, the power generation company found the problem persisted into the next release of the compiler.

By now it had become a crisis for the customer, with many hundreds of thousands of dollars at stake. Untold numbers of golf games were disrupted as Company Vice Presidents (ours and theirs) were called in to pronounce on the matter. The outcome was that the customer dispatched a senior engineer on an international flight to the U.S. to visit me and plead for the bug to be fixed. This was the first anyone in the compiler department had seen of the bug! We fixed it immediately and sent him home with a patched compiler. But I was also struck by the fact that they could easily have coded around the bug if they had invested a small amount of time in investigating exactly what caused it. The moral of this story is two-fold:

1. Report to customer support all the product defects that you find. We can only fix the bugs that we know about and can reproduce (another source of frustration for us is government agencies who report problems but "for security reasons" will not provide even sanitized versions of the code that reproduces them).

2. Zen and the art of software maintenance suggests that you should spend a little time investigating any bugs you find; there may be an easy workaround.

What we really want is the ability to grow a table as needed, so the only limit is the overall amount of memory. And this is indeed possible if you don't declare your arrays directly, but instead allocate them at runtime on the heap. There is a library call, `realloc()`, that reallocates an existing block of memory to a different (usually larger) size, preserving its contents while doing this. Whenever you want to add an entry to your dynamic table, the operation becomes:

1. Check whether the table is already full.
2. If it is, `realloc` the table to a larger size. Check that the reallocation succeeded.
3. Add the entry.

In C code, this looks like:

```
int     current_element=0;
int     total_element=128;
char    *dynamic = malloc(total_element);

void add_element(char c) {
    if (current_element==total_element-1) {
        total_element*=2;
        dynamic = (char *) realloc(dynamic, total_element);
        if (dynamic==NULL) error("Couldn't expand the table");
    }
    current_element++;
    dynamic[current_element] = c;
}
```

In practice, don't assign the return value from **`realloc()`** directly to the character pointer; if the reallocation fails, it will nullify the pointer, and you'll lose the reference to the existing table!

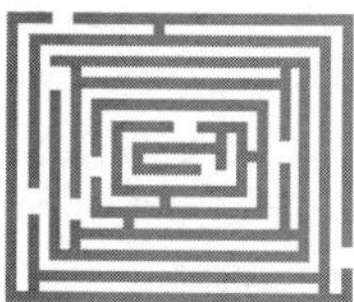

Programming Challenge

Dynamically Growing Your Arrays
Write a `main()` routine to go with the above function, check the original storage array, and fill it with enough elements that you cause a reallocation to take place. Extra Credit: Add a couple of statements to `add_element()` so that it is also responsible for the initial memory allocation of the dynamic area. What are the advantages and disadvantages of doing this? How could you use `setjmp()/longjmp()` to gracefully cope with an error in growing the table?

This technique of simulating dynamic arrays was extensively applied to SunOS in version 5.0. All the important fixed-size tables (the ones that imposed limits which people hit in practice) were changed to grow as needed. It has also been incorporated in much other system software, like compilers and debuggers. The technique is not suitable for blanket use everywhere, for the following reasons:

- The system may slow down at unpredictable points when a large table suddenly needs to grow. The growth multiple is a vital parameter.
- The reallocation operation may well move the entire memory area to a different location, so addresses of elements within the table will no longer be valid. Use indices instead of element addresses to avoid trouble.
- All "add" and "delete" operations must be made through routines that preserve the integrity of the table— changing the table now involves more than just subscripting into it.
- If the number of entries shrinks, maybe you should now shrink the table and free up the memory. The shrinkage multiple is a vital parameter. Everything that searches the table had better know how big it is at any given instant.
- You may have to protect table access with locks to prevent one thread reading it while another thread is reallocating it. Locking may well be required for multithreaded code anyway.

An alternative approach for a dynamically growing data structure is a linked list, at the cost of no random access. A linked list can only be accessed serially (unless you start caching addresses of frequently accessed elements), whereas arrays give you random access. This can make a huge difference to performance.

Some Light Relief— The Limitations of Program Proofs

> *The problem with engineers is that they cheat in order to get results.*
>
> *The problem with mathematicians is that they work on toy problems in order to get results.*
>
> *The problem with program verifiers is that they cheat on toy problems in order to get results.*
>
> —Anonymous

Readers of the Usenet network's C language forum were somewhat surprised to see the following strident posting one summer day. The poster (name omitted to protect the guilty) demanded the universal adoption of formal program proofs, because "anything else is just engineering hacks." His argument included a 45-line proof of the correctness of a three-line C program. In the interests of brevity I've condensed the posting somewhat.

Table 10-3 Program Proofs Posting

```
From: A proponent of program proofs
Date: Fri May 15 1991, 12:43:52 PDT
Subject: Re: Swapping 2 values without a temporary.

Someone asks if the following program fragment (to swap 2 values) works:
        *a ^= *b;       /* Do 3 successive XORs */
        *b ^= *a;
        *a ^= *b;

Here's the answer.
Make the Standard Assumptions that (1) this sequence executes atomically, and
(2) it executes without hardware failure, memory limitations or math failure.
Then after the sequence
            *a ^= *b; *b ^= *a; *a ^= *b;

*a, and *b will have the values f3(a), and f3(b) where:
            f3 = lambda x.(x == a? f2(a) ^ f2(b): f2(x))
```

Table 10-3 Program Proofs Posting (Continued)

```
            f2 = lambda x.(x == b? f1(b) ^ f1(a): f1(x))
            f1 = lambda x.(x == a? *a ^ *b: *x)

or in more readable terms:
            f3(a) = f2(a) ^ f2(b), f3(x) = f2(x) else
            f2(b) = f1(b) ^ f1(a), f2(x) = f1(x) else
            f1(a) = *a ^ *b, f1(x) = *x else
(provided that *a and *b are defined, i.e. a != NULL, b != NULL).

This leads to only two solutions (derived by beta reduction), namely:
            if a and b are the same: f3(a) = f3(b) = 0
            if a and b are different: f3(a) = b, f3(b) = a.

And about reliable verification and debugging:
mathematical verification and proof is the only reliable technique.
Everything else is engineering hacks. And contrary to the commonly
received myth, all of C is easily tractable in this way by
mathematical analysis.
```

Alert readers were even more startled to see the same poster follow up a few minutes later...

Table 10-4 Program Proofs Follow-Up Posting

```
From: A proponent of program proofs
Date: Fri May 15 1991, 13:07:34 PDT
Subject: Re: Swapping 2 values without a temporary.

Where I previously wrote:
        This leads to only two solutions (derived by beta reduction),
namely:
                if a and b are the same: f3(a) = f3(b) = 0
                if a and b are different: f3(a) = b, f3(b) = a.

I actually meant to write
                f3(a) = *b, and f3(b) = *a...
```

Not only did the proof have two errors, but the C program that he "verified" was not in fact correct to start with! It is a quite well known result in C that it is impossible to swap two values (in the general case) without the use of a temporary. In this case, if a and b point to overlapping objects, the algorithm fails. Additionally, the algorithm can't even be applied if one of the values to be swapped is in a register or is a bitfield, since you can't take the address of a bitfield or a register. The algorithm doesn't work if *a or *b are of different-sized types, or if either of them points to an array.

In case anyone is not convinced and still believes that program proofs are ready for prime time, reproduced below is a typical single verification clause from an actual program proof that is believed correct. The clause arises in the proof of a Fourier transform (a clever kind of signal waveform analysis), and was presented in a 1973 report, "On Programming," by Jacob Schwartz of New York University's Courant Institute.

If you find anyone who still believes that program proving is practical, offer them this challenge. We have made a simple change to this proof; please find it. It is possible to identify the amendment from the information that is there. The answer is given at the end of the chapter.

A single verification condition from the proof of a Fast Fourier Transform program

Programmer Health Warning: Don't actually study this!
The purpose of this horrible looking program proof
is to convince you of the impracticality of program proofs!

How would you like to spend your day poring over pages and pages like that? There's a substantial probability that the mere act of reproducing the condition here has introduced errors. How could an entire proof based on reams of conditions like these ever be written out accurately, let alone proved for completeness, consistency, and correctness?

Some people suggest that the complicated notation can be managed by having automated program provers. But how can we be sure that such a program prover has no bugs in it? Perhaps feed the verifier into itself for verification? A moment's reflection reveals why that is not adequate. It's like asking a possible liar, "Do you tell lies?" You cannot trust a denial.

Further Reading

For more detail on the problems with program verification, there's a very readable paper in *Communications of the ACM*, vol. 22, no. 5, May 1979, called "Social Processes and Proofs of Theorems and Programs," written by Richard de Millo, Richard Lipton, and Alan Perlis. It provides the background on why program proofs are not practical now, and probably won't ever be. The primary point that program proofs prove is that the present process of program proving is not a practical proposition. Phew! Let's stick with the "engineering hacks" for now.

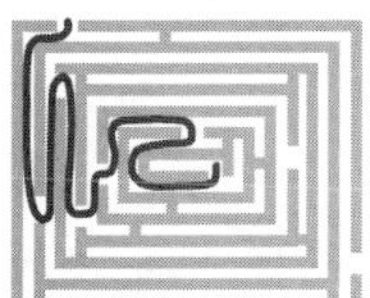

Programming Solution

Answer to Change in Program Proof

OK, I confess. I didn't change anything in the proof. But how can anyone reviewing that complicated text be sure one way or the other? Program proofs are not practical because most programmers find them too inaccessible.

P

You Know C, So C++ is Easy! 11

C++ will do for C what Algol-68 did for Algol.[1]

—David L. Jones

If you think C++ is not overly complicated, just what is a ***protected abstract virtual base pure virtual private destructor****, and when was the last time you needed one?*

—Tom Cargill, *C++ Journal*, Fall 1990

allez-OOP!...abstraction—extracting out the essential characteristics of a thing...encapsulation—grouping together related types, data, and functions...showing some class—giving user-defined types the same privileges as predefined types...constructors and destructors... inheritance—reusing operations that are already defined... multiple inheritance—deriving from two or more base classes... overloading—having one name for the same action on different types... input/output in C++...polymorphism—runtime binding... other corners of C++...if I was going there, I wouldn't start from here... it may be crufty, but it's the only game in town... some light relief—the dead computers society

Allez-OOP!

You know C, so C++ is easy, right? Well, maybe. Most C++ books are three or four hundred pages of densely packed text. It's easy to get lost in a forest of detail, and not be able

1. Algol-68 was a monster-sized language that built on the small and successful Algol-60. It was hard to understand (it had a formal specification written in denotational semantics), hard to implement, and hard to use. But it was "very powerful" or so everyone said. Algol-68 effectively killed Algol-60 by replacing it, before self-destructing in a wave of impracticality. Some people see parallels between the two Algols and the two C's.

to see the semantic wood for the binary trees. On the other hand, for most practical purposes C++ is a superset of ANSI C. Some of the places where it's not are listed in a table at the end of this chapter. But to benefit from the language, or even understand it fully, you have to understand the underlying concepts. This is what people mean when they talk about the "object-oriented paradigm" and the "shift in thinking" needed to program in C++. We strip away the mystique, and describe C++ in simple English, relating it to familiar C features.

It's similar to the window-interface paradigm, when we learned to rewrite our programs for the window system point of view. The control logic was turned inside-out to cope with window_main_loop. Object-oriented programing is in the same vein, but rewriting for the datatype point of view.

Object-Oriented Programming (OOP) is not a new idea; the concept has been around since Simula-67 pioneered it more than a quarter of a century ago. Object-oriented programming (naturally) involves the use of objects as the central theme. There are lots of ways to define a software object; most of them agree that a key element is grouping together data with the code that processes it, and having some fancy ways of treating it as a unit. Many programming languages refer to this type of thing as a "class." There are some ten-dollar definitions of object-oriented programming, too. You can usually follow them only if you already know what OOP is. They generally run something like:

> Object-oriented programming is characterized by inheritance and dynamic binding. C++ supports inheritance through class derivation. Dynamic binding is provided by virtual class functions. Virtual functions provide a method of encapsulating the implementation details of an inheritance hierarchy.

Well, duh! Here we'll make a lightning tour of C++, and describe only the highlights. We'll try to bring the framework of the language into sharp relief by leaving out many less important details. Our approach is to look at the key concepts of OOP, and summarize the C++ features that support each. The concepts build on one another in the logical order in which they appear here. Some of the programming examples deliberately relate to everyday actions like squeezing juice from an orange. Juice-squeezing is not usually achieved by software. We call functions to do it here, to focus attention on the abstraction rather than the lowest-level implementation details. First, let's summarize the terminology and describe it in terms of concepts we already know from C (see Table 11-1).

C++ was known by the name "C with classes" up until about 1985, but it now includes much, much more than this. It was quite a reasonable extension to C at that point, easy to explain, implement, and teach. Then it got caught up in a wave of enthusiasm that has not yet crested, and a lot of other features (including the metaphorical kitchen sink) were added. To halt this, it has been suggested that C++ should have "conservation of featurism": new features in C++ should be subject to growth curtailment rules, like those that apply to pub licenses in the Republic of Ireland—anyone proposing an additional one must surrender two existing ones to be withdrawn from use. You want multiple inheritance? Sure—but you have to give up exceptions and templates!

Table 11-1 The Key Concepts of Object-Oriented Programming

Term	Definition
Abstraction	The process of refining away the unimportant details of an object, so that only the essential characteristics that describe it remain. Abstraction is a design activity. The other concepts are the OOP features that provide it.
Class	A user-defined type, just as int is a built-in type. The built-in types have well-defined operations (arithmetic etc.) on them, and the class mechanism must allow the programmer to specify operations on the class types he or she defines, too. Anything in a **class** is known as a **member** of the class. Member functions of a class (the operations) are also known as **methods**.
Object	A specific variable of a class type, just as `j` may be a specific variable of type `int`. An **object** is also known as an **instance** of a class.
Encapsulation	Grouping together the types, data, and functions that make up a class. In C, a header file provides a very weak example of encapsulation. It is a feeble example because it is a purely lexical convention, and the compiler knows nothing about the header file as a semantic unit.
Inheritance	This is the big one—allowing one class to receive the data structures and functions described in a simpler base class. The derived class gets the operations and data of the base class, and can specialize or customize them as needed. It can also add new data and function members. There's no example in C that suggests the concept of inheritance. C does not have anything resembling this feature.

Now C++ is a rather large language. As a concrete example, the size of a C compiler front-end might be around 40,000 lines; a C++ compiler front-end might be twice as big, or more.

Abstraction—Extracting Out the Essential Characteristics of a Thing

Object-oriented programming starts with object-oriented design. And object-oriented design starts with abstraction.

What's an "object"? Using our new-found skill of "abstraction", consider the similarities between real-world objects, say, a car and a software object. The attributes they share are shown in Table 11-2.

Software Dogma

The Key Idea: Abstraction

Abstraction is the notion of looking at a group of "somethings" (such as cars, invoices, or executing computer programs) and realizing that they have common themes. You can then ignore the unimportant differences and just record the key data items that characterize the thing (e.g., license number, amount due, or address space boundaries). When you do this, it is called "abstraction", and the types of data that you store are "abstract data types". Abstraction sounds like a tough mathematical concept, but don't be fooled—it's actually a simplification.

Table 11-2 Abstraction Example

Automobile Example	Object Characteristic	Software example: A Sorting Program
"Car"	Has a name for the whole thing	"sort"
Input: fuel & oil Output: transportation	Well-defined inputs and outputs	Input: an unordered file Output: a file of ordered records
Engine, transmission, pumps, etc.	Composed of smaller self-contained objects	Modules, header files, functions, data structures
There are many cars and many different types of cars	Can have many instantiations of the object	The implementation should allow several users to sort at once, for example, not rely on one global temporary working space.
The fuel pump doesn't rely on or affect the windshield washer	Those smaller, self-contained objects don't interact except through well-defined interfaces	The routine to read records should be independent of the key comparison routine.
Advancing the timing is not a normal driving task, so there is no control accessible to the driver that directly achieves this.	Can't directly manipulate, or even see, the implementation details	The user should not need to know or be able to take advantage of the specific sort algorithm used (quicksort, heapsort, shellsort, etc.)
Can fit a larger engine without changing the driver's controls	Can change the implementation without changing the user interface	The implementor should be able to substitute a better sort algorithm without affecting any users.

Notice that many of the software attributes are "shoulds." OOP languages like C++ provide the features needed to move these goals from being a desired state to an easily-accomplished fact. Abstraction is useful in software because it allows the programmer to:

- hide irrelevant detail, and concentrate on essentials.
- present a "black box" interface to the outside world. The interface specifies the valid operations on the object, but does not indicate how the object will implement them internally.
- break a complicated system down into independent components. This in turn localizes knowledge, and prevents undisciplined interaction between components.
- reuse and share code.

C supports abstraction through allowing the user to define new types (`struct`, `enum`) that are almost as convenient as the predefined types (`int`, `char`, etc.), and to use them in a similar way. We say "almost as convenient" because C does not allow the predefined operators (`*`, `<<`, `[]`, `+` etc.) to be redefined for user-defined types. C++ removes this barrier. C++ also provides automatic and controlled initialization, cleanup at the end of data's lifetime, and implicit type conversion. All of this is either missing from C, or not present in so convenient a form.

Abstraction creates an abstract data type, and C++ uses the class feature to implement it. This is a view from the top down, looking at the attributes of data types. It is also possible to approach this from the bottom up, and view it in terms of encapsulation: grouping together the various data and methods that implement a type.

Encapsulation—Grouping Together Related Types, Data, and Functions

When you bundle together an abstract data type with its operations, it is termed "encapsulation". Non-OOP languages don't have adequate mechanisms for doing this. There is no way to tell a C compiler, "These three functions are the only valid operations on this particular struct type." There is no way to prevent a programmer from defining additional functions that access the struct in an unchecked or inconsistent manner.

Software Dogma

The Key Idea—
A *Class* Encapsulates (Bundles Together) Code with Its Related Data

When programming first evolved, assembler programs could only operate on bits and words. As high-level languages developed, they provided easy access to the growing variety of hardware operands: floats, doubles, longs, chars, and so on. Some high-level languages enforced strong typing to ensure that only operations appropriate to a variable's type could be done. This was a rudimentary form of class, as it tied together data items with the permissible operations on them. The operations were typically restricted to individual hardware instructions, like "floating-point multiply".

The next development allowed programmers to group together various data types into user-defined records (structs in C), but there was no way to restrict the functions that could manipulate the data or control access to the individual fields. If a struct was visible at all, any part of it could be modified in any way. There was no way to tie the functions to the types so that it was clear they belonged together.

The Key Idea—
A *Class* Encapsulates (Bundles Together) Code with Its Related Data

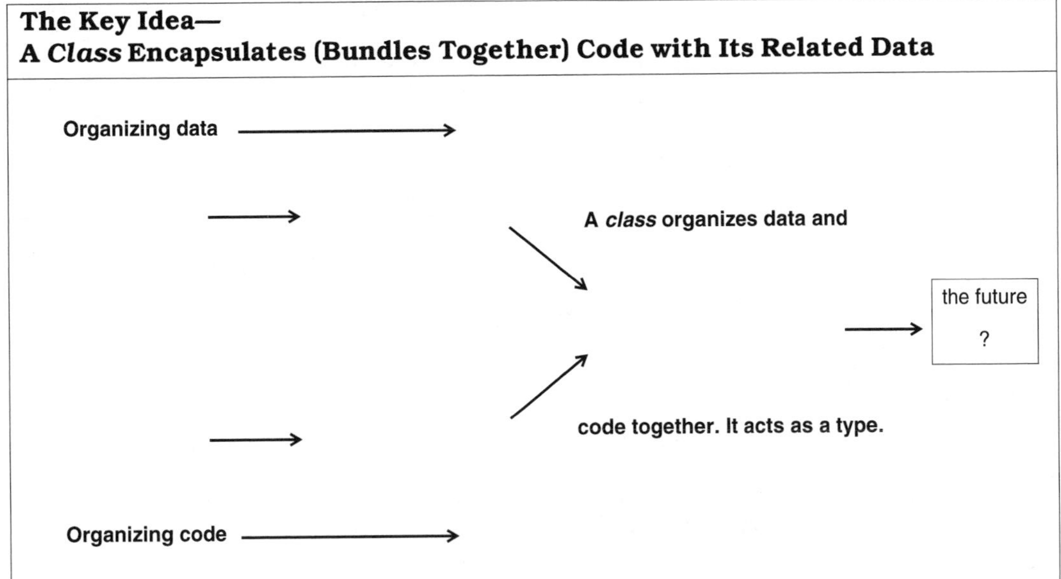
Organizing data
A *class* organizes data and
code together. It acts as a type.
the future
?
Organizing code

The current state of the art is object-oriented programming languages that enforce data integrity by bundling together the user-defined data structures plus the user-defined functions that are allowed to operate on them. No other functions are allowed to access the data. This extends strong typing from built-in data types to user-defined data types.

Showing Some Class—Giving User-Defined Types the Same Privileges as Predefined Types

The C++ class mechanism provides OOP encapsulation. A class is the software realization of encapsulation. A class is a type, just like `char, int, double,` and `struct rec *` are types, and so you must declare variables of the class to do anything useful. You can do pretty much anything to a class that you can do to a type, such as take its size, or declare variables of it. You can pretty much do anything to an object that you can do to a variable, for example, take its address, pass it as an argument, receive it as a function return value, make it a constant value, and so on. An object (variable of a class type) can be declared just like declaring any other variable:

```
Vegetable carrot;
```

Here `Vegetable` is the name of a class (more about how to create the class itself shortly), and `carrot` is an object of that class. It's a helpful convention to start class names with a capital letter.

A C++ class allows user-defined types to:

- group together user-defined types and the operations on them.
- have the same privileges and appearance as built-in types.
- build up sophisticated types out of more basic ones.

Software Dogma

The Key Idea: A Class

A class is just a user-defined type with all the operations on it.

A class is often implemented as a struct of data, grouped together with pointers-to-functions that operate on that data. The compiler imposes strong typing—ensuring that these functions are only invoked for objects of the class, and that no other functions are invoked for the objects.

The C++ class accomplishes all this. It can be compared to a struct, and indeed can be conveniently implemented as a struct. The general form is:

```
class classname {
                availability: declarations
                     . . .
                availability: declarations
            };
```

Availability

The *availability* is a keyword that says who can access the declarations that follow. The *availability* will be one of the following:

`public:`	The declarations that come after are visible outside the class and can be set, called, and manipulated as desired. It's preferred to not make data public. This is because leaving data private keeps the metaphor complete: only the object itself can change things; outside functions have to use member functions, which ensures the data is only updated in a disciplined way.
`protected:`	The declarations that come after are visible to functions inside this class, and to functions in classes derived from this class.
`private:`	The declarations that come after can only be used by the member functions of this class. Private declarations are visible outside the class (the name is known), but they are not accessible.

There are two other keywords, `friend` and `virtual`, that affect availability. These keywords apply to individual declarations, rather than whole groups of them as the ones above. Unlike the other three availability controls, `friend` and `virtual` are not followed by a colon.

`friend`	This says that the function is not a member of the class, but can access private and protected data just as though it were. A friend can be another function or another class.
`virtual`	We have not yet covered the concepts that motivate this, so we'll postpone explaining it till later.

I submitted a formal paper (document number X3J16/93-0121) to the C++ standardization committee, suggesting that all five of the availability keywords should begin with "p", by renaming `friend` to `protégé` (this would also promote internationalization and express the asymmetry of the relationship in a way that `friend` doesn't). The keyword `virtual` should be renamed to `placeholder`, and the descriptive term "pure," which has nothing to do with availability, should be renamed to "empty." This would slightly increase the lexical orthogonality in the language, and if the committee liked the experiment they could extend it to more significant semantic areas of the language.[2] No word yet on whether they'll go for it...

Declarations

The *declarations* are just regular C declarations of functions, types (including other classes), or data. The class binds them together. Each function declaration in the class

2. This is not a facetious suggestion: the misnamed `const` keyword in standard C causes very real problems. Here is an opportunity to avoid similar problems and bring consistency to a thorny area in C++.

needs an implementation, which can be inside the class or (usually) separated out. So the whole thing may look like:

```
class Fruit { public: peel(); slice(); juice();
              private: int weight, calories_per_oz;
            };


// an instance of the class
Fruit melon;
```

Remember, C++ comments start with // and go to the line end.

Programming Challenge

Try Compiling and Running a C++ Program...

It's time to try a C++ program. C++ source files usually have an extension of `.cpp` or `.cc` or `.C`. Create such a file, type in the above code, and add a "hello world" main program. Declare a couple of objects of the fruit class.

On many systems, you invoke the C++ compiler by:

```
CC fruit.cpp
```

Compared with C, it seems you have to shout at the C++ compiler to invoke it. Compile, and run the a.out file. Congratulations—it may not do much, but you have successfully written a C++ class.

The implementation of a member function, when placed outside its class, has some special syntactic sugar on the front.

The syntactic sugar `::` says "Hey! I'm important! I refer to something in a class."

So instead of looking like the regular C function declaration,

```
return-type            functionname(parameters) { . . . };
```

member functions (also known as "methods") will have the form

```
return-type Classname ::      functionname(parameters) { . . . };
```

The `::` is called "the scope resolution operator." The identifier that precedes it is a class to look in. If there's no preceding identifier, it means global scope. If the implementation of `peel()` is put inside the class, it might look like this:

```
class Fruit { public: void peel(){ printf("in peel"); }
                           slice();
                           juice();
              private: int weight, calories_per_oz;
 } ;
```

And, if you separate it out, it will look like this

```
class Fruit { public: void peel();
                           slice();
                           juice();
              private: int weight, calories_per_oz;
} ;

void Fruit::peel(){ printf("in peel"); }
```

The two approaches are semantically equivalent, but the second is more usual and provides benefits for organizing the source more cleanly using include files. The first approach is commonly used for very short functions, and it makes the code automatically expand in line instead of causing a function call.

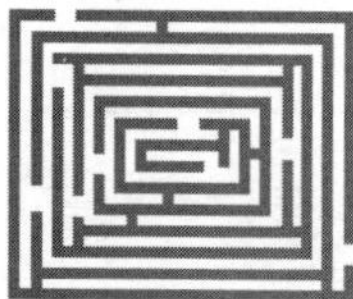

Programming Challenge

Write the Method Bodies

Write similar bodies for `slice()` and `juice()` for the `Fruit` class. Copy the body of peel to start with.

1. In a real system, these methods would presumably operate a robot arm to carry out the desired fruit preparation. In this training exercise, just make each method print out the fact that it has been invoked.
2. Give these methods likely parameters and return types. For example, `slice()` should take an integer parameter indicating the desired number of slices, `juice()` should return a float value representing the number of cc's of juice obtained, and so on. The prototypes in the class definition will have to match the function definitions, of course.
3. Try accessing data in the private part of the class, from inside a method and then from outside.

How to Call a Method

Look at the interesting way to call a function within a class. You have to prefix it with the instance, or class variable, you want it to operate on.

```
Fruit melon, orange, banana;

main() {
        melon.slice();
        orange.juice();
        return 0;
}
```

Then the object does that operation on itself. It's quite similar to some predefined operators; when we write `i++` we are saying "take the `i` object and do the post-increment operation on it." Invoking a member function on a class object is equivalent to the "sending a message to that object" terminology that other object-oriented languages use.

Every method has a `this` pointer parameter implicitly passed to it, allowing an object to refer to itself inside a method. Note how the explicit use of the `this` pointer can be omitted when inside a member function, and it is assumed.

```
class Fruit { public: void peel();
 private: int weight, calories_per_oz;
} ;

void Fruit::peel(){ printf("this ptr=%p", this);
                    this->weight--;
                    weight--;}

Fruit apple;
printf("address of apple=%x",&apple);
apple.peel();
```

Programming Challenge

Call the Methods

1. Make calls to the methods `slice()` and `juice()` that you wrote in the previous exercise.
2. Experiment with accessing the `this` pointer that is the implicitly-passed first argument to every method.

Constructors and Destructors

Most classes have at least one constructor. This is a function that is implicitly called whenever an object of that class is created. It sets initial values in the object. There is also a corresponding clean-up function, called a "destructor," which is invoked when an object is destroyed (goes out of scope or is returned to the heap). Destructors are less common than constructors, and you write the code to handle any special termination needs, garbage collection, and so on. Some people use destructors as a bulletproof way to ensure that synchronization locks are always released on exit from appropriate scopes. So they not only clean up an object, but also the locks that the object held. Constructors and destructors are needed because no one *outside* the class is able to access the private data. Therefore, you need a privileged function *inside* the class to create an object and fill in its initial data values.

This is a bit of a leap from C, where you just initialize a variable with an assignment in its definition, or even leave it uninitialized. You can define several different constructor functions, and tell them apart by their arguments. Constructor functions always have the same name as the class, and look like this:

```
Classname :: Classname (arguments) { . . . };
```

In the fruit example:

```
class Fruit { public: peel(); slice(); juice();
              Fruit(int i, int j); // constructor
              ~Fruit(); // destructor
            private: int weight, calories_per_oz;
            } ;


// constructor body
Fruit::Fruit(int i, int j) { weight=i; calories_per_oz=j; }


// object declarations are initialized by the constructor.
Fruit melon(4,5), banana(12,8);
```

Constructors are needed because classes typically contain structs with many fields, requiring sophisticated initialization. An object's constructor function will be called automatically whenever an object of that class is created, and should never be invoked explicitly by the programmer. For a global, static object, its constructor will be automatically called at program start-up, and its destructor will be called at program exit.

Constructors and destructors violate the "nothing up my sleeve" approach of C. They cause potentially large amounts of work to be done implicitly at runtime on the programmer's behalf, breaking the C philosophy that nothing in the language should require implementation by a hidden runtime routine.

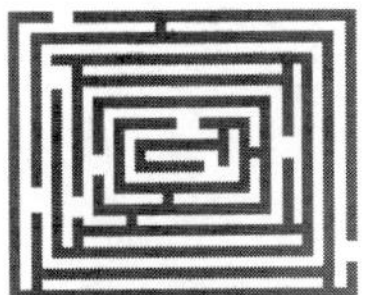

Programming Challenge

Do Something Destructive

Write a body for the `Fruit` destructor including a `printf()` statement, and declare a `Fruit` object in an inner scope. You will need to `#include <stdio.h>` at the start of your program. Then recompile and run the a.out file, checking that the destructor is called when the object goes out of scope.

Inheritance—Reusing Operations that Are Already Defined

Single inheritance occurs when a class specializes, or refines, the data structures and methods of a single base class. That creates a hierarchy, similar to a scientific taxonomy. Each level is a specialization of the one above. Type inheritance is an essential part of OOP, and it is a concept that doesn't really exist in C. Get ready to spring forward with that "conceptual leap"!

Software Dogma

The Key Idea: Inheritance

Deriving one class from another such that all of the other's characteristics are automatically available. Being able to declare types which share some or all of the characteristics of previously-declared types. Being able to share some characteristics from more than one parent type.

Inheritance usually provides increasing specialization as you go from a simple base class (e.g. vehicle) to a more specific derived class (e.g. passenger car, fire truck, or delivery van). It could equally subset or extend the available operations, though. The `shape` class seems to be the popular example of choice in the C++ literature. From a basic `shape`, more specialized configurations of `circle`, `square`, and `pentagon` can be derived. We think it makes more sense if we first consider a real-world example of "class inheritance" in the Linnaean taxonomy of the animal kingdom (see Figure 11-1), and a similar example showing how it relates to the existing C type model.

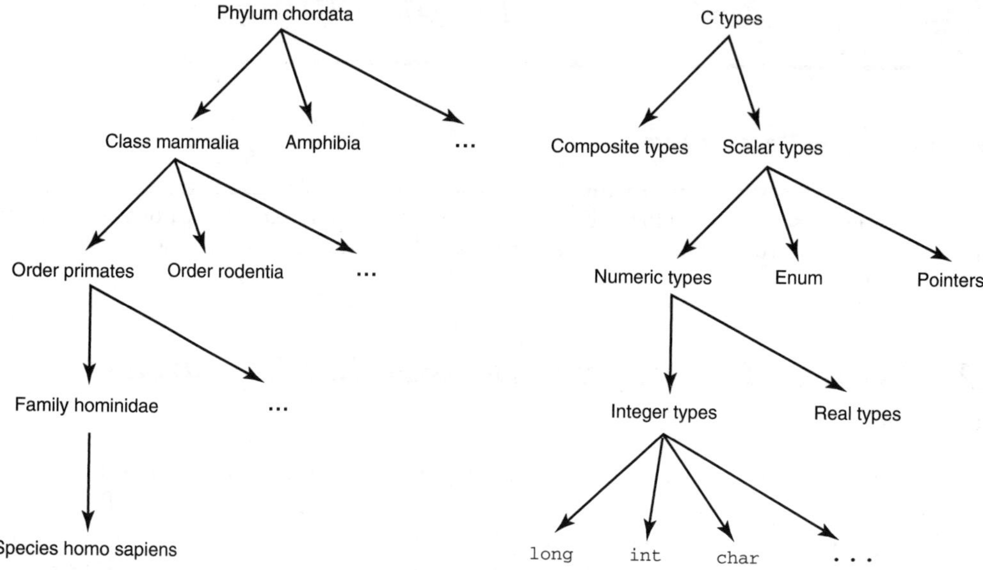

Figure 11-1 Two Real-World Examples of an Inheritance Hierarchy

In the example above:

- The phylum chordata contains every creature that has a notochord (roughly, a spinal cord), and only those creatures. There are 32 phyla in the animal kingdom in all.
- All mammals have a spinal cord. They inherit it by virtue of being "derived" from the chordata phylum. Mammals also have specialized characteristics: they feed their young milk, they have only one bone in the lower jaw, they have hair, a certain bone configuration in the inner ear, two generations of teeth, and so on.
- Primates inherit all the characteristics of mammals (including the quality of having a spinal cord, which mammals inherited from chordates). Primates are further distinguished by forward-facing eyes, a large braincase, and a particular pattern of incisor teeth.
- The hominidae family inherits everything from primates and more distant ancestors. It adds to the class the unique specialization of a number of skeletal modifications suitable for walking upright on two feet. The homo sapiens species is now the only species alive within this family. All other species have become extinct.

To be a little more abstract, the hierarchy of types in C can be similarly analyzed:

- All types in C are either composite (types like arrays or structs, which are composed of smaller elements) or scalar. Scalar types have the property that each value is atomic (it is not composed of other types).
- The numeric types inherit all the properties of scalar types, and they have the additional quality that they record arithmetic quantities.
- The integer types inherit all the properties of numeric types, and they have the additional characteristic that they only operate on whole numbers (no fractional quantities).

The type `char` is a smaller range within the values in the integer family.

Although we can amuse ourselves by showing how inheritance can theoretically be applied to the familiar C types, we note that this model is of no practical use to a C programmer. C does not allow the programmer to create first class new data types, much less data types that inherit attributes from other data types. So a programmer cannot use the type hierarchy in real programs. An important part of OOP is figuring out the hierarchies of the abstract data types in your application. The major novelty that C++ provides, which cannot easily be accomplished by disciplined use of C, is inheritance. Inheritance allows the programmer to make the type hierarchies explicit, and to use the relationships to control code.

Let's invent a class `Apple` that has every characteristic of fruit, and two specialized operations of its own. The two things that are done with apples that are not generally done with other kinds of fruit, are:

- bobbing for apples. You can't bob for pears, for example, as they are denser than apples and sink. Apple bobbing is implemented by the method `bob_for()`.
- making candy apples ("toffee apples" to the British). People don't make caramel-covered grapes, not even in California. Making candy apples is implemented by the method `make_candy_apple()`.

So we make `Apple` a derived class that inherits all the `Fruit` class operations and adds these two specializations of its own. Don't get hung up on how these methods might be implemented. Obviously, they are far removed from usual computing. Remember, we're concentrating on the new concepts, without getting caught up in specific algorithms.

Software Dogma

How C++ Does Inheritance

Inheritance takes place between two classes (and not between individual functions).

An example of a base class is:

```
class Fruit { public: peel(); slice(); juice();
              private: int weight, calories_per_oz;
              } ;
```

An example of class inheritance is:

```
class Apple : public Fruit {
    public:
        void make_candy_apple(float weight);
        void bob_for(int tub_id, int number_of_attempts);
}
```

An example object declaration is:

```
Apple teachers;
```

The example says that `class Apple` is a specialization of the base class `Fruit`. The `public` keyword on the first line of the inherited Apple class controls accessibility into the base class from outside the derived class. It is one of several possibilities too detailed to cover fully here.

The syntax for inheritance is uncomfortable at first. The derived class name is followed by a colon followed by the base class name. It's terse, it doesn't provide much of a hint which is the base class and which the derived, and it doesn't convey any suggestion of specialization. It's not based on an existing C idiom, so orthogonality can't guide us.

Don't confuse nesting one class inside another with inheritance. Nesting just brings one class into another with no special privileges or relationship. Nesting is often used to bring in a container class (a class that implements some data structure, like a linked list, hash table, queue, etc.). Now that templates have been added to C++, these are being used for container classes, too.

Inheritance says *the derived class is a variation of the base class* and there are many detailed semantics governing how they can access each other. It's the difference between a smaller object being one part of many in a larger object (nesting), and one object being a specialization of a more general parent object (inheritance). We wouldn't say that a mammal is nested in a dog; we may say that dogs inherit mammalian characteristics. Figure out which situation you have, and use the appropriate idiom.

Multiple Inheritance—Deriving from Two or More Base Classes

> *C makes it easy to shoot yourself in the foot. C++ makes it harder, but when you do, it blows away your whole leg.*
>
> —Bjarne Stroustrup

Multiple inheritance allows two classes to be combined into one, so that objects of the resulting class would behave as objects of either class. It turns a tree hierarchy into a lattice.

Continuing our `Fruit` metaphor, we might also have a `class Sauces`, and note that some objects that are fruits can also be used as sauces. This gives a type hierarchy featuring multiple inheritance that can be represented as:

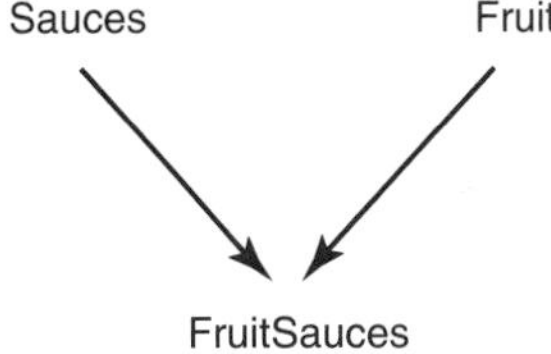

Some likely object declarations would be:

```
FruitSauce orange, cranberry; // Instances that are sauce and fruit
```

Multiple inheritance is much less common than single inheritance, and has been the subject of considerable debate as to whether it should be in the language at all. It's not in other OOP languages like Smalltalk. It is in other OOP languages like Eiffel. We should note that, in practice, type hierarchies tend to look much more like Figure 11-2 than like Figure 11-3.

Multiple inheritance seems a difficult, error-prone feature in both implementation and use. Some people say that no convincing examples have been produced where there was no alternative design avoiding multiple inheritance.

Figure 11-2 Direct Inheritance

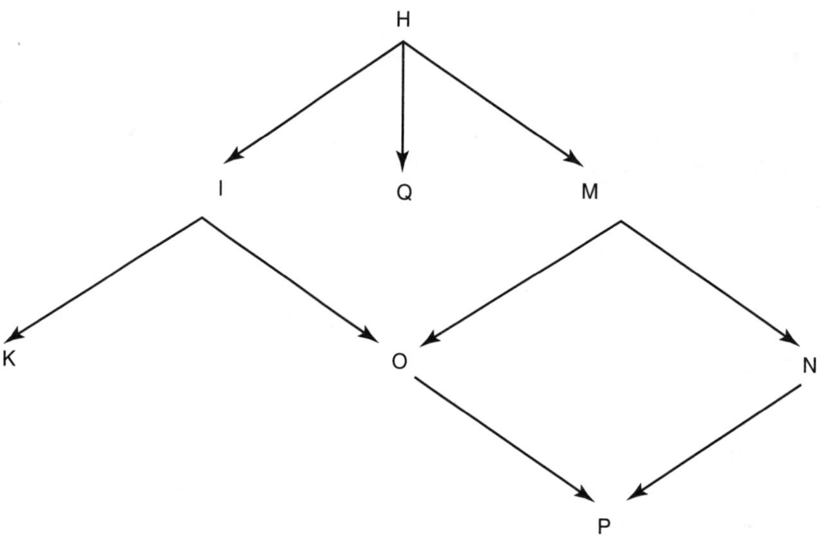

Figure 11-3 Multiple Inheritance

Overloading—Having One Name for the Same Action on Different Types

Overloading simply means reusing an existing name, but using it to operate on different types. The name can be the name of a function, or it can be an operator symbol. Operator overloading is already present in C in a rudimentary way. Virtually all languages overload operators for built-in types.

```
double e,f,g;
int i,j,k;
 . . .
e = f+g;    /* floating-point addition */
i = j+k;    /* integer addition */
```

The + operation is different in the two cases. The first will generate a floating-point add instruction, and the second an integer add instruction. Since the same conceptual operation is being performed, the name or operator should be the same. Since C++ allows the creation of new types, the programmer is given the ability to overload names and operators for those new types too. Overloading allows programmers to reuse function names and most operators, `+`, `=`, `*`, `-`, `[]`, and `()`, giving them additional meanings for user-defined class types. This is all part of the OOP philosophy of treating objects as a composite whole.

Overloading (by definition) is always resolved at compile time. The compiler looks at the types of the operands, and checks that it has seen a declaration of that operator for those types. In order to conserve programmer sanity, you should only overload an operator for a similar operation; don't overload `*` so that it now does division.

How C++ Does Operator Overloading

As an example, let's overload the "+" operator, and define addition for the `Fruit` class. First add the prototype for the operator to the class:

```
class Fruit { public: void peel(); slice(); juice();

                    int operator+(Fruit &f); // overload "+" operator

             private: int weight, calories_per_oz;
            } ;
```

Then provide a body for the overloaded operator function:

```
int Fruit::operator+(Fruit &f) {

        printf("calling fruit addition\n"); // just so we can see

        return weight + f.weight;
}
```

As before, every method is passed an implicit `this` pointer, allowing us to reference the left operand of the operator. The right operand of the addition is the parameter called `f` here; it is an instance of Fruit, and the preceding ampersand indicates it is passed by reference.

The overloaded function can be called like this:

```
Apple apple;
Fruit orange;

int ounces = apple+orange;
```

The precedence and number of operands ("arity" in compiler jargon) remain the same for the overloaded operator as for the original operator. So, you see, C++ says you *can* add apples to oranges, if you define it first. C++ gives the phrase "operator error" a whole new class of meanings. Overloading is also very convenient in C++ I/O, described in the next section.

Input/Output in C++

As well as having the stdio library of C, C++ features some new I/O routines and concepts of its own. There is an I/O interface known as `iostream.h` that helps to make I/O more convenient[3] and more in tune with the object-oriented philosophy.

The operators << (to put, or "insert") and >> (to get, or "extract") are used instead of functions like `putchar()` and `getchar()`.

3. Don't confuse the C++ iostream (formerly known as streams) I/O interface with the unrelated UNIX kernel STREAMS framework for communicating between a device driver and a user process.

The << and >> operators are still used for shift left and right as in C, but they are overloaded for C++ I/O. The compiler looks at the types of their operands to decide whether to generate code for a shift, or for I/O. If the leftmost operand is a stream, I/O was intended. Using operators, not functions, has four big advantages:

- The operators can be defined for every type. Thus, we do not need an individual function or (equivalently) a string format specifier like "`%d`" for each different type.

- There is some notational convenience in using an operator rather than a function when you wish to output multiple messages. Just as you can write an expression `i + j + k + l`, the left-associativity of the operator ensures that you can sensibly chain multiple I/O operands together:

```
cout << "the value is " << i << endl;
```

- It provides an additional layer that simplifies format control and the use of functions like `scanf()`. Let's face it, the `scanf()` family could certainly use a bit of simplifying (despite the fact that the manual for it is quite short).

- It is possible, and desirable, to overload the extract and insert operators (as these double chevrons are called) for reading and writing an entire object as a single operation. This is just an application of overloading as shown in the previous section.

You can make do with C's `stdio.h` functions in C++, but it's worthwhile to switch to the C++ features at an early point.

Polymorphism—Runtime Binding

Everyone has played nethack, so everyone knows that polymorphism is Greek for "many shapes." In C++ it means supporting different methods for related objects, and allowing runtime binding to the appropriate one. The mechanism by which this is supported in C++ is *overloading*—all the polymorphic methods are given the same name, and the runtime system figures out which one is the appropriate one. This is needed when you inherit: sometimes it's not possible to tell at compile time whether you have an object of the base class or the inheriting class. The process of figuring this out and calling the right method is called "late binding," and you tell the compiler you want it by applying the `virtual` keyword to a method.

With ordinary compile-time overloading the signature of the functions must differ enough so that the compiler can tell by looking at the argument types which function is intended. With virtual functions the signatures must be identical and the polymorphism is resolved at run time. Polymorphism is the last highlight of C++ that we will cover, and it is easier to explain with a code example than with text.

Software Dogma

The Key Idea: Polymorphism

Polymorphism refers to the ability to have one name for a function or an operator, and use it for several different derived class types. Each object will carry out a different variant of the operation in a manner appropriate to itself. It starts with "overloading" a name—reusing the same name to represent the same concept with different objects. It is useful because it means that you can give similar things similar names. The polymorphism comes in when the runtime system selects which of these identically named functions is the right one.

Let's start by considering our familiar base class of `Fruit` and adding a method to peel a fruit object. Once again, we won't fill in the details of peeling, just have it print a message.

```
#include <stdio.h>
class Fruit { public: void peel(){printf("peeling a base class fruit\n");}
                      slice();
                      juice();
            private: int weight, calories_per_oz;
           } ;
```

When we declare a fruit object, and invoke the `peel()` method like this,

```
Fruit banana;
banana.peel();
```

we will get the message

```
peeling a base class fruit
```

So far, so good. Now consider deriving our apple class, and *giving this its own method for peeling!* After all, apples are peeled somewhat differently than bananas: you can peel a banana with your thumbs, but you need a knife to peel an apple. We know we can have methods with the same name, as C++ can cope with overloading.

```
class Apple : public Fruit {
        public:
            void peel() {printf("peeling an apple\n");}
            void make_candy_apple(float weight);
};
```

Let's declare a pointer to a fruit, then make it point to an apple object (which inherits from the fruit class), and see what happens when we try peeling.

```
Fruit * p;
p = new Apple;
p->peel();
```

Whoa! If you try it, you'll get output like this:

```
% CC fruits.cpp
% a.out
peeling a base class fruit
```

In other words, the `Apple`-specific method `peel()` wasn't called, the base class's `peel()` was!

Explanation

The reason is that C++ demands that you warn it when you start supplanting base class methods with derived class ones. You warn it by adding the keyword `virtual` to the base class method that you might be replacing. You can see now why we were reticent about explaining `virtual` back on page 301 where we first discovered it. You needed a lot of background information, which we have now covered.

Handy Heuristic

Virtually Impractical

Why isn't `virtual` the default? After all, you can always get the method from the base class by saying:

```
p->Fruit::peel();
```

It's pretty much for the same reason that C originally used the `register` keyword—it's a dumb optimization. So that every method call doesn't involve an extra indirection at runtime, you have to tell the compiler which ones do.

The word `virtual` is a bit of a misnomer in this context. Elsewhere throughout computer science, "virtual" means letting the user see something that is not really there, and supporting the illusion by some means. Here, it means *not* letting the user see something that *is* really there (the base class method). A more meaningful (though impractically long) keyword would be

```
choose_the_appropriate_method_at_runtime_for_whatever_object_this_is
```

or more simply, `placeholder`.

How C++ Does Polymorphism

Adding the keyword `virtual` to our base class method, and making no other changes results in

```
#include <stdio.h>
class Fruit {
    public:  virtual void peel(){printf("peeling a base class fruit\n");}
             slice(); juice();
    private: int weight, calories_per_oz;
 } ;
```

And the compilation and execution is

```
% CC fruits.cpp
% a.out
peeling an apple
```

Exactly as desired. So far, this could all have been achieved at compile time, but polymorphism is a runtime effect. It refers to the process of C++ objects deciding at runtime which function should be called to carry out a particular operation.

The runtime system looks at the object that has called the overloaded method, and chooses the method that goes with that class of object. If this is a derived object, we don't want it to call the base class version. We want it to call the derived class version, but this may not have been seen by the compiler when the base class was compiled. Therefore, this must be done dynamically at runtime, or, in C++ terminology, "virtually."

Single inheritance is usually implemented by having each object contain a pointer `vptr` to a vector `vtbl` of function pointers. There is one of these vectors for each class, and there is one entry in the vector for each method in the class. In this way, the implementation code is shared by all objects of a given class. The vector is laid out so that a given function pointer lies at the same offset in the virtual tables for all subclasses of a class. Each method call can be mapped to a `vtbl` offset at compiletime. At runtime, the call is made indirectly through the pointer at the appropriate offset. Multiple inheritance requires a slightly more complicated scheme with another layer of indirection. If that didn't make sense, draw yourself a picture of it; it's the end of the line for this particular bus.

Fancy Pants Polymorphism

There are a lot more fancy tricks that you can pull with polymorphism, and sometimes it's downright essential. It makes a derived class's method preferred over those of the base class, but still allows the base class ones to be used if no derived ones have been defined. Sometimes a method does not know at compiletime whether it is operating on an object of its own class or one derived from it. Polymorphism says this has to work correctly.

```
main() {
    Apple apple;
    Fruit orange;
     Fruit * p;
```

```
    p=&apple;
    p->peel();

    p=&orange;
    p->peel();
}
```

At runtime, the results will be:

```
% a.out
peeling an apple
peeling a base class fruit
```

Software Dogma

Deep Thought—Polymorphism Has Something in Common with Interposing

Polymorphism and interposing both allow multiple functions to have the same one identifier. Interposing is a bit of a blunt instrument, as it binds every occurrence of the name to the same one definition at compile time. Polymorphism is a little more discerning, as it makes the binding decision on an object-by-object basis at runtime.

Other Corners of C++

There are plenty of smaller C++ concepts not covered in this brief review of the high points. And there are plenty more detailed rules that apply to the concepts mentioned here. However, if you master the material in this chapter you will have a basic understanding of the OOP concepts and how they are expressed in C++. You will have enough of a head start to begin writing experimental C++ programs. And that is the real way, the only way, to learn any programming language.

Among the concepts not covered here, C++ also has:

- Exceptions: borrowed from Ada and also from Clu (an experimental language developed at MIT, in which the key idea is a "cluster"). These are for changing the flow of control for error-handling. They simplify some kinds of error-handling by automatically diverting processing to a part of the program that can process the error.
- Templates: support parameterized types. Like the class/object relationship, a template/function can be thought of as providing a "cookie-cutter" approach to algorithms. Once you get the basic algorithm down, you can plug different types into it. They are similar to the `generic` facility in Ada and parameterized modules in Clu. They have quite complicated semantics. This code:

```
template <class T> T min (T a, T b) { return (a < b) ? a : b; }
```

  allows one to assign any arbitrary type T (for which the < operator has been defined) to the variables a and b and the function min. Some people refer to templates as providing compiletime polymorphism. It's a bit of a stretch, but they mean that a stated operation can be done on a variety of different types, and it's all figured out at compiletime.

- In-lining of functions: a programmer can stipulate that a particular function should be expanded in-line (as though it were a macro) in the instruction stream rather than generating a function call.
- The operators `new` and `delete`, to replace `malloc()` and `free()` function calls. The operators are slightly more convenient (the `sizeof` calculation is done implicitly for example, and the proper constructor/destructor is called). `new` truly creates an object, whereas `malloc` just allocates memory.
- Call-by-reference: C uses only call-by-value (except for arrays). C++ brings call-by-reference into the language.

Software Dogma

C++ Design Goals: That Was Then. This Is Now.

From *SIGPLAN Notices*, vol. 21, no. 10, October 1986
"An Overview of C++," by Bjarne Stroustrup

Section 6. What is Missing?

C++ was designed under severe constraints of compatibility, internal consistency, and efficiency: no feature was included that

[1] would cause a serious incompatibility with C at the source or linker levels.

[2] would cause run-time or space overheads for a program that did not use it.

[3] would increase run-time or space requirements for a C program.

[4] would significantly increase the compile time compared with C.

[5] could only be implemented by making requirements of the programming environment (linker, loader, etc.) that could not be simply and efficiently implemented in a traditional C programming environment.

Features that might have been provided but weren't because of these criteria include garbage collection, parameterized classes, exceptions, multiple inheritance, support for concurrency, and integration of the language with a programming environment. Not all of these possible extensions would actually be appropriate for C++, and unless great constraint is exercised when selecting and designing features for a language, a large, unwieldy, and inefficient mess will result. The severe constraints on the design of C++ have probably been beneficial and will continue to guide the evolution of C++.

Ah, What years those were! The Reagan years, when tomato ketchup was a vegetable, trees were the major source of pollution, and C++ was assured of remaining unencumbered by parameterized classes, exceptions, and multiple inheritance.

If I Was Going There, I Wouldn't Start from Here

There is a property of programming languages known as orthogonality. This refers to the degree to which different features follow the same underlying principles. For example, in Ada, a programmer who learns how packages work will be able to apply this knowledge to generic packages, too. Unhappily, much of C++ is quite unorthogonal. Mastering one feature in C++ provides no clue or mental model that can be applied to other features. Most programmers will take the approach of only using a simpler subset of C++.

Software Dogma

A Simple Subset of C++

C++ features to use:

- classes
- constructors and destructors, but only with very simple bodies
- overloading, including operator overloading and C++ I/O
- single inheritance and polymorphic functions

C++ features to avoid using:

- templates
- exceptions
- virtual base classes
- multiple inheritance

The major purpose of a programming language is to provide a framework for expressing problem solutions in terms which a computer can process. The better a language is at representing this discourse, the more successful it will be. The Fortran language, one of the first high-level languages, provided a powerful means of expressing mathematical formulae (the name "Fortran" means "*For*mula *tran*slation"). The COBOL language addressed itself to file processing, decimal arithmetic and output editing. And it is highly successful in that domain. C gave systems programmers access to many hardware-supported operators. The language didn't "get in the way" with many layers of abstraction.

A language will be successful if its constructs are useful "building blocks" for solving problems in a given domain. Deciding on the "building blocks" of the language is the most important part of language design; the details, like choosing whether a semicolon is a terminator or a separator, cannot be ignored, but the building blocks are critical. How good a language C++ is will be decided on the basis of whether its features are good "building blocks" for solving interesting problems and whether the language can be reliably used by normal programmers.

Some people claim that C++ classes will revolutionize software reuse. Reuse is a nebulous goal in software. Inheritance is not necessarily the panacea that it seems. Those with long memories are reminded of inflated claims made for Ada a decade ago. Let's make an analogy by saying that a computer program is like a book. Then you have libraries of both. And you want to reuse some routines in one of your programs. This corresponds to some paragraphs in the book.

Software Dogma

Design Challenge: The C++ Machine

In the past, some people have built special-purpose computer hardware that would be very efficient at executing a particular language:

Algol-60:	early Burroughs processors
Lisp:	Symbolics Inc.
Ada:	Rational Computers

What would a C++ machine look like? Why have all special language processors come to a sticky end?

This is a trick question—there's no common theme. The market for a single language is always less than for a general machine. Workstations ate the Lisp machine for lunch. The end of the Cold War killed the Ada machine. Burroughs ploughs on as part of Unisys.

The problem is that you can't create any kind of new worthwhile text by cutting and pasting entire paragraphs from other books. The level of abstraction is wrong. You can share text on the level of individual words or letters (this corresponds to individual lines of code or characters), but the effort involved in laboriously cutting them out is higher than the effort involved in deriving them afresh for the new work. And in just the same way, software reuse at the library level has empirically turned out to be less than originally envisioned.

There is a small number of special-purpose routines that can be and are shared: mathematical libraries, a few data structure routines, and sorting and searching libraries. That's about it. These correspond to diagrams or reference tables in a book, which can be lifted wholesale and understood somewhere else.

C++ may be more successful at software reuse than previous languages because its style of inheritance, based on objects, allows data to be inherited as well as code. Ada generics allow this too, but the Ada feature is cumbersome and too abstract for most programmers. To continue the analogy above, C++ makes it easier to check books out from the library, but you still have the problem of copying the relevant parts sensibly.

It May Be Crufty[4], but It's the Only Game in Town

Having seen some of the serious failings in C in the first few chapters of this book, it would be really nice to say that C++ addresses these while retaining the flavor of C. It would be really nice, but it isn't going to happen, because it isn't true. C++ has some point improvements, but it retains many of the flaws of C, and piles up another big layer of complexity on top. The original C philosophy of "no features that need invisible runtime support" has been compromised.

Software Dogma

Improvements in C++ Over C

- The error-prone construct of initializing a char array without enough room for the trailing nul is regarded as an error. `char b[3]="Bob";` will cause an error in C++, but not in C.
- A typecast can be written in the more normal-looking format of `float(i)` as well as the strange-looking C style of `(float)i`.
- C++ allows a constant integer to define the size of an array.

```
const int size=128;
char a[size];
```

  is allowed in C++, but will generate an error message from C.

- Declarations can be intermingled with statements, dropping the C requirement that all declarations precede all statements in a block. It's great that this arbitrary rule was dropped. Since this fix causes an incompatibility with C, why not go the whole way and provide a simpler alternative that fixes the horrible C declaration syntax, too?

Although C++ may be crufty, it's the only game in town. All the major players are behind it. All new development at AT&T is said to be in C++ now. The graphics part of Windows NT (which was later, slower and bigger than expected) was written in C++. Most new software development tools, applications libraries, and advanced technologies are now written in C++, or at least the ANSI C subset of it. But how long will it be before we start to see spectacular bugs like the AT&T network shutdown, caused or aggravated by features in C++ rather than C?

It doesn't matter. C++ will become widely used in spite of its flaws, and we hope it will eventually lead the way to something better.

4. "Crufty */kruhf'tee/* [origin unknown] adj. possibly over-complex"—*The New Hacker's Dictionary*, ed. Eric Raymond, Cambridge, MA, MIT Press, 1991.

Handy Heuristic

Transitioning from C to C++

The best way to get started with C++ is to start programming in its ANSI C subset. Avoid the early translators based on cfront, which generated C code rather than machine code. Using C as a portable machine language really complicated linking and debugging, as cfront mangled all the function names to encode argument information. Name-mangling is a horrible kludge which will likely live on in C++ for a long time. Contrast this with Ada, which does it properly and does not define the semantics by a hacked implementation. Name-mangling is a hack for doing type checking between different files. But it implies that all your C++ rules must be complied with the same compiler as the name-mangling scheme may differ among compilers. This is a big defect in the C++ reuse model as it effectively prevents reuse at the binary level.

Here is a representative sample of the ways that C is not a C++ subset, to give an idea of potential trouble spots.

Restrictions in C++ that are not in C:

- The main() routine may not be called by user code in C++. This is permitted (but most unusual) in C.
- Function prototypes are mandatory in C++, but optional in C.
- Typedef names cannot clash with struct tags in C++, but they can in C (they belong to separate namespaces).
- A cast is required to assign a `void *` pointer to another pointer type in C++; no cast is required in C.
- Features in C++ that mean something different in C:
- There are more than a dozen new keywords in C++. These may be used as identifiers in a C program, but such use will usually generate an error message from a C++ compiler.
- A declaration can appear anywhere a statement can in C++; in C, declarations must appear before statements in a block.
- A struct name in an inner scope will hide an object name in an outer scope in C++, but not in C.
- Character literals have type `char` in C++, but type `int` in C. That is, `sizeof('a')` yields 1 in C++ and a larger value in C.
- Pathological cases involving the `//` comment convention of C++ (as shown in Chapter 2).

There are many more differences, but you now know enough to be dangerous. So go out there and be dangerous. When you're comfortable with the compiler and all the tools working in the ANSI C subset, then spread your wings and start defining your own classes. Choose a good C++ book—look at several, and choose one in a style you like. Make sure it is current with the language, which is still evolving. Make sure it covers exceptions and templates, which were the latest two things added.

Just as with C, C++ standardization is now a joint effort of ISO (Working Group 21), and ANSI X3J16. The most optimistic estimates predict that it will take around six years to standardize the language, finishing in 1996, but make sure your C++ book mentions the ANSI C++ direction.

So What Is a *Protected Abstract Virtual Base Pure Virtual Private Destructor?*

Let's break this down and take it a little bit at a time. The phrase actually decomposes into two parts: a *pure virtual private destructor* that is inherited from a *protected abstract virtual base.*

- A *private destructor* is the function called when an object goes out of scope. "Private" means that it can only be called by a member or friend of the class.
- A *pure virtual* function contains no code itself, but is used to act as a guide for other derived functions through inheritance.
- A *pure virtual destructor* only makes sense if defined by a derived class. Since a destructor automatically does default clean-up actions on a class, like call member or base destructors, there is often no need to explicitly write any code in the destructor definition.

Simple enough. Tackling the second phrase

- An *abstract virtual base* means that the base class is shared by the multiply-inherited classes (it's a "virtual base"), and that it contains at least one pure virtual function, from which other classes derive through inheritance (an "abstract base"). Virtual base classes also have special initialization semantics.
- A *protected abstract virtual base* class is one we inherited "protectedly," so our children know our parentage, but outsiders don't.

So, putting it all together, a *protected abstract virtual base pure virtual private destructor* is

a destructor function, that

- can only be called by members or friends of the class, and
- has no definition in the base class that declares it, but will be defined later in a derived class,
- that (refering to the derived class) shares the multiply inherited base
- which (refering to the base class) is inherited in a protected way.

So What Is a
Protected Abstract Virtual Base Pure Virtual Private Destructor?

And the last time we needed one was...well, we haven't yet! Does this start to remind anyone of the program proof of the Fast Fourier Transform? It certainly ranks alongside it in complexity.

In C++ code, this might look like:

```
class vbc {
 protected: virtual void v()=0;
 private: virtual ~vbc()=0; // private destructor
};
// vbc is an abstract class because it contains pure virtual functions


class X : virtual protected vbc {
 // X inherits vbc virtually, and does it in a way such that
 // vbc's protected members are protected members of X.
 // So vbc is a "protected abstract virtual base" class of X.
    protected: void v() {}
 ~X() { /* do some X destruction */ }
};


// When an X object is destroyed, X::~X is called, and then...
// X's "protected abstract virtual base pure virtual private destructor"
// is called too. So even though it's declared pure, it must be defined.
```

These are the kind of semantics that gives C++ a reputation for being overly complicated. The problem is not any one feature, but rather the complexity of how all the different features interact. We'll stop at this point, and allow the reader to form his or her own conclusions.

Some Light Relief—The Dead Computers Society

There are many and varied computer-related organizations, but the prize for most unusual surely goes to The Dead Computers Society!

Modeled after the "Dead Poets Society," which was actually an appreciation group for classical rhymesters, the Dead Computers Society is an appreciation group for computer architectures that no longer exist. It started as an informal discussion panel at the 1991 ASPLOS ("Architecture Support for Programming Languages and OS's") conference in

Santa Clara, California. A group of friends and colleagues attending the conference noticed that many of them had worked on systems that were now discontinued.

They decided to make light of this by forming the Dead Computers Society and holding an open forum round table on the issues involved. The hope was that an intelligent retrospective would allow future designers to learn from the lessons of the past. Membership of the Dead Computers Society is open to anyone who has helped design, build, or program a computer system that no longer exists, ideally for a company that no longer exists. There are a lot of these; a partial list is shown in Table 11-3.

Table 11-3 Dead Computers

The Dead Computers Honor Roll	
• American Supercomputer Inc.	• Intel iPSC/1
• Ametek/Symult	• Intel iPSC/2
• Astronautics	• Intel/Siemens BiiN
• Burroughs BSP	• Masscomp/Concurrent
• CDC 7600, Cyberplus	• Multiflow
• CHoPP	• Myrias
• Culler Scientific	• Niche
• Cydrome	• Prisma
• Denelcor	• SCS
• Elxsi	• SSI
• Evans & Sutherland CD	• Star Technologies
• ETA/CDC	• Supertek
• FLEX (Flexible Computer)	• Suprenum/Siemens
• Goodyear Aerospace/Loral DataFlow Systems	• Texas Instruments ASC
• Guiltech/SAXPY	• Topologix
• Floating Point Systems AP-line and T-series	• Unisys ISP
• Intel 432	

On the other hand, membership is also open to anyone who just thinks it's a kind of neat idea. At the inaugural meeting, there were over 350 attendees.

The panel moderator tried to draw the members out on the "one single thing that, more than anything else, was responsible for your dead computer." The Elxsi designer said that they had tried to push the technology too much and used ECL (emitter-coupled logic) before it was ready for prime time. However, the chief architect from Multiflow, which went down the tubes around the same time as Elxsi, felt that their decision not to use ECL was one of several factors that ultimately caused Multiflow's demise!

About the only consensus was that management and market conditions were responsible for many, many more bankruptcies than were technical failures. This is understandable; companies that don't listen to their customers *always* go out of business. Companies that try to push the state of the art often succeed.

There were some minor technical themes, like making your product hard to program (e.g. the CDC7600 with two-level memory, or one's complement arithmetic, or the cruel and unusual punishment of 60-bit words) doesn't help. It's not too surprising that no major common technical theme emerged. Maybe there isn't one. One thing is certain, though: we all learn far more from our mistakes than from our successes.

Some Final Light Relief—Your Certificate of Merit!

[Instructions: cut out from book, write your name in, and hand to boss]

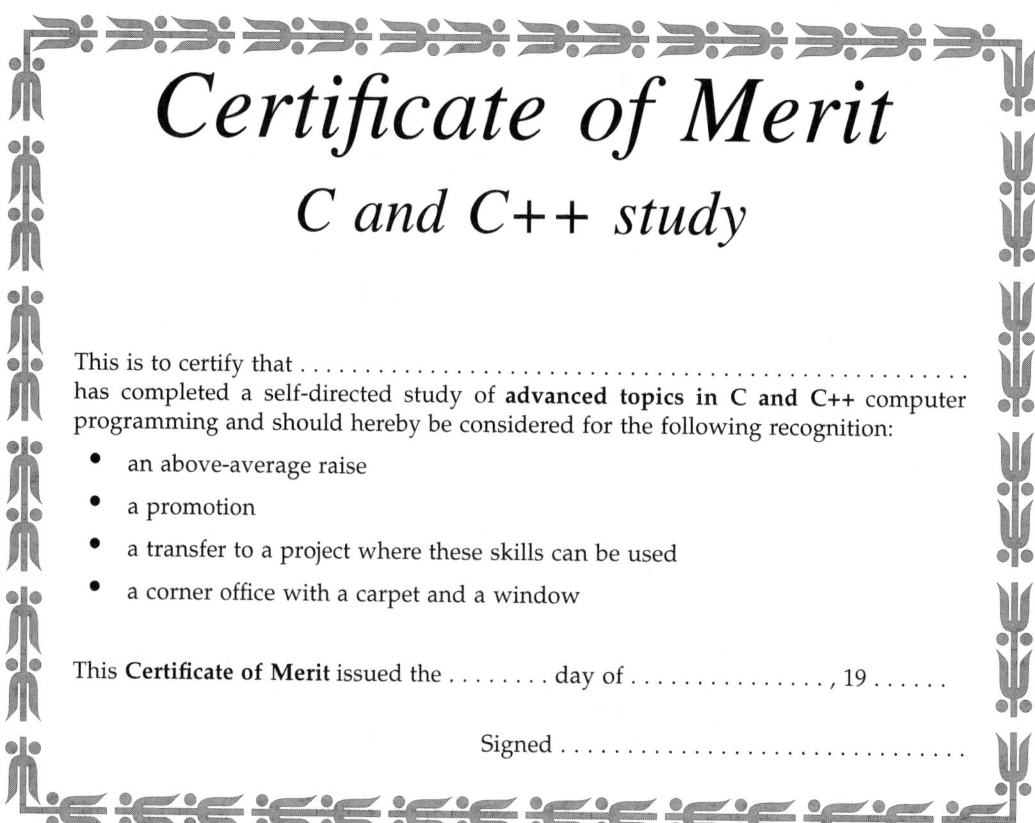

Certificate of Merit

C and C++ study

This is to certify that . . . .
has completed a self-directed study of **advanced topics in C and C++** computer programming and should hereby be considered for the following recognition:

- an above-average raise
- a promotion
- a transfer to a project where these skills can be used
- a corner office with a carpet and a window

This **Certificate of Merit** issued the . . . . day of . . . . , 19 . . . . . .

Signed . . . .

Further Reading

One C book I have found very helpful is *C, A Reference Manual,* written by Samuel P. Harbison and Guy L. Steele, (Englewood Cliffs, Prentice Hall, 1991). Harbison and Steele wrote this book based on their experience developing a family of C compilers for a wide range of different architectures, and their practical insights shine off every page.

Appendix: Secrets of Programmer Job Interviews

A little hardware knowledge is a dangerous thing. One programmer dismantled one of those novelty Christmas cards that plays a carol, and retrieved the piezoelectric melody chip. He secretly installed it into his boss's keyboard, and connected it to one of the LEDs. It turns out that the voltage over a lighted LED is sufficient to drive one of these chips.

Then I, oops, I mean "he", amended the system editor, so it turned on the LED when it started and turned it off when it exited. Result: the boss's terminal played continuous Christmas carols whenever he used the editor! The people in neighboring offices formed a lynch mob after half-an-hour and made him stop all work until the cause was uncovered.

—The Second Official Handbook of Practical Jokes[1]

Silicon Valley programmer interviews...how can you detect a cycle in a linked list?...what are the different C increment statements for?... how is a library call different from a system call?...how is a file descriptor different from a file pointer?...write some code to determine if a variable is signed or not...what is the time complexity of printing the values in a binary tree?...give me a string at random from this file... some light relief—how to measure a building with a barometer

Silicon Valley Programmer Interviews

This appendix provides some hints about the interview process for C programmers looking for a position with the top companies. One of the best things about the sharp end of the computer business is the unusual way we choose new employees to join the team. In a lot of industries, the supervisor or manager makes all the hiring decisions; indeed, is often the only one who even meets the job applicants. But on the leading edge of software

1. By Peter van der Linden, © 1991 by Peter van der Linden. Used by permission of Dutton Signet, a Division of Penguin Books USA Inc.

development, and especially in high-tech start-ups, programmers are sometimes more qualified than managers to judge which of the candidates has the best technical skills as an "individual contributor." The talent needed to do some systems programming is so rare and specialized that sometimes technical ability is the single most important characteristic that you look for in an interview.

So a distinctive style of interview has evolved. The manager follows company policies to select the pool of candidates to interview. These prospects are then given a technical grilling by every person on a development team, not just the manager. A typical job interview will last all day, involving successive hour-long sessions with six or seven different engineers—and all of them need to be convinced of how well the applicant can program before a job offer is made.

Engineers often develop some favorite questions, and this chapter contains a collection of favorites. There's no harm in revealing these "secrets"—the kind of person who reads this book probably already knows enough to be hired by a good software company. Many of these problems had their origins in real algorithms we were trying to program, and have since been replaced by other, newer problems. Of course, part of what you look for when you interview people is not just *what* they respond with, but *how* they respond. Do they think carefully about a question and come up with several possibilities, or do they just blurt out the first response that comes into their head? How persuasively do they argue the case for their ideas? Are they insistent on an obviously wrong strategy, or do they have the flexibility to adapt their answer? Some of the following interview questions have yielded the strangest answers. Try them for yourself, and see how you fare!

How Can You Detect a Cycle in a Linked List?

This starts off as the simple question, "How can you detect a cycle in a linked list?" But the questioner keeps adding extra constraints, and it soon gets quite fiendish.

Usual first answer:

Mark each element as you visit it; keep traversing; if you reach an already marked element, the list has a cycle in it.

Second constraint:

The list is in read-only memory, and you cannot mark elements.

Usual second answer:

As you visit each element, store its address in an array; check each successive element to see if it is already in the array. Sometimes poor candidates get hung up at this point on the details of hash tables to optimize array lookup.

Third constraint:

Uh-oh! There is a limited amount of memory, and it is insufficient to hold an array of the necessary size. However, you can assume that if there is a cycle, it is within the first *N* elements.

Usual third answer (if the candidate gets this far):

Keep a pointer at the beginning of the list. Check this pointer for a match against the next N - 1 elements in the list. Then move the pointer on one, and check against the next N - 2 elements. Keep doing this until a match is found, or all N elements have been compared to each other.

Fourth constraint:

Oh no! The list is arbitrarily long, and the cycle might be anywhere in it. (Even good candidates can get stuck at this point).

Final answer:

First, eliminate the pathological case of a 3-element list with a cycle from element 2 to 1. Keep two pointers. One at element 1 and the next at element 3. See if they are equal; if not, move P1 by one and P2 by two. Check and continue. If P1 or P2 is null, there is no loop. If there is one, it will definitely be detected. One pointer will eventually catch up with the other (i.e., have the same value), though it might take several traversals of the cycle to do it.

There are other solutions, but the ones above are the most common.

Programming Challenge

Knocked for a Loop

Convince yourself that the algorithm in the final answer above will detect a loop, if there is one. Make a loop; dry run your code; make the loop longer; dry run again; repeat until the induction condition jumps out at you. Also, convince yourself that the algorithm will terminate if there is no loop.

Hint: write the program, and extrapolate from there.

What Are the Different C Increment Statements For?

Consider the four C statements below:

```
x = x+1;     /* regular */
++x;         /* pre-increment */
x++;         /* post-increment */
x += 1;      /* assignment operator */
```

Clearly, these four statements all do the same thing, namely, increase the value of x by one. As shown here, with no surrounding context, there is no difference between any of them. Candidates need to (implicitly or explicitly) supply the missing context in order to answer the question and distinguish between the statements. Note that the first statement is the conventional way of expressing "add one to x" in an algorithmic language. Hence, this is the reference statement, and we need to find unique characteristics of the other three.

Most C programmers can immediately point out that `++x` is a pre-increment that adds one to x *before* using its value in some surrounding expression, whereas `x++` is a post-increment that only bumps up x *after* using its original value in the surrounding expression. Some people say that the "++" and "--" operators were only put in C because `*p++` is a single machine instruction on a PDP-11 (the machine for which the first C compiler was written). Not so. The feature dates from the B language on the PDP-7, but it turns out that the increment and decrement operators are incredibly useful on all hardware.

Some programmers give up at this point, overlooking that `x += 1` is useful when x is not a simple variable, but an expression involving an array. If you have a complicated array reference, and you want to demonstrate that the same index is used for both references, then

```
node[i >> 3] += ~(0x01 << (i & 0x7));
```

is the way to go. We took this example statement directly out of some code in an operating system. Only the data names have been changed to protect the guilty. A good candidate will also point out that the l-value (compiler-talk for an expression that locates an object—usually an address, but it may also be a register, or either of these plus a bit-field) is only evaluated once. It makes a difference because the statement

```
mango[i++] += y;
```

is treated as

```
mango[i] = mango[i] + y; i++;
```

and *not*

```
mango[i++] = mango[i++] + y;
```

Once, when we were interviewing applicants for a position on Sun's Pascal compiler team, the best candidate (and he ultimately got the job—Hi, Arindam!) explained these differences in terms of compiler intermediate code, for example "++x" means *take the location of x, increment the contents there, put this value in a register;* "x++" means *take the location of x, load the contents into a register, increment the value of x in memory,* and so on. By the way, how would the other two statements be described in compiler terms like these?

Though Kernighan and Ritchie say that incrementing is often more efficient than explicitly adding one (K&R2, p. 18), contemporary compilers are by now usually good enough to make all methods equally fast. Modern C compilers should compile these four statements into exactly the same code in the absence of any surrounding context to bring out the differences. These should be the fastest instructions for incrementing a variable. Try it with your favorite C compiler—it probably has an option to produce an assembler listing. Set the compiler option for debugging, too, as that often makes it easier to check the correspondence between assembler and C statements. Don't switch the optimizer on, as the statements may be optimized out of existence. On Sun workstations, chant the magic incantation "`-S`" so the command line will look like

```
cc -S -Xc banana.c
```

The `-S` causes the compilation to stop at the assembler phase, leaving the assembly language in file `banana.s`. The latest compilers, SPARCompilers 3.0, have been improved to cause the source to appear interspersed in the assembler output when this option is used. It makes it easier to troubleshoot problems and diagnose code generation.

The `-Xc` tells the compiler to reject any non-ANSI C constructs. It's a good idea to always use this option when writing new code, because it will help you attain maximum program portability.

So sometimes the difference is a question of what looks better in the source. Something short can be simpler to read than something long. However, extreme brevity is also difficult to read (ask anyone who has tried to amend someone else's APL code). When I was a graduate student teaching assistant for a systems programming class, a student brought me some code that had an unknown bug in it, but the code was so compressed that it could not be found. Amid jeers from some of the upperclassmen C programmers, we methodically expanded one statement from something like:

```
frotz[--j + i++] += --y;
```

into the equivalent, but longer,:

```
--y;
--j;
frotz[j+i] = frotz[j+i] + y;
i++;
```

To the chagrin of the kibitzers, this quickly revealed that one of the operations was being done in the wrong place!

Moral: Don't try to do too many things in one statement.

It won't make the generated code any more efficient, and it will ruin your chances of debugging the code. As Kernighan and Plauger pointed out, "Everyone knows that debugging is twice as hard as writing a program in the first place. So if you're as clever as you can be when you write it, how will you ever debug it?"[2]

How Is a Library Call Different from a System Call?

One question we sometimes use to see if a candidate knows his or her way around programming is simply, "What is the difference between a library call and a system call?" It's amazing how many people never figured it out. We haven't seen many books that describe the difference, so this is a good way to determine if a candidate has done much programming and has the intellectual curiosity to find out about issues like this.

The short answer is that library calls are part of the language or application, and system calls are part of the operating system. Make sure you say the keyword "trap". A system call gets into the kernel by issuing a "trap" or interrupt. A comprehensive answer will cover the points listed inTable A-1.

Table A-1 Library Call versus System Call

Library Call	System Call
The C library is the same on every ANSI C implementation	The systems calls are different in each OS
Is a call to a routine in a library	Is a call to the kernel for a service
Linked with the user program	Is an entry point to the OS
Executes in the user address space	Executes in the kernel address space
Counts as part of the "user" time	Counts as part of the "system" time
Has the lower overhead of a procedure call	Has high overhead context switch to kernel and back

2. Brian W. Kernighan and P.J. Plauger, *The Elements of Programming Style*, Second Edition, p.10, New York, McGraw-Hill, 1978, p. 10.

Table A-1 Library Call versus System Call

Library Call	System Call
There are about 300 routines in the C library libc	There are about 90 system calls in UNIX, (fewer in MS-DOS)
Documented in Section 3 of the UNIX OS manual	Documented in Section 2 of the UNIX OS manual
Typical C library calls: system, fprintf, malloc	Typical system calls: chdir, fork, write, brk

Library routines are usually slower than in-line code because of the subroutine call overhead, but system calls are much slower still because of the context switch to the kernel. On a SPARCstation 1, we timed the overhead of a library call (i.e., how fast a procedure call is made) at about half a microsecond. A system call took seventy times longer to establish (35 microseconds). For raw performance, minimize the number of system calls wherever possible, but remember, many routines in the C library do their work by making system calls. Finally, people who believe that crop circles are the work of aliens will have trouble with the concept that the `system()` call is actually a library call.

Programming Challenge

Professor Perlis's Gut-Busting Homework Assignment

Caution: This Programming Challenge may be too intense for some viewers.

Some graduate schools also use programming questions to test their new students. At Yale University, Professor Alan Perlis (one of the fathers of Algol-60) used to set the following assignment (due in one week) to his incoming class of graduate students.

Program each of the following problems:

1. Read a string and output all combinations of its characters.
2. The "8-queens" problem (print all the chess configurations where eight queens can be placed on a board without attacking each other).
3. Given N, list all the prime numbers up to N.
4. Write a subroutine to multiply two arbitrary-sized matrices together.

Professor Perlis's Gut-Busting Homework Assignment (Continued)

in each of the following languages:

1. C
2. APL
3. Lisp
4. Fortran

Any *one* of these programming problems would have been a pretty reasonable assignment for a class that was just one of several that a graduate student took. But here we were being asked to do *all* of them in just one week, in *all* of a variety of languages that some of us had never even seen before!

Of course, we didn't know that Perlis was just testing us, and that he wasn't actually going to nail anyone. Most of the new graduate students spent a frantic week of late nights hunched over a terminal, only to find that, back in class, Alan asked for volunteers to present a single language/problem combination on the board.

Some of the problems could be solved by idioms, like the APL one-liner[1] for problem 3:

```
(2=+.0=T≤.|T)/T← ⍳N
```

Thus, anyone who attempted any part of the assignment had the opportunity to show it. Anyone who was so overwhelmed by the problem that they didn't even try the smallest part of it learned that they were probably not cut out for graduate school. It was a week of furious activity, in which I learned more about APL and Lisp than I have done in the dozen years before or since.

1. You can see why they don't have an "Obfuscated APL Competition" —there's no need, it already comes that way

How Is a File Descriptor Different from a File Pointer?

This question follows naturally from the previous one. All the UNIX routines that manipulate files use either a *file pointer* or a *file descriptor* to identify the file they are operating on; what are each of these, and when is each used? The answer is actually straightforward, and gives you an idea of how familiar a person is with UNIX I/O and the various trade-offs.

All the system calls that manipulate files take (or return) a "file descriptor" as an argument. "File descriptor" is somewhat of a misnomer; the file descriptor is a small integer (usually between 0 and 255) used in the Sun implementation to index into the per-process table-of-open-files. The system I/O calls are `creat()`, `open()`, `read()`, `write()`, `close()`, `ioctl()`, and so on, but these are not a part of ANSI C, won't exist in non-UNIX environments, and will destroy program portability if you use them. Hence, a set of standard I/O library calls were specified, which ANSI C now requires all hosts to support.

To ensure program portability, use the stdio I/O calls `fopen()`, `fclose()`, `putc()`, `fseek()`—most of these routine names start with "f". These calls take a pointer to a `FILE` structure (sometimes called a stream pointer) as an argument. The `FILE` pointer points to a stream structure, defined in <stdio.h>. The contents of the structure vary from implementation to implementation, and on UNIX is typically an entry in the per-process table-of-open-files. Typically, it contains the stream buffer, all the necessary variables to indicate how many bytes in the buffer are actual file data, flags to indicate the state of the stream (like ERROR and EOF), and so on.

- So a file descriptor is the *offset* in the per-process table-of-open-files (e.g., "3"). It is used in a UNIX system call to identify the file.
- A `FILE` pointer holds the *address* of a file structure that is used to represent the open I/O stream (e.g. hex 20938). It is used in an ANSI C stdio library call to identify the file.

The C library function fdopen() can be used to create a new `FILE` structure and associate it with the specified file descriptor (effectively converting between a file descriptor integer and the corresponding stream pointer, although it does generate an additional new entry in the table-of-open-files).

Write Some Code to Determine if a Variable Is Signed or Not

One colleague, interviewing with Microsoft, was asked to "write some code to determine if a variable is signed or not." It is actually a pretty tough question because it leaves too much open to interpretation. Some people wrongly equate "signed" with "has a negative sign" and assume that what is wanted is a trivial function or macro to say if a value is less than zero.

That isn't it. The question has to do with whether or not a given *type* is signed or unsigned in a particular implementation. In ANSI C, "char" can be either signed or unsigned as an implementation desires. It is useful to know which when writing code that will be ported to many platforms, and ideally the result will be a compiletime constant.

You can't achieve this with a function. The type of a function's formal parameter is defined within the function, so it cannot be passed via the call. Therefore you have to write a macro that will operate on its argument according to the *declaration* of that argument.

The next point is to clarify whether the macro's argument is to be a type or a value of a type. Assuming the argument is a value, the essential characteristic of an unsigned value is that it can never be negative, and the essential characteristic of a signed value is that complementing its most significant bit will change its sign (assuming 2's complement representation, which is pretty safe). Since the other bits are irrelevant to this test, you can complement them all and get the same result. Therefore, try the following:

```
#define ISUNSIGNED(a) (a >= 0 && ~a >= 0)
```

Alternatively, assuming the argument is to be a type, one answer would use type casts:

```
#define ISUNSIGNED(type) ((type)0 - 1 > 0)
```

The correct interpretation is key here! Listen carefully, and ask for a better explanation of any terms that you don't understand or weren't well defined. The first code example only works with K&R C. The new promotion rules mean it doesn't work under ANSI C. Exercise: explain why, and provide a solution in ANSI C.

Most Microsoft questions have some element of determining how well you can think under pressure, but they are not all overtly technical. A typical nontechnical question might be, "How many gas stations are there in the U.S.?" or "How many barber shops are there in the U.S.?" They want to see if you can invent and justify good estimates, or suggest a good way of finding more reliable answers. One suggestion: call the state licensing authorities. This will give you exact answers with only 50 phone calls. Or call half-a-dozen representative states, and interpolate from there. You could even respond as one environmentally-conscious candidate did, when asked "How many gas stations?" "Too many!" was her annoyed response.

What Is the Time Complexity of Printing the Values in a Binary Tree?

This question was asked during an interview for a position on a compiler team with Intel. Now, the first thing you learn in complexity theory is that the notation O(N) means that as N (usually the number of things being processed) increases, the time taken increases at most linearly. Similarly, $O(N^2)$ means that as N increases, the processing time increases much, much faster, by up to N-squared in fact. The second thing that you learn in complexity theory is that *everything* in a binary tree has O(log(n)), so most candidates naturally give this answer without even thinking about it. Wrong!

This turned out to be a question similar to Dan Rather's famous "What is the frequency, Kenneth?" question—an enquiry designed to discomfit, confuse, and annoy the listener rather than solicit information. To *print* all the nodes in a binary tree you have to *visit* them all! Therefore, the complexity is O(n).

Colleagues have reported similar chicanery in an interview question for electronic engineers at Hewlett-Packard. The question is posed in the form of a charged and uncharged capacitor suddenly connected together, in an ideal circuit with no resistance. Mechanical engineers were asked the same question about two massless springs displaced from equilibrium and then released. The interviewer then derives two inconsistent end-states using two different physical laws (i.e., conservation of charge and conservation of energy in the case of the capacitors), and queries the hapless prospect on the cause of the inconsistency.

The trick here is that at least one expression of the end-state uses a formula that involves integration over the event separating the start and end conditions. In the real world this is fine, but in the theoretical experiment posed it causes integration over a discontinuity (since the moderating effects have been idealized away); hence, the formula is useless. Engineers are most unlikely to have encountered this before. Yep, those massless springs and circuits without resistance will get you every time!

Yet another curve ball was pitched in an interview for a position as a software consultant with a large management consulting company. "What does the *execve* system call return, if successful?" was the question. Recall that execve() replaces the calling process image with the named executable, then starts executing it. There is no return from a successful *execve* hence there is no return value. Trick questions are fun to pose to your friends, but they don't really belong in an interview.

Give Me a String at Random from This File

Another favorite Microsoft question. The interviewer asks the applicant to write some code that selects one string at random from a file of strings. The classic way of doing this is to read the file, counting the strings and keeping a record of the offset at which each begins. Then pick a random number between 1 and the total number, go to the corresponding offset in the file, and that's your string.

What makes it very hard to solve is that the interviewer sets the condition that you can only make one sequential pass through the file, and you may not store any additional information like a table of offsets. This is another of those questions where the interviewer is mostly interested in seeing how you solve problems. He or she will feed you hints if you ask for them, so most people eventually get it. How well you do depends on how quickly you get it.

The basic technique is to pick survivors, and recalculate as you go along. This is so computationally inefficient that it's easy to overlook. You open the file and save the first string. At this point you have one candidate string with a 100% probability of picking it. While remembering the first string, you read the next string. You now have two candidates, each with a 50% probability. Pick one of them, save it, and discard the other. Read the next string, and choose between that and the saved string, weighting your choice 33% toward the new string and 67% toward the survivor (which represents the winner of the previous two-way selection). Save the new survivor.

Keep on doing this throughout the entire file, at each step reading string N, and choosing between that (with probability 1/N) and the previous survivor, with probability (N - 1)/N. When you reach the end of the file, the current survivor is the string picked at random!

This is a tough problem, and you either have to figure out the answer with the minimum of hints, or have cleverly prepared yourself by reading this book.

Some Light Relief—How to Measure a Building with a Barometer

We find these kinds of questions so much fun that we even pose them to ourselves in a non-computing context. Sun has a "junk mail" e-mail alias for employees to share thoughts of random interest; occasionally people will pose problems on this alias, and challenge other engineers to compete in submitting the best answer. Here is one such puzzle, recently set.

There is an old story about a physics student finding novel ways to measure the height of a building using a barometer. The story is retold by Alexander Calandra in *The Teaching of Elementary Science and Mathematics*.[3]

> A student failed an exam after he refused to parrot back what he had been taught in class. When the student protested, I was asked to act as arbiter. I went to the professor's office and read the examination question: "Show how it is possible to determine the height of a tall building with the aid of a barometer."
>
> The student had answered: "Take the barometer to the top of the building, attach a long rope to it, lower the barometer to the street and then bring it up, measuring the length of the rope. The length of the rope is the height of the building."
>
> A high grade is supposed to certify competence in physics, but the answer did not confirm this. I suggested that the student have another try at answering the question. I gave the student six minutes, with the warning that his answer should show some knowledge of physics. In the next minute he dashed off his answer, which read: "Take the barometer to the top of the building and lean over the edge of the roof. Drop the barometer, timing its fall with a stopwatch. Then, using the formula for the distance travelled by a falling object, $S = 1/2\ a\ t^2$ calculate the height of the building." At this point, I gave the student full credit.
>
> The student went on to propose three other methods of measuring a building's height with a barometer:
>
> Take the barometer out on a sunny day and measure the height of the barometer, the length of its shadow, and the shadow of the building. By the use of a simple proportion, determine the height of the building.
>
> Take the barometer and begin to walk up the stairs. As you climb the stairs, mark off the length of the barometer along the wall. Then count the number of marks, and this will give you the height of the building in barometer units.
>
> Last (and probably least) offer the barometer as a gift to the building superintendent if he will just tell you how high the building is.

When this old story was rehashed at Sun as a "science puzzler," 16 more ingenious new methods for barometric building measurement were suggested! The new responses were of the following types:

3. St. Louis, Washington University, 1961.

The Pressure Method: Measure the air pressure at the bottom and top of the building, then compute the height of the building from the pressure difference. This is the only method that actually uses the barometer for its designed purpose of measuring air pressure. Although aircraft altimeters often work by this principle, it is one of the least accurate methods for measuring a building's height.

The Pendulum Method: Go onto the building's roof, and lower the barometer on a string until it almost reaches the ground. Swing the barometer and measure the pendulum's period of oscillation. From this the length of the pendulum, and hence the building, can be calculated.

The Avarice Method: Pawn the barometer to raise seed money for a chain letter campaign. Then stack the currency thus obtained against the building, measuring it in units of currency thickness. No comment on how to stay ahead of the police long enough to measure the building.

The Mafia Method: Extort the building's height from the superintendent, using the barometer as a weapon.

The Ballistic Method: Fire the barometer from ground level with a mortar, just high enough to reach the top of the building. You may need to take some ranging shots to get the explosive charge and firing elevation just right. A table of standard ballistic calculations will then yield the height reached by the projectile.

The Paperweight Method: Use the barometer as a paperweight while looking over the building plans.

The Sonic Method: Drop the barometer from the top of the building, and time the interval between seeing the barometer hit the ground and hearing it. For practical distances, the sight will be instantaneous, and the sound will travel at the speed of sound (1150 feet/second at standard temperature-pressure and mean sea level), giving the height.

The Reflective Method: Use the glass face of the barometer as a mirror and time the interval it takes light to traverse the round trip between the top of the building and the ground. Since the speed of light is a known quantity, the distance can be calculated.

The Mercantile Method: Sell the barometer, and buy some proper equipment.

The Analog Method: Attach the barometer to a string, wind the string around the shaft of a small generator, and measure the amount of electrical energy produced as the barometer falls from the top of the building to the ground. The generated energy is proportionate to the number of revolutions of the shaft, and hence the distance to the ground.

The Trigonometric Method: Pick a spot on the ground a known distance from the building, go to the top of the building with the barometer and a protractor level, and wait for the sun to reach the horizon. Then, using the barometer as a mirror, aim a spot of sunlight at the place you previously picked and measure the angle of the mirror with the level. Use trigonometry to calculate the building's height.

The Proportion Method: Measure the height of the barometer. Bring a friend and a tape measure. Stand at a known distance from the building and sight past the barometer to the building. Move the barometer toward or away from you until the top and bottom of the barometer line up with the top and bottom of the building. Then have your friend measure the distance from the barometer to your eye. Compute the building height by proportion.

The Photographic Method: Set up a tripod with a camera at a known distance from the building. Hold the barometer a known distance from the camera and take a picture. From the relative heights of the barometer and the building in the picture, you can compute the height of the building.

The Gravitational Method I: Suspend the barometer from a yard of string. Measure the oscillation period of the pendulum thus formed at the top and bottom of the building. Compute the building's height from the difference in gravitational acceleration.

The Gravitational Method II: Weigh the barometer at the top and bottom of the building with a spring balance (a beam balance won't work for this!). Differences in the readings will be due to the different gravitational acceleration, due to the differing distances from Earth. (A reader tells me that the Lacoste Romberg gravimeter provides a practical way of getting the required accuracy.) Compute the building's height from the two measurements.

The Calorific Method: Drop the barometer from the roof into a container of water covered with a narrow slit to minimize splashing. The rise in temperature of the water is an analog of the energy that the barometer had on impact, and hence the height it fell from.

And you thought questions like this only came up in algebra problems!

Further Reading

If you have enjoyed this book you might also enjoy the text *Bartholomew and the Oobleck*, by Dr. Seuss, (New York, Random House, 1973).

As Dr. Seuss explains, Oobleck "squiggles around in your fist like a slippery potato dumpling made of rubber." He doesn't tell you how to make it, so I will here.

How to make Oobleck

1. Take one cup of cornstarch.
2. Add some drops of green food coloring; Oobleck should always be green in color.
3. Slowly knead in up to half a cup of water.

Oobleck has some extremely strange, non-Newtonian properties. It flows like water through your fingers, except when you work it like dough—then it immediately assumes a solid consistency. Except when you stop kneading it, it turns back to liquid. If you strike it quickly with something hard, you can shatter it!

Like all Dr. Seuss books, *Bartholomew and the Oobleck* can be read and enjoyed on several levels. For example, *One Fish Two Fish, Red Fish Blue Fish* can be deconstructed as a searing indictment of the narrow-minded binary counting system. Software engineers can benefit from a sophisticated reading of *Bartholomew and the Oobleck.*

The world would be a better place if every programmer would just play with Oobleck occasionally. The good programmers would be more rested and refreshed and the bad programmers would probably get their heads stuck to the table. But always remember, no matter how lowly or exalted a hacker you are, you are a child process of the universe, no less than the disk controller, or the stack frame mechanism (explained at such length in Chapter 6).

They say that when you stare deeply into an abyss, the abyss also stares into you. But if you stare deeply into this book, well, it's rude to stare, plus you might get a headache or something.

I can't think of a job I'd rather do than computer programming. All day, you create patterns and structure out of the formless void, and you solve dozens of smaller puzzles along the way. The wit and ingenuity of the human brain is pitted against the remorseless speed and accuracy of the electronic one.

Thus has it ever been. Humanity's higher purpose is to strive, to seek, to create. Each and every computer programmer should seek out and grasp opportunities to—whoa! That's your 75,000 words already—

Index

D

E

F

G

H

I

R

S

T

U

V

W

X

Y